THE FORM (DATA VIEW) SPEE

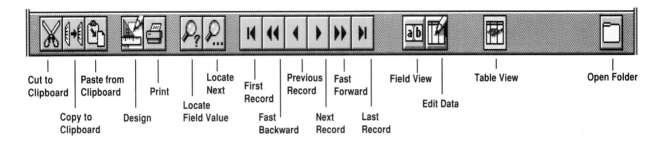

Cut to Clipboard

Copy to Clipboard

Paste from Clipboard

Design

Print

Locate Field Value

Locate Next

First Record

Fast Backward

Previous Record

Next Record

Fast Forward

Last Record

Field View

Edit Data

Table View

Open Folder

THE REPORT (VIEW DATA) SPEEDBAR

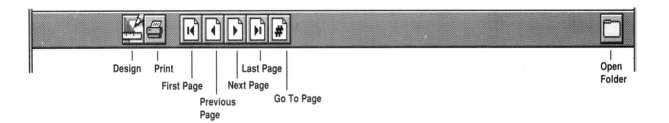

Design

Print

First Page

Previous Page

Next Page

Last Page

Go To Page

Open Folder

THE SCRIPT SPEEDBAR

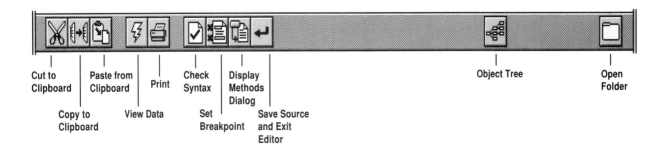

Cut to Clipboard

Copy to Clipboard

Paste from Clipboard

View Data

Print

Check Syntax

Set Breakpoint

Display Methods Dialog

Save Source and Exit Editor

Object Tree

Open Folder

SYBEX *Running* **START** BOOKS

The SYBEX *Running Start* series offers busy, computer-literate people two books in one: a quick, hands-on tutorial guide to program essentials, and a comprehensive reference to commands and features.

The first half of each *Running Start* book teaches the basic operations and underlying concepts of the topic software. These lessons feature trademark SYBEX characteristics: step-by-step procedures; thoughtful, well-chosen examples; an engaging writing style; valuable Notes, Tips, and Warnings; and plenty of practical insights.

Once you've learned the basics, you're ready to start working on your own. That's where the second half of each *Running Start* book comes in. This alphabetical reference offers concise instructions for using program commands, dialog boxes, and menu options. With dictionary-style organization and headings, this half of the book is designed to give you fast access to information.

SYBEX is very interested in your reactions to the *Running Start* series. Your opinions and suggestions will help all of our readers, including yourself. Please send your comments to: SYBEX Editorial Department, 2021 Challenger Dr., Alameda, CA 94501.

PARADOX FOR WINDOWS *Running* START

PARADOX® FOR WINDOWS™ *Running* START

GORDON PADWICK

SYBEX® San Francisco . Paris . Düsseldorf . Soest

Acquisitions Editor: David Clark
Developmental Editor: David Peal
Editor: James A. Compton
Technical Editor: Maryann Brown
Book Series Designer: Claudia Smelser
"Running Start" Icon Designer: Alissa Feinberg
Production Artists: Ingrid Owen, Claudia Smelser, and Lucie Živny
Screen Graphics: John Corrigan
Desktop Publishing Specialist: Ann Dunn
Proofreader/ Production Coordinator: Catherine Mahoney
Indexer: Ted Laux
Cover Design and Illustration: Archer Design
Screen reproductions produced with Collage Plus.

Library of Congress Card Number: 92-85246
ISBN: 0-7821-1047-9

Manufactured in the United States of America
10 9 8 7 6 5 4 3 2 1

To Kathy
wife, friend, and partner

ACKNOWLEDGMENTS

This is my opportunity to acknowledge the many people who have contributed to this book. There would be no book without their enthusiastic cooperation.

High on my list of contributors are the many Borland people who created Paradox for Windows, particularly the technical support people who have so patiently answered my many questions during the almost 12 months that I have been working with pre-release versions of Paradox.

A great deal of credit must go to David Peal and Jim Compton, SYBEX developmental and copy editors, for their guidance and many helpful suggestions. Their firm, yet gentle, prodding kept me on track and almost on schedule.

While the responsibility for any remaining technical errors in this book is mine, there would have been many more if it had not been for the eagle eye of Maryann Brown, the technical editor who reviewed all the step-by-step procedures.

As always, Dianne King and the whole SYBEX acquisitions team deserve thanks for conceiving this book project and getting it started.

I have been fortunate to have a 80486-based computer from Gateway 2000 running MS-DOS 5.0 and Windows 3.1 from Microsoft as an excellent high-performance platform on which to run Paradox. Microsoft's Word 5.0 running on a 80286-based Zenith computer has been my faithful friend during many hours of writing and revising. All the screen captures were made with the help of Collage Plus from Inner Media. Additional graphics were created with the help of CorelDRAW 3.0 from Corel Systems.

My thanks go to all, those named and unnamed, who have contributed to this project.

TABLE*of*CONTENTS

lesson 3   **USING CUSTOM DATA ENTRY FORMS**   **47**

PART II ALPHABETICAL REFERENCE

INTRODUCTION

This is the book you need if you want to start using Paradox for Windows, but don't have the time to wade through extensive and detailed manuals. I assume you have some experience with databases and are already using Windows. And I assume you are ready to start working with Paradox for Windows and want to see some positive results—fast.

The book focuses on using Paradox for Windows interactively. By that, I mean that you will be giving mouse and keyboard commands to direct Paradox to perform specific tasks. The book does not cover ObjectPAL, the programming language you can use to automate database operations. But don't discard this book if you intend to develop ObjectPAL applications. You need to learn about using Paradox interactively before you are ready to explore ObjectPAL.

This book is about Paradox for Windows so, from now on, the word *Paradox* used by itself refers to Paradox for Windows. On the few occasions when reference is made to the DOS version of Paradox, that is explicitly stated.

WHO IS THIS BOOK FOR?

This book is primarily for readers who have some previous experience with database programs, are acquainted with Windows, and want a fast way of getting started with Paradox for Windows.

You certainly don't have to be a database expert before starting this book, but it will help if you have previously used another database program.

You don't need to be a Windows expert either, but it will help if you have some Windows experience.

This is a getting-started book. After you have read it, you will have a good basic understanding of Paradox, but you will not be an expert. To learn more you will need to dig into the Paradox manuals and, perhaps, study a more comprehensive book such as Alan Simpson's *Mastering Paradox for Windows*.

WHAT YOU WILL LEARN IN THIS BOOK

This book has two parts. The first part is a fast-paced, six-lesson tutorial that will familiarize you with Paradox essentials. The second part is an alphabetical reference that provides step-by-step instructions for more than 200 of the operations you will most often perform within Paradox, along with concise explanations of many of the most important underlying concepts.

The six lessons in Part I, the Step-by-Step Tutorial, use a hands-on example of a database that lists software used within a company. Three separate tables provide information about each software package, about suppliers, and about users. By the time you have worked through these lessons, you will be familiar with many of Paradox's capabilities and you will have a database you can use.

Lesson 1 starts by introducing database concepts in Paradox terms. As the lesson continues, it provides information about the tables Paradox uses to store data, the many types of fields you can use, and the built-in facilities to enhance data integrity. The last few pages of the lesson invite you to see Paradox on your monitor, and introduce you to the Desktop components.

We start using Paradox seriously in Lesson 2. This lesson takes you through the process of creating the structure for a table and the mechanics of entering data directly into a table. The lesson also introduces you to forms that you can use to simplify data entry.

Lesson 3 focuses on forms. It guides you through the process of creating custom data entry forms, including arranging the layout of fields, adding text, enhancing forms with graphics, and using color. The lesson shows you how to use a form to enter new data and how to locate and edit existing data.

The important concept of linking tables is introduced in Lesson 4. The lesson first deals with linking tables in one-to-one relationships, and then moves to one-to-many relationships. It also shows how a table can be linked to a lookup table as a means of simplifying data entry. The final pages of the lesson cover many-to-many relationships between tables.

The first four lessons are primarily concerned with creating tables and entering data into them. In Lesson 5, we move on to the subject of creating printed reports based on data in tables. The lesson shows how to design a report based on linked tables and how to prepare a multirecord report suitable for printing mailing labels.

Lesson 6 deals with queries—the way you can use Paradox interactively to get information from a database. This lesson shows you how to ask queries by creating an example of the answer you want—the Query By Example (QBE) technique pioneered by Borland. This lesson leads you through many of the ways Paradox can provide answers tailored to specific queries.

Part II, the Alphabetical Reference, is arranged alphabetically by major topics. Within each major topic, specific tasks are also arranged alphabetically. Rather than attempt to include every possible operation, I have tried to focus on the tasks you are likely to encounter as you begin to use Paradox.

An appendix lists the hardware and software you must have before you can install and use Paradox. It also explains the installation procedure.

GETTING STARTED

Welcome to Paradox for Windows. Refer to the Appendix if you need help in installing Paradox, turn to Lesson 1, and you're on your way.

I hope you enjoy exploring and working with Paradox as much as I have.

Gordon Padwick

PART I

Step-by-Step
Tutorial

1

GETTING STARTED

This lesson gets you started with Paradox for Windows. Read it carefully if you are new to databases because it explains basic concepts that are developed throughout the rest of this book. Even if you have considerable experience with other databases, scan through this lesson to become familiar with Paradox terminology.

The topics introduced here are all covered in more detail in subsequent lessons and in Part II of this book.

UNDERSTANDING PARADOX DATABASES

Paradox for Windows allows you to create and work with databases in several different formats. In addition to its native format Paradox for Windows can handle the DOS Paradox, dBASE III Plus, and dBASE IV formats. This book deals only with the native Paradox for Windows format.

The next few pages briefly review databases to make sure you are familiar with Paradox terminology.

WHAT IS A DATABASE?

A *database* is a collection of data. Usually this data consists of text and numbers but, in the case of Paradox for Windows, it may also include other types of information such as sound and pictures. Like most databases, Paradox databases have a specific structure of tables, records, and fields.

DEFINING BASIC TERMS

All data in a Paradox database is contained in *tables*, each table containing information about similar items. For example, one table may contain information about people; another may contain information about items in an inventory. Very simple databases consist of only one table, but most consist of two or more *related* tables. This book starts with a single-table database and then leads you into working with multitable databases.

A table consists of *records*, each containing information about a single item. In a table containing information about customers, clients, or employees, each record has data about one person; in an inventory table, each record has information about one inventory item. A small table may contain only a few records, whereas a large table may contain thousands or even millions of records.

Each record consists of named *fields*. Each field contains a specific piece of information, which is its *value*. A field's name describes this value. For people records, individual fields contain last names, first names, addresses, and telephone numbers;

for an inventory, fields contain item names, descriptions, part numbers, prices, and so on. In most tables, records have a relatively small number of fields, typically 10 to 20, although Paradox allows up to 255 fields.

You can visualize a table as a matrix of information, as shown in Figure 1.1. The labels at the top are the field names. Each row corresponds to a single record. Notice that every record contains the same fields and that, for a given field, each record occupies the same space regardless of the length of individual field values.

When you create a table, you have to define each field by giving it a name and a data type (Alphanumeric, Number, etc.). As you will soon see, there are several other characteristics you can define for fields.

The majority of fields in most tables are Alphanumeric—they hold letters and numbers. You can also define fields that will hold only numeric values, only dates, or several other types of information.

Throughout the rest of this book, Paradox for Windows *is referred to simply as* Paradox.

In Paradox, you decide the size of Alphanumeric fields according to the values you expect them to contain, from one character to 255. If it becomes necessary, you can easily change field sizes while you are developing a database.

The sizes of some types of fields, such as Number and Date fields, are predetermined by Paradox. Other types, Memo fields for example, can contain almost any amount of information, limited only by the space available on your hard disk.

FIGURE 1.1:

A database as a matrix of information.

Co. No.	Name	Address	City	State	Zip
1	Strong Software	126 East Street	Ansel	CA	
2	Best Systems	895 Better Blvd.	Goodtown	OR	
3	Lookyer Company	897 Optimist Ave.	Goldtown	CA	
4	Success, Inc.	59 Down Avenue	Uptown	CA	
5	Letdoit	41156 Enterprise Dr.	Bigcity	MA	
6	Winning Company	7 Aldes Street	Oldtown	WI	

A Paradox table can contain almost any type of data, including graphics and sounds. Virtually anything that can be represented digitally can be stored in a Paradox table.

CREATING A PARADOX DATABASE

There are three stages involved in creating a usable database: planning, implementing, and testing. Planning must come first! The more thoroughly you plan how a database will be used, the fewer problems you will have implementing and testing it. However, you will inevitably find that you want to modify your original plans as you progress through the implementation and testing stages. Paradox is flexible enough to allow you to do this quite easily.

PLANNING A DATABASE

Planning starts with writing a precise statement of the purpose of the database. Remember that the purpose of any database is to make information available in useful formats. Before you get started with implementation, make sure you know what information you or other people will want from the database and how you will want it to appear.

DEFINING REQUIREMENTS

The database used in this book's examples provides information about software packages used in a small company. We can define its purpose more specifically by stating what questions the database should be able to answer. Once we know what we expect from the database, we can plan it properly.

The database should be able to:

- ◆ Provide a printed report showing what software each person in the company is using.

- ◆ Provide a printed report showing who uses each software package.

- ◆ Provide a list of the software used in each department.

◆ Provide the name, address, and telephone number of the manufacturer of each software package.

This might be your initial list of expectations. Before getting on with implementation, it is a good idea to ask everyone who will be using the database for other requirements. It is much easier to incorporate additional requirements during the planning stage than after you've built the database.

CHOOSING TABLES

In the list of requirements, you can see that our database contains three types of information:

◆ people who use software;

◆ software packages;

◆ companies that supply software.

A single table recording all the information about every software package would contain redundant data and would be difficult to update. It makes sense, therefore, to create separate tables for these three types of information and link them together to provide the reports we need. We will call these three tables People, Software, and Company.

IMPLEMENTING THE DATABASE

The first task in implementing a database is to create structures for the tables. We can use the Company table as an example.

CREATING A TABLE STRUCTURE

To create a structure, you must determine what fields are required, give each field a name, and decide what type each should be. In the case of Alphanumeric fields, you must also define each field's size.

DEFINING FIELD NAMES AND TYPES

Paradox allows you to use ten types of fields, which are described in detail in Part II under Fields. The Company table used here as an example has only Alphanumeric, Number, and Memo fields.

The fields needed for this table are:

FIELD NAME	TYPE	SIZE
Co. No.	Number	
Name	Alphanumeric	25
Address	Alphanumeric	25
City	Alphanumeric	15
State	Alphanumeric	2
ZIP code	Alphanumeric	10
Phone	Alphanumeric	12
Fax	Alphanumeric	12
Notes	Memo	25

Each field in a table must have a unique name consisting of no more than 25 characters. Names must not start with a blank space but may contain spaces. You can use uppercase and lowercase characters in field names, but Paradox will not recognize, e.g., FAX and Fax as different file names.

TIP

You can use the same field name in different tables, as you will frequently do when you plan to link tables. To avoid confusion, fields with the same names in different tables should be of the same type and size.

Most of the fields in this example are Alphanumeric. Why not use Number fields for the telephone numbers and ZIP codes? First, Number fields are normally used only for data that is to be used in calculations. Also, some ZIP codes start with a zero; and Paradox normally does not display leading zeros in number fields. By using an Alphanumeric field for ZIP codes, you avoid this problem.

The purpose of all the fields except the first and the last should be obvious. The first field, Co. No., contains a number that is unique for every company. We will be using this field to link one table to another. The principal reason for using a number rather than a name for this purpose is that numbers are always unique and names sometimes aren't. You may need two or more records for the same company.

The last field, Notes, is a catch-all field in which we can enter comments or miscellaneous information about a company that does not fit into the other specific fields. Notice that Notes is a Memo field, in which the number of characters is limited only by the space available on your hard disk.

DEFINING FIELD SIZES

You have to choose a size for each Alphanumeric field. This is quite easy for fields that will contain values in a standard format, such as ZIP codes and telephone numbers. For fields that will contain names or addresses, it is more difficult to choose field sizes. Fortunately, Paradox allows you to change field sizes after you have created table structures, so initially make your best guess about the field sizes you need. When you test your database with real data, you will soon discover whether you need larger fields or are wasting storage space.

Notice that no size is shown for the Co. No. field, because Paradox automatically assigns the size of Number fields.

Although Notes, a Memo field, can contain virtually any number of characters, you still have to assign a size to it. Assigning a size of 25 characters will allow you to see the first 25 characters of information in the field when you display it as a table. This does not limit the actual number of characters you can place in the field.

MINIMIZING DATA ENTRY ERRORS

When creating a table structure, you can take several steps to minimize errors in the data that will be entered:

- Make a field *required*. Paradox will not accept a record unless data is provided for every field that has the Required property.

- Provide *maximum and minimum values*. Paradox will not accept a record if data entered into a field is outside these values.

- Provide *default data*. Paradox automatically enters the default data into every record unless other data is entered.

- Provide a format, known as a *picture*, for the data. This ensures a consistent format for each record.

- Make use of *referential integrity*. Paradox will only accept data into a field if that data already exists in another table.

You do not necessarily have to choose these properties at the time you create a table structure. You can subsequently modify a table's structure by changing its properties.

You will see how you can use these properties as you progress through this book.

GETTING TO WORK WITH PARADOX

Now you have a general idea about where we are going, so let's start working with Paradox.

USING THE MOUSE

Like most Windows applications, Paradox is intended to be controlled by a mouse. Although you can use the keyboard for most, but not all, Paradox tasks, most people find it is faster and easier to work with the mouse.

Most Paradox operations are selected by pressing the left mouse button. Throughout the rest of this book, references to the mouse button mean the left button unless the right button is specifically mentioned.

The *cursor*, or *mouse pointer*, moves around the screen as you move your mouse. Most of the time the cursor is an arrow pointing up and to the left, as shown in Figure 1.2. At other times, the cursor changes shape to indicate what it is ready to do. As you work with Paradox, you use the cursor to select objects already on the screen, to place new objects, and to activate Paradox functions.

This book frequently asks you to *click* an object on the screen. This means that you should move the cursor onto the object and then quickly press and release the left button once. The term *right-click* means that you should point onto the object and then quickly press and release the right mouse button once.

To *double-click* an object is to place the cursor on the object and quickly click the left mouse button twice.

To move an object on the screen, you place the cursor on that object, press and hold down the mouse button, move the mouse to drag the object to a new position, then release the mouse button. This book uses the common shorthand term *drag* to describe the entire operation.

OPENING PARADOX

Paradox must be installed before you can use it. If you have not already installed Paradox, see the appendix for a brief summary of the procedure.

> *If your computer is part of a network, and several users have access to the same Paradox files, you must install the DOS command SHARE before you open Windows.*

Take the following steps to start Paradox:

1. Start Windows and display the Program Manager window.

2. Double-click the Paradox for Windows program group icon. (If you don't see this icon, it means the program has not been installed, or it has been installed in a different program group.)

3. In the Paradox for Windows group window, double-click the icon labeled Paradox for Windows.

After a few seconds you will see an information box that tells you Paradox is being loaded. After several more seconds, your screen will show the *Paradox Desktop*, shown in Figure 1.2. This is where you start.

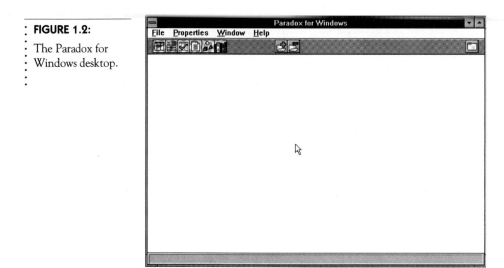

FIGURE 1.2:

The Paradox for Windows desktop.

THE PARADOX DESKTOP

When you first see the Paradox Desktop window, it is almost empty. It consists of the following components.

TITLE BAR

The *title bar* at the top of the screen is similar to those in most Windows applications. It contains the name of the application in the center, the Control-menu box at the left, and the Minimize and Maximize buttons at the right.

MENU BAR

The second line of the Paradox window is the *menu bar*, which initially offers File, Properties, Window, and Help. As you work with Paradox, additional menu titles become available. Click on any menu item to open a list of commands. For example, if you click on File you will see the drop-down menu shown in Figure 1.3. Notice that some items are dimmed. This means that the items are not available, because they are not relevant to the current situation.

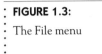

FIGURE 1.3:

The File menu

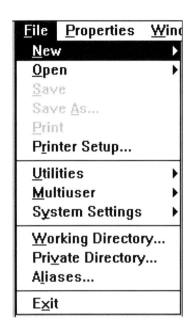

Refer to Part II for detailed information about the File and other menus.

After you have taken a look at the File menu, point to any unoccupied part of the screen and click to make the menu disappear.

If you click on Help in the menu bar, you'll see a Help menu similar to that in many other Windows applications. See "Getting Help" below for more information about Help.

SPEEDBAR

The *Speedbar*, the line below the menu bar, contains buttons that represent frequently used tasks. As you move the mouse to point onto a button in the Speedbar, the Status bar at the bottom of the screen tells you what task the button represents.

The buttons in the Speedbar vary according to the current Paradox status. Each window has a different set of Speedbar buttons.

You'll use many of these buttons in the lessons that follow. The first time a button is mentioned in the text, you'll see it in the margin.

You may not always want the Speedbar to be across the top of your screen. To change its shape and position:

1. Click Properties in the Menu bar. A single-item menu containing Desktop appears.

2. Click Desktop. The Desktop Properties dialog box (Figure 1.4) appears.

In this book, steps are presented as follows: Choose Properties ➤ Desktop, which means "Choose Desktop from the Properties menu."

You can use the Desktop Properties dialog box to change what appears in the title bar, to choose a background pattern for your screen, or to change the shape and position of the Speedbar.

FIGURE 1.4:

The Desktop Properties dialog box

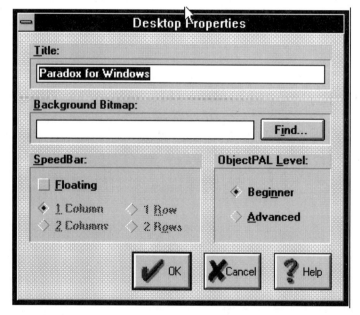

To change the appearance of the Speedbar:

1. Click the Floating button. A check mark appears, and four choices become available.

2. Click one of the four buttons to choose between one or two columns, or one or two rows.

3. Click OK. The Desktop reappears with the Speedbar in the new format.

4. Point onto the white rectangle at the top right of the Speedbar, then drag the Speedbar to where you want it on the screen.

 To restore the Speedbar to its original position and shape, Choose Properties ➤ Desktop and click the Floating button.

WORKSPACE

The remainder of the screen, apart from the bottom line, is the *Workspace* where you work with your database.

STATUS BAR

The *status bar* at the bottom of the screen provides information about the current status of Paradox. The Status Window at the left shows current information such as the name of a Speedbar button, and which record of a table is being accessed. Three smaller mode windows at the right provide information about current modes. From time to time, the remaining lessons in this book will draw your attention to information in the status bar.

GETTING HELP

Paradox has an extensive Help system you can refer to while working. Each dialog box has a Help button you can click to get information about the various parts of the box. To get more general help, press F1 or choose Help ➤ Contents to display a Table of Contents.

CLOSING PARADOX

Use any of the following methods to close Paradox:

- ◆ Choose File ➤ Exit.
- ◆ Click the Control-menu box, then choose Close.
- ◆ Double-click the Control-menu box.
- ◆ Press Alt+F4.

Alt+F4 means that you should press and hold down the Alt key while you tap the F4 key. This convention is used throughout this book.

FOR MORE INFORMATION

You will find more information about the following related topics in Part II.

Desktop

Fields in a Document

Fields in a Table

Help

Password Protection

Queries

Reports

Tables

CREATING A DATABASE TABLE

After reading Lesson 1, you are familiar with basic Paradox terminology and have a plan for a multitable database. In this lesson, you will create one of the tables and enter some records into it.

USING WORKING
AND PRIVATE DIRECTORIES

The Paradox installation procedure automatically creates two directories named WORKING and PRIVATE on your hard disk. Unless you specify otherwise, all the database and associated files you create while you are working with Paradox are written into the WORKING directory.

It is a good idea to create a separate working directory for each Paradox project, so we will create a directory named SWLIST and use that instead of the default for our files.

Paradox creates temporary files when it performs certain tasks. Unless you choose otherwise all these files are written into the PRIVATE directory. This is no problem in a single-user environment. In a multiuser environment, however, each user should have a separate directory that Paradox can use for temporary files.

CREATING DIRECTORIES

You have to create working and private directories under DOS or Windows because you cannot create directories from within Paradox. The following procedure for creating a new subdirectory using the Windows File Manager assumes you have installed Paradox for Windows in a directory named PDOXWIN on your C drive.

1. With Windows running, open File Manager.
2. Scroll until you find the PDOXWIN directory.
3. Click PDOXWIN.
4. Choose File ➤ Create Directory. The Create Directory dialog box appears.
5. Type SWLIST as the name for the new directory, which will be your working directory for this book's examples.
6. Click OK. The File Manager window shows the new directory under PDOXWIN.
7. Choose File ➤ Exit to close File Manager.

Follow the same steps to create a private directory. You can use SYBEX or your last name (abbreviated to eight letters, if necessary) as its directory name.

DESIGNATING PRIVATE AND WORKING DIRECTORIES

Now you need to designate your new directories as private and working.

1. Open Paradox.
2. Choose File ➤ Private Directory. The Private Directory dialog box appears.
3. Replace the existing Private Directory name with, e.g., C:\PDOX-WIN\SYBEX, then click OK.
4. Choose File ➤ Working Directory. The Set Working Directory dialog box appears.
5. Replace the existing Working Directory name with C:\PDOX-WIN\SWLIST, then click OK.

Paradox remembers the names of your private and working directories, so you do not need to repeat these steps each time you start the program.

TIP

The Set Working Directory dialog box also lets you designate aliases. An alias is an alternative file name. Paradox automatically provides PRIV as an alias for the full path name of your private directory—C:\PDOXWIN\SYBEX, and WORK as an alias for the full path name of your current working directory. Aliases start and end with a colon. To select your working directory by its alias rather than its full path, you simply type **:WORK:**. *You will see these alias names on the screen from time to time as you work with Paradox. You can provide additional aliases for file names if you wish, to save yourself a lot of typing, particularly if you have complex directory structures. See Aliases in Part II for information.*

CREATING A TABLE

Creating a table structure involves naming fields and specifying their type, size (where required), and various optional properties for individual fields.

Let's get started creating the Company table.

CREATING A NEW TABLE

The first step in creating a new table is to open the Create Paradox Table dialog box. With the Paradox Desktop displayed:

1. Choose File ➤ New. A pop-up menu of object types appears, as shown in Figure 2.1.

2. Click Table in the list of object types. The Table Type dialog box appears.

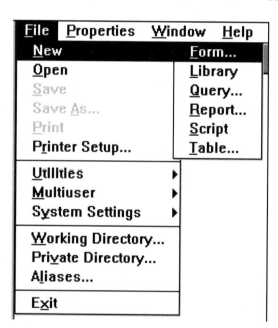

The Table Type dialog box lets you specify the database format you want to use (Paradox for Windows, DOS Paradox, dBASE, and so on). In this book, we are only concerned with the native Paradox for Windows format, which is the default suggestion in the dialog box, so:

3. Click OK. The Create Paradox for Windows Table dialog box, shown in Figure 2.2, appears.

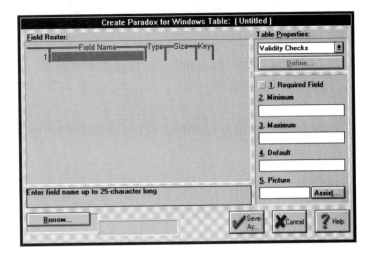

FIGURE 2.2:

The Create Paradox for Windows Table dialog box.

Now you are ready to start creating a table structure.

CREATING A TABLE STRUCTURE

In the Field Roster area of this dialog box, you provide names for fields and assign their types and sizes.

The unnamed column at the left, initially containing the number 1, automatically numbers fields in order.

The second column is where you enter field names. Notice that this field is initially highlighted, and that the information box near the bottom of the dialog box tells you to *Enter a field name up to 25 characters long*. The information box guides you as you create a table structure.

The third column is where you define field type, and the fourth is where you define field size. For the present, let's ignore the Key column.

Do the following to start creating the Company table structure:

1. Type **Co. No.** The characters appear in the first row of the Field Name column as you type them. If you make a typing mistake, press Backspace to delete one character at a time, then retype the correct characters.

2. When the field name is correct, press Tab or ↵. The highlight moves to the Type column.

3. Press the spacebar (or right-click the highlighted area). A list of field types appears.

4. Click Number to designate this field's type. An N appears in the Type column.

The first letter of each field type is underlined in the displayed list of types. Instead of using Steps 3 and 4, you can just type the appropriate single character, such as N for number, to assign a type to the current field. An uppercase character is displayed whether you type it as uppercase or lowercase.

5. Press Tab. The highlight skips over the Size column to the Key column because Paradox automatically assigns a size to Number fields.

6. Ignore the Key column for the present. Press Tab and a new, blank line appears in the Field Roster.

Use the same method to create the remaining fields (refer to the completed table shown in Figure 2.3 for field names, types, and sizes to use). Notice that when you press Tab after selecting an Alphanumeric field, the highlight moves to the Size column because you must assign a size to Alphanumeric fields. Also, when you press Tab after assigning a field size, the highlight moves immediately to the Field Name column for the next field. You will see why this happens when we look at key fields later in this lesson.

FIGURE 2.3:

Completed Field Roster for the Company table.

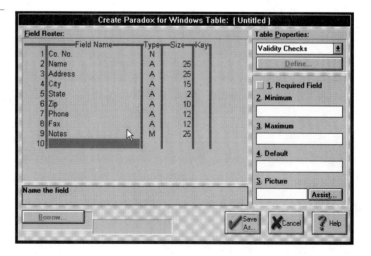

Saving the Table Structure

To save the table structure you have just completed:

1. Click Save As at the bottom of the dialog box. The Save Table As dialog box appears, as shown in Figure 2.4. Notice the flashing insertion point in the New Table Name text box.

2. Type **COMPANY** as the table name, then click OK. The file is saved under the name COMPANY.DB in your working directory, and the screen clears to the Paradox desktop.

CHANGING A TABLE'S STRUCTURE

You can change the structure of a table at any time. When a table contains data, however, some changes to its structure, such as deleting a field or reducing its size, may cause data to be lost. Paradox warns you if this is about to happen.

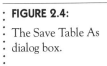

FIGURE 2.4:
The Save Table As dialog box.

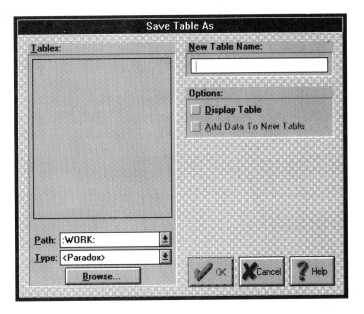

DELETING A FIELD

To illustrate how we can change the structure of a table, we will temporarily delete the Fax field:

1. Starting at the Paradox desktop, choose File ➤ Utilities. The pop-up menu shown in Figure 2.5 appears.

2. Click Restructure in the pop-up menu. The Select File dialog box appears.

3. Click the appropriate table (COMPANY.DB in this case) and click OK. The Restructure Paradox for Windows Table dialog box appears. Apart from the title, this box is identical to the Create Paradox for Windows Table dialog box you used previously.

4. To delete a field, point to its number in the left column of the Field Roster and click. The field number becomes highlighted.

FIGURE 2.5:

The Table Utilities pop-up menu.

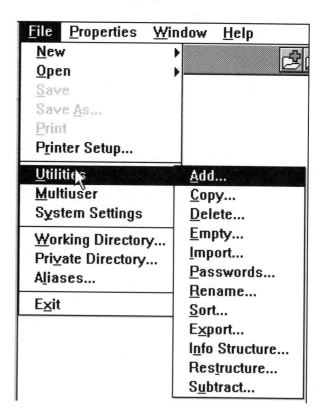

5. Press Ctrl+Delete. The field disappears from the roster and the Notes field is renumbered.

6. Click Save to save the structure with the same name as it had before. Because you have deleted a field, a Restructure Warning dialog box appears, asking you to confirm that you want to save the structure with the field deleted.

7. In this exercise, click Cancel because you do not want to change the table structure permanently. Normally you'll choose OK.

8. Click Cancel to leave the Restructure dialog box.

INSERTING A FIELD

Follow these steps to insert a field in the Company table.

1. Choose File ➤ Utilities ➤ Restructure. The Select File dialog box appears.

2. Double-click COMPANY.DB. The Restructure dialog box appears, with the structure of COMPANY.DB displayed.

3. Click the number of the field above which you want to insert the new field.

4. Press Insert. An empty row appears in the Field Roster with the Field Name position highlighted.

5. Define the new field in the same way as when you created the structure.

6. In this exercise, click Cancel because you do not want to keep the table with an added field. Normally, you'll choose Save.

CHANGING THE ORDER OF FIELDS

You can easily change the order of fields in a table's roster. To see how this works, we will reverse the order of the Phone and Fax fields in the Company table.

Close the Company table if it is open on your screen, and then display its structure in the Restructure dialog box.

1. With the Restructure dialog box on screen, point onto the desired field number (in this example, 8, the Fax field) in the left column.

2. Press and hold down the mouse button. The cursor changes to a double-headed arrow and two horizontal gray lines mark the selected field.

3. Drag the cursor over the field number position where you want the selected field to be (in this case, 7).

4. Release the mouse button. The roster now has the fields in the new order. Fax is field 7 and Phone is field 8.

5. Click Cancel at the bottom of the dialog box because in this example you do not want to save the change.

Changing a Field Name, Type, or Size

When there is no data in a table, you can freely change field names, types, and sizes. If a table contains data that could be erased by a change, Paradox will warn you.
To change the name of a field (for example, ZIP to ZIP Code):

1. With the Restructure dialog box on screen, click the desired field name (in this example, ZIP). The field becomes highlighted.

2. Begin typing the new entry (ZIP Code). As soon as you type the first character, the original field name disappears and is replaced by what you type.

TIP

Instead of typing a complete field name, you can edit an existing one. To do this, click to highlight the field name. Then point to the place within the name where you want to edit and click again. Now you can use normal editing techniques to delete and insert characters.

You can change field types and sizes in the same way.
If you have made changes to the table structure, click Cancel to leave the Restructure dialog box without saving your changes.

ADDING PROPERTIES TO FIELDS

Lesson 1 gave a brief preview of how assigning properties to fields can minimize data entry errors. You can assign properties when you first create a table structure or at any later time. Here we'll use the Restructure dialog box to make the Name field required, define a default value for the State field, and assign a picture to the ZIP field.

MAKING A FIELD REQUIRED

There are some fields for which data should be provided in every record. In the Company database, for example, there should be a name in every Name field. To make this field required:

1. In the Restructure dialog box, click anywhere within the definition of the Name field so that a part of the definition is highlighted.
2. In the Table Properties section of the dialog box, click the Required Field box. A check mark appears in the check box.

When you enter data into the table, you will see the effect of making this field required. Paradox will not accept a record unless data is provided for every required field.

DEFINING A DEFAULT VALUE FOR A FIELD

If you define a default value for a field, Paradox will automatically put that value into every record unless you enter a different value. If most of the companies from whom you buy software are in California, for example, giving the State field a default value of CA will save typing and reduce the chance of errors. Here's how:

1. In the Restructure dialog box, click anywhere within the definition of the State field.
2. In the Table Properties section of the dialog box, click the Default text box. A flashing insertion point appears in the text box.
3. Type **CA**.

Now the State field has a default value.

DEFINING A PICTURE FOR A FIELD

A picture is a pattern of characters that define a format. Assigning a picture to a field can simplify data entry in two ways. The picture restricts the type of data you can enter into a field, and it can also automatically enter certain characters into the field or change capitalization. Paradox offers a set of predefined pictures you can select; you can also define your own pictures. (The Pictures entry in Part II lists the special characters you can use and shows how to define a picture.)

In the Company table, we want to make sure that entries in the ZIP Code field consist of either five numeric digits or nine digits, with the last four preceded by a hyphen. Paradox has defined a picture for just that purpose, so we will select it in this exercise.

1. In the Restructure dialog box, click anywhere within the definition of the ZIP field.

2. If you know how to define pictures, you can click the Picture text box, and then type the picture. For this exercise, click Assist. You'll see the Picture Assistance dialog box, shown in Figure 2.6.

3. Open the Sample Pictures list box. A list of sample pictures appears.

4. Click the sample *5{#}[-*4{#}]. This is the picture for a five- or nine-digit ZIP code, as indicated in the center of the dialog box.

5. Click Use. The picture appears in the Picture text box.

6. Click Verify Syntax. The message *The picture is correct* appears.

7. Click OK. The Restructure dialog box appears with the ZIP field highlighted and the Picture text box showing the picture you selected.

8. Click Save to save the changes you have made. For each change, a dialog box asks whether to enforce the new properties on data already in the table.

9. Click OK.

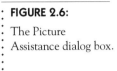

USING KEY FIELDS

The Key column in the Field Roster is used to identify one or more fields as a *key*. A table's key field controls the order in which records are stored on disk, prevents duplication of records, and links tables together. The key field is sometimes known as a *primary index* field; you can also designate *secondary index* fields for sorting and linking.

RULES FOR KEY FIELDS

Each table may have only one key, and its value must be different in every record. You can, however, combine two or more fields to form a *composite* key. In that case, only the combined value has to be unique.

A single key must be the first field in a roster, and the fields for a composite key must be consecutive, beginning with the first field.

Because the value in a key field must be different for every record, only one record in a table with a single key field can have an empty key field. For a table with a composite key, any of the key fields can be empty in any record, as long as the composite value of all the key fields is different for every record.

To ensure uniqueness, a key field should normally contain ID numbers or codes rather than data. That's one reason we assign numbers to companies in our software database and use Co. No. as the key field.

DESIGNATING A KEY FIELD

The Co. No. field in the Company table was created for the sole purpose of being a key field, and it is already at the top of the Field Roster. To make this field a key, return to the Restructure dialog box and take the following steps:

1. In the Key column of the Field Roster, point into the Co. No. row and click. A highlight appears in that position.

2. Either double-click or press any key. An asterisk appears in the Key column, indicating that the field is now a key field.

If you decide not to have a key field, just repeat the two steps above to remove the asterisk.

CONTROLLING RECORD DISPLAY ORDER WITH SECONDARY INDEXES

Unless you choose differently, Paradox displays records in key order. To display records in a different order, you can designate almost any field as a secondary index and use that field to control the display order. You can designate two or more fields as secondary indexes to display your data in several different orders.

Secondary indexes serve another very important purpose. They allow you to use any fields, not just key fields, for linking tables. (You'll learn how to link tables in Lesson 4.)

Let's use the Company table as an example of creating secondary indexes. Without a secondary index, this table is always displayed in the order controlled by the Co. No. field. We also want to be able to display the table in alphabetical order of company names.

Paradox requires that a table have a key before any field can be used as a secondary index. The Company table already has a key field, so we can proceed as follows:

1. With the Restructure dialog box displaying the structure of the Company table, open the Table Properties list box by clicking the arrow next to Validity Checks.

2. Click Secondary Indexes.

3. Click Define. You'll see the Define Secondary Index dialog box, shown in Figure 2.7. The Fields box shows all the fields in the table. Notes is dimmed because it is a Memo field and cannot be used as a secondary index.

4. In the Fields list, click the field you want for a secondary index (in this case, Name).

5. Click the arrow pointing from the Fields list to the Indexed Fields list. Name is copied into the Indexed Fields list.

6. Click OK. The Save Index As dialog box appears.

7. Type a name, such as **Name Order**, and then click OK. The Restructure dialog box reappears with Name Order listed as a secondary index.

8. Click Save to save the new structure.

Later in this lesson, you'll use the secondary index to display the records alphabetically by company name.

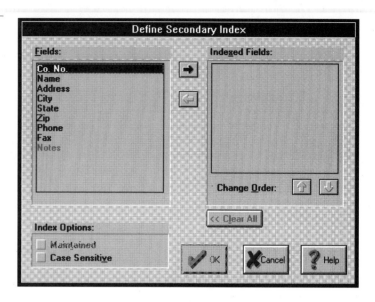

If you see the error message invalid restructure operation when you try to save the restructured table, you have not followed the rules correctly. This message occurs, for example, if you designate a secondary index for a table that does not have a key.

PRINTING A STRUCTURE

Whenever you close a structure after creating, viewing, or restructuring it, Paradox saves it as a table with the name STRUCT.DB in your Private subdirectory. It's a good idea to make a printed copy of every table structure for convenient reference. Here's how to open the STRUCT.DB table and print it.

1. From the Paradox desktop, choose File ➤ Open ➤ Table. The Open a Table dialog box appears, showing the table names COMPANY.DB and :PRIV:STRUCT.DB.

2. Double-click :PRIV:STRUCT.DB. A Table window opens, showing the structure of the most recent table you worked with, in this case the Company table, as shown in Figure 2.8. As you can see, there is one record for each field in the original table, and one field for each column of the Field

FIGURE 2.8:

The Table window showing part of a STRUCT.DB file.

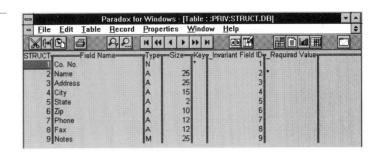

Roster. The table also shows any properties you have assigned to fields. Scroll to the right and notice, for example, that the Name field is marked as required, the State field has a default value, and the Zip field has a picture.

3. Choose File ➤ Printer Setup. The Printer Setup dialog box appears.

4. Make whatever changes are necessary to your printer setup. You will probably want to select Landscape orientation.

5. Click OK to save the printer setup.

6. Choose File ➤ Print. The Print File dialog box appears.

7. In the Overflow Handling section of the dialog box, click the Create Horizontal Overflow Page button so the entire contents of the table are printed.

8. Click OK. An information box appears to tell you Paradox is preparing a report. After a short delay, the table is printed.

Take a few moments to examine the printed copy of the structure, which occupies four pages. You will see that each field is listed, showing:

- field name

- field type

- field size, where appropriate

- whether it is a key field

- whether a value is required

- any minimum value

- any maximum value
- any default value
- any picture
- any table lookup
- any table lookup type

With the exception of table lookup, covered in Lesson 4, we have already discussed all of these field attributes.

ENTERING DATA INTO A TABLE

There are three ways to enter data into a table:

- by displaying the table and typing data into each field
- by displaying a data entry form and typing data into each field
- by importing data from an existing file

We will use the first two methods to enter some data into the Company table in this lesson. See Exporting and Importing Data in Part II for the third method.

ENTERING DATA DIRECTLY INTO A TABLE

Starting with the Paradox desktop:

1. Choose File ➤ Open ➤ Table. The Open a Table dialog box appears.
2. Double-click COMPANY.DB to open that table. The table appears in a fairly small window.
3. Click the Maximize button in the Paradox for Windows title bar so that Paradox occupies the entire screen.
4. Click the Maximize button in the Table:COMPANY.DB title bar, so that it occupies as much of the screen as possible.

When you first open a table, it is in View mode, in which you can look at data but cannot enter or edit it. To enter data or make any changes to existing data, you must select the Edit mode.

5. Choose Table ➤ Edit Data. The word *edit* appears in the mode section of the Status bar. The record number of the first record is highlighted. Press Tab to highlight the first field (Co. No.).

6. Type **1** and press Tab. The highlight moves to the Name column, and the number in the Co. No. column changes to 1.00 because the default format for number fields is to show two decimal places. You will change the number format later in this lesson.

7. Proceed to enter the following values in the record. After you complete each field, press Tab or ↵ to move to the next. Notice that you do not have to enter a value in the State field because you previously provided a default value for that field. If you make a mistake while you are typing, use the backspace key to erase characters, and then retype.

FIELD	VALUE
Name	Strong Software
Address	126 East Street
City	Ansel
State	CA
ZIP	93784
Phone	510-824-5355
Fax	510-822-3745

8. Try to type something into the memo field. A message in the status bar tells you to press Shift+F2.

9. Press Shift+F2. Now you have almost the whole screen to type the notes. Type the text shown in Figure 2.9. Press Shift+F2 again to return to Edit mode. Notice that you see the first few words of the Notes field.

10. Press Tab to complete the first record. Now Paradox is ready for you to type another record.

If you attempt to enter data that is incompatible with a field's type, the computer beeps and the Status bar displays the message Illegal Character. *This happens, for example, if you try to enter an alphabetic character into Co. No., a Number field. Once you highlight a required field you cannot leave that field until you have entered some data into it.*

DISADVANTAGES OF ENTERING RECORDS DIRECTLY

As you have seen, it is somewhat inconvenient to enter values directly into a table because:

- ◆ you cannot see all the fields in a record at one time;
- ◆ it is impractical to enter values in any other sequence than the order in which fields appear in the table;
- ◆ if you want to use a Memo-type field, you have to keep switching into and out of memo view.

For these reasons, we will not enter more records directly into the table. Instead we will use a data entry *form*.

ENTERING DATA INTO A FORM

Paradox automatically provides a Quick Form that we can use for data entry. We can also create a custom form. In this lesson you'll use the default Quick Form. You'll learn about custom forms in Lesson 3.

One of the following steps gives you the option of clicking a Speedbar button. Now is a good time to get into the habit of pointing at buttons and looking at the Status bar to see what they do.

To display a Quick Form:

1. If the Status bar shows that you're in Edit mode, choose Table ➤ End Edit.

2. Choose Table ➤ Quick Form. Alternatively, press F7 or click the Quick Form Speedbar button. A Quick Form window appears on the screen with a record displayed, as shown in Figure 2.9. The status bar shows the name of the table, the number of records, and which of them is currently displayed in the form.

3. If the Quick Form is not large enough to display the entire record, use standard Windows methods to enlarge it. Notice that there is much more space to display what is in the Notes field than there was when the table was displayed.

Notice that the menu bar and Speedbar change when you switch from a Table window to a Form window.

So far, you have used a Quick Form to display a record. Now you will use it to enter additional records.

1. Choose Form ➤ Edit Data to enable editing. Alternatively, press F9 or click the Edit Data Speedbar button. *Edit* in the status bar tells you that editing is enabled. Also, the form's title bar now contains the words *Data Entry*.

FIGURE 2.9:

Quick Form displaying an entire record.

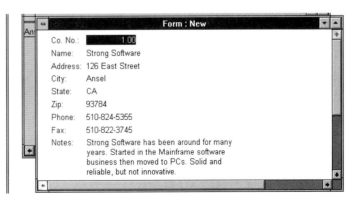

2. Press Page Down. The form now shows the field names and the status bar indicates *Empty record*.

3. Add data for this record and subsequent records, using the values shown in Table 2.1 and giving consecutive numbers to the records in the Co. No. field. Press Tab or ↵ to proceed from one field to another. When you have completed each record, press Page Down to display the next empty record. Type some comments into the notes field for some of the records. You do not have to press Shift+F2 before you can enter data into the Notes field when you are using a form.

4. After you have completed all ten records, turn off Edit mode.

5. Choose Form ➤ Table View. Alternatively, press F7 or click the Table View Speedbar button. All the records you typed are in the table.

TABLE 2.1: Values for the Company Table

NAME	ADDRESS	CITY	STATE	ZIP	PHONE	FAX
Strong Software	126 East Street	Ansel	CA	93784	510-824-5355	510-822-3745
Best Systems, Inc.	895 Better Blvd.	Goodtown	OR	98765	503-988-1211	503-988-8675
Lookyer Company	897 Optimist Avenue	Goldtown	CA	95743	805-593-6655	805-594-8953
Success, Inc.	59 Down Avenue	Uptown	CA	91254	609-543-5944	609-543-1696
Letdoit	41156 Enterprise Drive	Bigcity	MA	09876	617-894-7788	617-894-6796
Winning Company	7 Aldes Street	Oldtown	WI	53564	414-892-8888	414-892-7438

TABLE 2.1: Values for the Company Table (continued)

NAME	ADDRESS	CITY	STATE	ZIP	PHONE	FAX
Checksright Company	999 Chapter Street #11	Snowtown	WA	99876	206-495-1234	206-496-8235
Bugfree Software, Inc.	1565 Spider Street	Anytown	ME	04295	207-653-1122	207-653-7482
CanDoItAll	1199 Wantobe Lane	Easytown	CA	96423	510-945-1244	510-945-8921
Browning Company	4440 Main Street	Wayne	LA	71277	318-894-7272	318-894-7649

EDITING DATA IN A RECORD

You have already seen that you can correct a data entry error by using Backspace to delete characters, but you can only do this before you move to the next field. After leaving a field, you must switch to Edit mode to make corrections. You can either replace the entire value or change individual characters.

To try out both methods using the Company table, you can change Strong Software to String Software and then reverse the change.

REPLACING THE VALUE IN A FIELD

Take the following steps to replace the value in a field:

1. Check the status bar to make sure Edit mode is selected. If it is not, choose Table ➤ Edit Data.

2. Click the field you need to correct (in this example, Name in the first record).

3. Begin typing. Your new entry (*String Software*) replaces the old contents (*Strong Software*).

4. Press ↓ to accept the new name.

EDITING THE VALUE IN A FIELD

Take the following steps to edit within a field value (in this example, changing *String* back to *Strong*).

1. Make sure Edit mode is selected.

2. Select the field to be corrected (Name).

3. Click exactly where you need to edit (between *i* and *n*), then move the cursor away. A flashing vertical bar, an insertion marker, appears where you clicked. Also, the word *Field* appears at the right end of the status bar to indicate that Paradox is ready for you to edit a field.

4. Insert or delete characters as needed. (Here, delete the *i* and insert an *o*.)

5. Press ↓ to accept the change and move to the next record. The word *Field* disappears from the status bar, indicating that you are no longer editing a field.

CHANGING A VALUE'S PROPERTIES

Everything you work with in Paradox is known as an *object*. For example, tables, fields, and values are all different kinds of objects. Each type of object has certain characteristics, known as *properties*.

The properties of the value in a field include such things as:

- horizontal and vertical position within the field,

- background and character colors,

- typeface,

- type size,

- type style,

- number format (Number fields).

Paradox uses a set of default properties unless you choose otherwise. For example, the values you enter into a Number field appear in a table with two decimal places. You saw this when you typed 1 into the Co. No. field and it was displayed on your screen as 1.00.

> *The default number format is provided by Windows. If someone has changed the Windows number format on your computer, the default Paradox number format will be something different from two decimal places.*

Let's see how we can change some properties.

CHANGING THE FORMAT OF A NUMBER FIELD

To change any object's properties, you click on the object with the right mouse button, choose the properties you want to change, and make the necessary changes. To change the format of numbers in the Co. No. field, for example, do the following:

1. Point onto the Co. No. value of 1.00 in the first record and right-click. The Properties pop-up menu for the field appears, as shown in Figure 2.10.

2. In the Properties menu, point onto Number Format and left-click. A list of available number formats appears with a check mark beside the current format, as shown in Figure 2.11.

FIGURE 2.10:

The Properties menu for a number field.

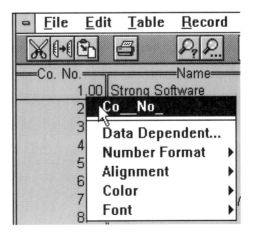

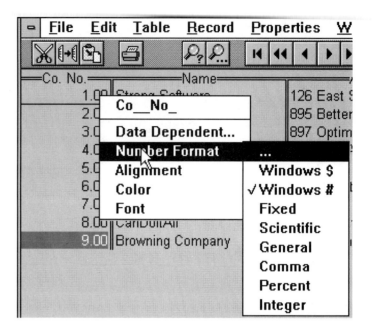

3. Click Integer. The pop-up menus disappear and the number in the Co. No. field changes to an integer value (a number without any decimals).

After you have changed the format of a field value in one record, Paradox applies that format to the same field in all other records.

CHANGING THE ALIGNMENT OF A FIELD

By default, Paradox aligns all values in Number fields at the right side of the field, and all values in Alphanumeric fields at the left. In both cases, it aligns values at the top of the field. If you wanted to align the two-letter state abbreviations in the center of the State field, for example, you would do the following:

1. Right-click CA in the State field to display the pop-up Properties menu.

2. Left-click Alignment in the pop-up menu. The list of possible alignments appears with those currently selected checked, as shown in Figure 2.12.

FIGURE 2.12:

The Alignment pop-up menu.

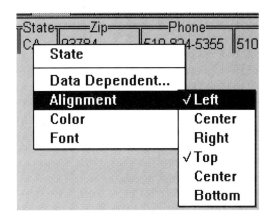

3. Left-click Center (between Left and Right). The pop-up menu disappears and CA in the State field moves to the center of the field.

DELETING A RECORD FROM A TABLE

You can delete a record from either a table or a form. As an example, you can delete the Letdoit record from the Company table.

1. With the Company table displayed, switch to Edit mode.

2. Select the Letdoit record by clicking any one of its fields.

3. Choose Record ➤ Delete. Alternatively, press Ctrl+Delete. The record disappears from the table.

After you have deleted the record, scroll to the extreme left and notice that Paradox has renumbered the records after the one you deleted.

SAVING FIELD VALUES

Paradox automatically saves the values you enter into a table, or the values you edit, whenever you move from one record to another, so you do not have to save a table. In fact, when you have a table window active, Save and Save As in the File menu are dimmed to show they are not available.

DISPLAYING RECORDS IN SECONDARY INDEX ORDER

Paradox normally displays records in the order determined by the key field, if there is one. Otherwise, records are displayed in the order they are added to a table. You can display records in the order determined by any other field by making that field a secondary index. Remember, though, that a table must have a key field before it can have secondary indexes.

DISPLAYING A TABLE IN A SECONDARY INDEX ORDER

We have already designated the Name field as a secondary index, so we can use this index to display the records in alphabetical order by company name.

1. Choose Table ➤ Order/Range. The Order/Range dialog box, shown in Figure 2.13, appears. The Index List list box shows the available indexes. Co. No. is highlighted as the field that currently controls the display order. The asterisk indicates that it is a key field. Name Order is included in the list because that is the name we gave to the secondary index based on the Name field.

2. Click Name Order and then OK. The table reappears with the records listed in alphabetical order of company names.

MOVING FROM ONE RECORD TO ANOTHER

In our work so far we have dealt with only a few records, so it has been relatively easy to move from one record to another. Real databases, though, usually have many records. Paradox provides several ways to move around large tables by clicking speedbar buttons or by pressing keyboard keys.

FIGURE 2.13:

The Order/Range dialog box.

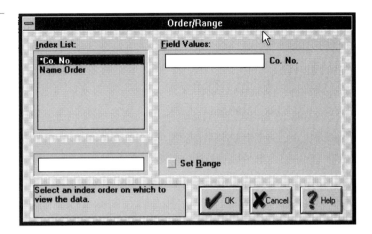

USING THE SPEEDBAR

The six navigation buttons in the center of the Speedbar displayed above a table, shown in Figure 2.14, allow you to move quickly from one record to another.

FIGURE 2.14:

Speedbar buttons used to move among records.

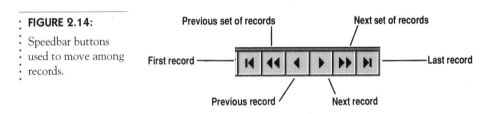

One set of records, in this context, consists of the records displayed in the current window, whatever its size.

USING THE KEYBOARD OR RECORD MENU

Refer to *Tables* in Part II for information about the keys and menu items you can use to move around a table.

FOR MORE INFORMATION

You will find more information about the topics covered in this lesson by referring to the following entries in Part II.

Directories

Fields in a Table

Forms

Help

Indexing

Tables

USING CUSTOM DATA ENTRY FORMS

INTRODUCING

Creating a custom form
Properties of a form
Selecting and arranging objects
Number formats
Formatting with graphics
Locating records
Folders

In Lesson 2, you created a table and then used a Quick Form to enter some more data into it. This experience showed that it is more convenient to enter data into a form than directly into a table. You will discover in this lesson how you can make data entry even more convenient by creating a custom data entry form.

CREATING A CUSTOM DATA ENTRY FORM

To demonstrate the tools Paradox provides for creating and using forms, this lesson's examples create a custom data entry form and use it to enter a new record into the Company table.

OPENING A NEW FORM

The first step is to open a new form that already contains the fields in the Company table.

1. From the Paradox desktop choose File ➤ New ➤ Form. A Data Model dialog box appears, as shown in Figure 3.1.

2. Click COMPANY.DB in the File Name list. A small box containing *company.db* appears in the right part of the dialog box. This brings the fields from the Company table into the new form.

3. Click OK. The Design Layout dialog box appears, as shown in Figure 3.2.

The Design Layout dialog box shows a proposed layout just like that in the Quick Form. The dialog box offers a number of choices about how fields should initially appear in the form. After looking at some of the possibilities, accept the default choices.

FIGURE 3.1:

The Data Model dialog box.

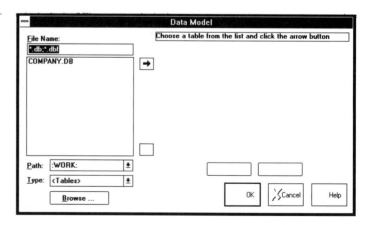

48

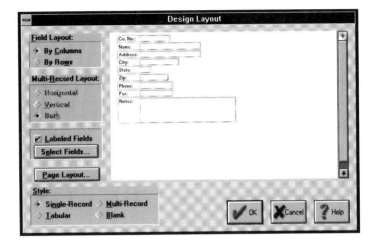

4. In the Style section of the dialog box, click Tabular and notice that the fields now appear as a table. Click Multi-Record to see a layout which has several records in one form. Click Blank to see a form with no records.

5. Click Single-Record to return to the default layout.

6. Click OK in the Design Layout dialog box. The Form Design window appears.

7. Maximize both the Paradox for Windows workspace and the Form Design window, as shown in Figure 3.3.

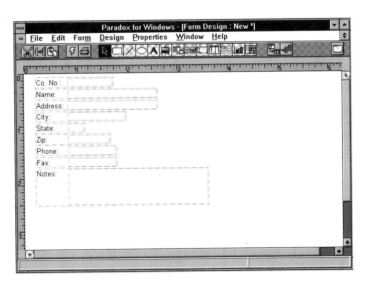

FIGURE 3.3:

The Form Design
window.

The Form Design window gives you the tools to design custom forms. The left side contains frames for each of the fields in the Company table. Each frame contains the field's label (its name), which is a text object, and an outline of the field object, which is where the field value is displayed. You can move each frame around on the form and change its appearance in many ways as you will soon see.

The Form Design window in the figure has optional horizontal and vertical rulers, to help position objects on the form. You will learn how to turn rulers on and off in a moment.

The Speedbar in Form Design contains several icons for placing objects on the form.

CUSTOMIZING THE FORM

You can do a lot to make the form attractive and easy to work with. The steps we are about to take will produce the form shown in Figure 3.4.

FIGURE 3.4:

A custom data input form.

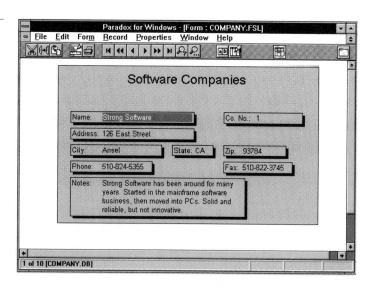

Selecting the Page Size
and Measurement Units

To select the page size and measurement units:

1. Choose Form ➤ Page ➤ Layout. The Page Layout dialog box appears, as shown in Figure 3.5.

2. If necessary, click the Screen button in the Design For section of the dialog box. The Screen Size section of the dialog box shows your screen size in pixels.

3. If necessary, click Inches in the Units section of the dialog box.

4. If necessary, click Landscape in the Orientation section of the dialog box.

5. Click OK. The Form Design window reappears.

FIGURE 3.5:

The Page Layout dialog box.

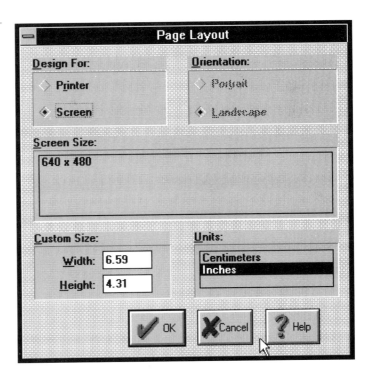

SELECTING PROPERTIES

In Paradox, properties control how an object behaves when you work with it and how it is shown on the screen or appears when printed.

Form design properties are controlled from the Properties menu, shown in Figure 3.6.

The bottom seven items in the Properties menu represent options you can turn on or off. When you click an option, the Properties menu disappears. The next time you open the menu, you see which options are currently on.

One property of the Form Design window is whether rulers are displayed.

Displaying Rulers The menu in Figure 3.6 has check marks by the side of Horizontal Ruler and Vertical Ruler. If the window on your screen does not have rulers, follow the steps below to turn them on.

1. Click Horizontal Ruler. The Properties menu disappears and the horizontal ruler is added to the Form Design window.

2. Choose Properties ➤ Vertical Ruler. The Properties menu disappears and the vertical ruler is added to the Form Design window.

FIGURE 3.6:

The Properties menu.

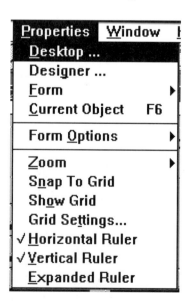

3. Choose Properties. The Properties menu appears with check marks by the side of Horizontal Ruler and Vertical Ruler.

Changing Magnification Now, take a look at Zoom in the Properties menu.

1. Click Zoom. The Zoom pop-up menu (shown in Figure 3.7) appears.

The Zoom pop-up menu allows you to reduce the size of the form so that you can see more of it, or increase its size to work more accurately on details.

2. Click 200%. The Form design window is enlarged.

3. Choose Properties ➤ Zoom ➤ 100% to go back to full size.

TIP

You can use Fit Width, Fit Height, or Best Fit commands in the Zoom menu to adjust the magnification so that you can see the entire width or entire height of a form, or the entire form.

FIGURE 3.7:

The Zoom pop-up menu.

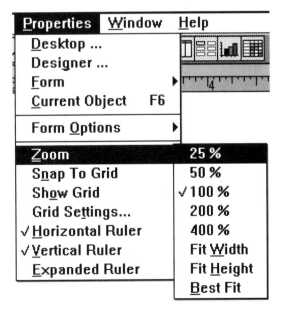

Showing the Grid Another way you can position objects accurately is to display a grid.

1. Choose Properties.

2. If the Show Grid option is unchecked, click it. If the check mark is already there, click an unoccupied part of the screen. In either case, the menu disappears and you see grid lines and dots in the Form Design window.

3. Choose Properties ➤ Grid Settings. The Grid Settings dialog box (shown in Figure 3.8) appears.

You can use the Grid settings dialog box to choose inches or centimeters as the measurement units for the rulers and the grid. You can also select the number of measurement units between the grid lines (the major division) and the spacing of grid dots between grid lines (the minor division). For the present, set the measurement units to inches with grid lines every inch and grid dots every 1/16 inch.

4. If necessary, open the Units list box and select Inches.

5. If necessary, click on the lower arrow in the Major Division text box until 1 appears.

6. If necessary, click on the appropriate arrow in the Minor Division text box until 16 appears.

7. Click OK. The Form Design window reappears.

: **FIGURE 3.8:**
: The Grid Settings
: dialog box.
:
:

8. Choose Properties. The menu reappears.

9. If there is no check mark by the side of Snap To Grid, click Snap To Grid. If a check mark is already there, point to an unoccupied part of the screen and click. In either case, the menu disappears.

TIP

Show Grid controls whether the grid appears on your screen or not. Snap To Grid, which works whether the grid is displayed or not, turns on a magnetic-like effect that pulls objects onto grid points. You'll see the advantage of using Snap to Grid when we move fields later in this lesson.

Saving Properties After you have chosen the properties you want, you can save them so that they will be available the next time you create a form.

1. Choose Properties ➤ Form Options. A pop-up menu appears.

2. Click Save Defaults.

USING FORM DESIGN TOOLS

The Speedbar for the Form Design window contains 13 buttons you can use when designing forms, as shown in Figure 3.9.

You will be using some of these buttons to place objects on your form.

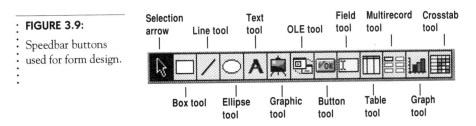

FIGURE 3.9:
Speedbar buttons used for form design.

WORKING WITH OBJECTS ON A FORM

Designing a form involves moving existing objects and placing new ones. To move an object, select it and then drag it to its new position. Selecting the correct object is important, so we will take a moment to understand how objects are selected.

OBJECTS WITHIN OBJECTS

The form we are dealing with is an object that consists of other objects. A form contains one or more pages, which are objects. A page, in turn, contains several fields, each consisting of a frame containing a label and a value. These are all objects, too. Figure 3.10 shows the structure of our form.

Paradox lets you display this structure on your screen as an *Object Tree*.

1. Press the Esc key. The rulers become completely blue, indicating that the entire form is selected. The right end of the Status bar, by *not* displaying the name of an object, confirms that the form itself has been selected. You may have to press Esc more than once.

2. Click the Object Tree button in the Speedbar. An Object Tree appears, as shown in Figure 3.11.

3. After you have looked at the Object Tree, remove it by double-clicking the Control-menu box in the Object Tree title bar.

It is important that you understand a form's structure when you select and move an object, and when you change an object's properties. Look at the City field in the Object Tree, for example. The field consists of a *text object* (the field name) and an *edit region* (the field value). To change a property of a field, you must select the entire field, not just one of the objects within it.

FIGURE 3.10:
The structure
of a form.

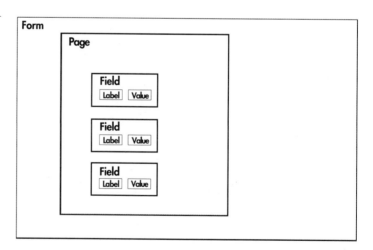

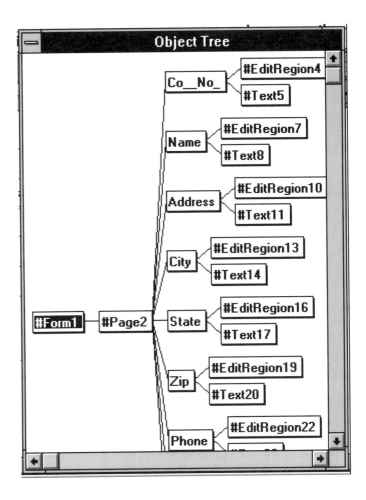

The Object Tree
representation of
a form.

SELECTING OBJECTS

In Paradox, as in other graphics applications, you select an object by pointing onto it and clicking. But because objects are nested within other objects, you need a way to select objects at any hierarchical level. Sometimes you'll need to select entire fields, and at other times select a field's label or value separately.

CONTROLLING THE WAY OBJECTS ARE SELECTED

Paradox uses the Select From Inside option to control object selection. By default, this option is off. To see the effect of this setting, first verify that it has not been changed:

- ◆ Choose Properties ➤ Designer to display the Designer Properties dialog box shown in Figure 3.12. Make sure the Select From Inside check box is cleared and the other three options are checked. Then click OK.

Back in the Form Design window, you can take the following steps to see how object selection works:

1. Click the value object within the Co. No. frame. Eight black squares (handles) appear around the field, showing that the entire field is selected. Red sections in the rulers show the size of the object. The Status bar shows that a field object is selected.

2. Click the value object again. Now the handles are around the value object within the field, and the Status bar indicates that an edit region is selected.

3. Click anywhere on the form outside a field object to deselect the value object. The Status bar shows that a page is selected, and the rulers become entirely red.

To see the alternative, return to the Designer Properties dialog box, put a check in the Select From Inside box, and select the Co. No. value object again. You'll see

FIGURE 3.12:
The Designer
Properties dialog box.

that only the value object is selected this time. Turn off Select From Inside before continuing with this lesson.

As you work with forms, you will sometimes find it difficult to select a particular object. Checking or unchecking Select From Inside will usually solve this problem.

SELECTING SEVERAL OBJECTS

Paradox offers two quick ways to select several objects at a time:

- ◆ **Shift-clicking:** Click the first object you want to select, hold down the Shift key, and click the other objects.

- ◆ **Outlining:** Holding down the Ctrl key, point above and to the left of the first object to select. Press the mouse button and drag to enclose all of your selection. Release first the mouse button and then the Ctrl key.

With several fields selected, you can deselect an individual field by holding down the Shift key and clicking that field.

As you work with Paradox, use whichever method of selecting multiple fields is convenient.

MOVING FIELDS ON A FORM

At present, the field frames are in a column at the left edge of the form. You can move the fields around to make the form easier to use. For example, it may be helpful to arrange the fields to match the way information is arranged on the paper forms often used in data entry. (Figure 3.4 could be printed out as such a form.)

First move all the fields down so that they are not in your way.

1. If the Selection Arrow in the Speedbar is not highlighted, click it.

2. Use the outline method to select all the fields on the form.

3. Point onto any field, then press and hold down the mouse button.

4. Drag down to move all the fields to the bottom of the screen.

5. Click anywhere outside a field to deselect the fields.

> *As you dragged the fields, you probably noticed that they moved in a jerky fashion. This is because Snap To Grid is on, and it forces the top-left corner of the moving object to grid points.*

Now, place the individual fields.

1. Point onto the Name field, press the mouse button and drag the field until its top-left corner is at the 1″ position on both rulers. With Snap to Grid on, you can easily place the field at an exact position.

2. Drag the Co. No. field so that its top-left corner is at 4″ on the horizontal ruler and 1″ on the vertical ruler.

3. Drag the remaining fields to the positions shown in Figure 3.13.

So far you have been looking at the Form Design, in which you adjust the positions of objects. Let's preview the form with actual data.

FIGURE 3.13:

Rearranged fields.

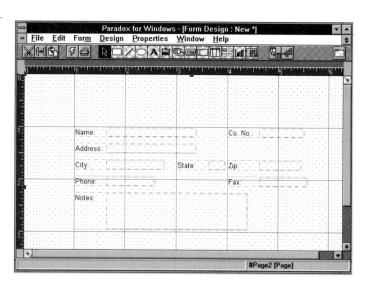

Viewing Data on a Form

To view data on the form, click the View Data button in the Speedbar. Figure 3.14 shows the form.

FIGURE 3.14:

Data displayed on the preliminary form.

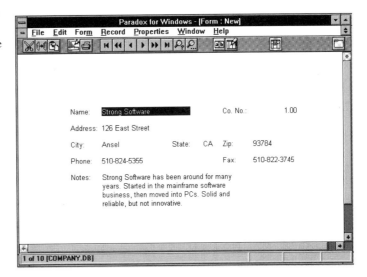

FIGURE 3.14:

Data displayed on the preliminary form.

As we continue with the design we will make several refinements. We will remove excessive space between labels and values, change the format of the company number, place boxes around each element and around the entire form, add color, and give the form a title.

First we will reduce the space in the ZIP field.

MOVING OBJECTS WITHIN A FIELD

To move objects within a field, you'll use the techniques you have just learned for selecting objects. In this case, we want to select the value object in the Zip field and move it to the left so that the ZIP code value is close to the label.

When we drag the value object to the left, we need to make sure that it remains horizontally aligned with the label. At present Snap To Grid is on. Because of this, as soon as we start to drag the object, it will move up or down to the nearest grid position. We don't want this to happen, so we could turn Snap To Grid off. But then we would need to have a very steady hand and sharp eye to move the object horizontally without allowing it to move vertically. The solution is to *pin* it vertically, as we shall now do.

PREVENTING VERTICAL MOVEMENT

Follow these steps to pin the Zip value object so that it cannot move vertically:

1. Click the Design button in the Speedbar to return to the Form Design window.

2. Click the value object within the Zip field twice, once to select the entire field, and again to select the value object. Handles around the object and a message in the status bar confirm that the correct object is selected.

3. Right-click the value object to inspect it. The properties pop-up menu appears.

4. Left-click Design in the pop-up. Another pop-up appears, as shown in Figure 3.15.

5. Click Pin Vertical to pin the object to its current vertical position. The pop-up menus disappear.

FIGURE 3.15:

A properties pop-up menu with Design selected.

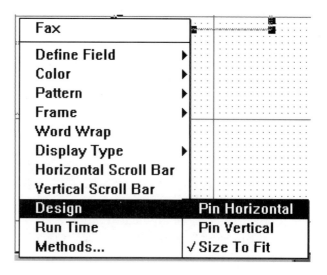

Now we can drag the object horizontally without any possibility that it will move vertically.

MOVING AN OBJECT WITHIN A FIELD

The value object with the Zip field is already selected so we can drag it closer to the label.

1. Point onto the value object within the Zip field then press and hold down the mouse button.

2. Drag to the left until the value object is about a quarter-inch from the label, then release the mouse button.

TIP *If objects become misaligned, you can select the objects and then choose Design ➤ Align to realign them.*

CHANGING NUMBER FORMAT AND ALIGNMENT

When you looked at data on the form, you saw that the company number was displayed with two decimal places. We already corrected this for the table, and we have to make the same correction for the form. Also, we need to reduce the space between the label and the number in the Co. No. field. This space occurs because number fields are aligned to the right by default.

1. Select the value object in the Co. No. field.

2. Right-click to inspect the object.

3. In the inspection pop-up menu, left-click Alignment.

4. In the alignment pop-up, left-click Left.

5. Inspect the object again.

6. Click Format, and then Number Format.

7. Click Integer.

When you return to View Data you will see that the company number is now left-aligned so that it is close to the label, and it is displayed without any decimal places.

SAVING A FORM

Save the form from time to time as you work with it.

1. With the form in Design mode, choose File ➤ Save. If you have not saved the form previously, the Save File As dialog box appears.

2. Type Company as the file name, then click OK. The file is saved as COMPANY.FSL.

CREATING BOXES AROUND OBJECTS

To make the form more attractive, let's place drop-shadow boxes around all the fields.

1. Use the outline method to select all the fields.

2. Right-click any field to inspect it. When two or more fields are selected and you inspect them, the inspection pop-up menu shows all the properties the selected fields have in common.

3. In the inspection pop-up menu, click Frame and then Style. The style menu (shown in Figure 3.16) appears.

4. Click the drop-shadow style, the third one from the bottom.

5. Click outside any field to deselect all fields.

Try applying other styles to the field to get a sense of your choices in creating a form.

ADDING A TITLE TO A FORM

Now we will use the Text tool to add a title to the form.

1. Click the Text tool in the Speedbar, then move the cursor onto the form. Notice that the cursor is now a cross with an A below it.

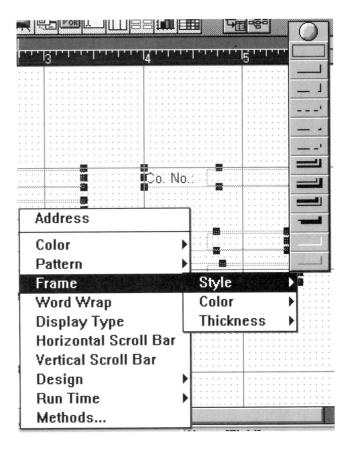

FIGURE 3.16:

A properties pop-up menu showing a choice of frame styles.

2. Place the center of the cross at 1″ on the horizontal cursor and at ¼″ on the vertical ruler.

3. Click and drag to 5-3/4″ on the horizontal ruler and 3/4″ on the vertical ruler, then release the mouse button. A rectangular text box appears with a flashing insertion marker.

4. Type **Software Companies**. The two words appear in the text box using the default font and alignment.

5. Click the Selection Arrow in the Speedbar.

6. Right-click the text to inspect it.

7. In the inspection pop-up menu, click Font and then Size. A list of available sizes is displayed, as shown in Figure 3.17.

8. Click 18 to select 18-point size. The title text appears in the larger size.

9. Right-click to inspect the text box again.

10. Click Alignment and then Center. The text is centered in the text box.

11. Click outside any field to deselect the text box.

FIGURE 3.17:

A pop-up menu showing the available font sizes.

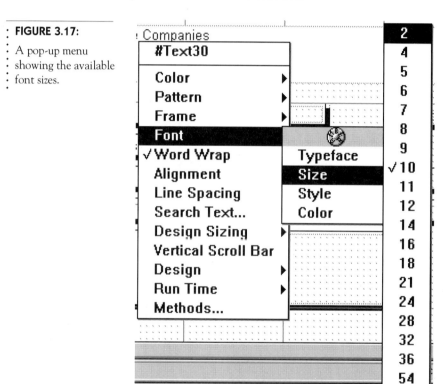

PLACING THE FORM IN A COLORED BOX

We will use the Box tool to enclose the form in a box.

1. Click the Box tool in the Speedbar.

2. Drag a box to enclose the form.

3. Right-click to inspect the box.

4. In the pop-up menu, click Color and a color selection palette appears, as shown in Figure 3.18.

5. Click light gray, or another color if you prefer, to fill the box.

6. Save the form as you did earlier.

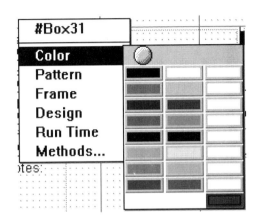

CHECKING THE FORM

To see what the form looks like now, click the View Data button in the Speedbar. Your form should look similar to the one in Figure 3.4, which you saw at the beginning of this lesson.

If you have ideas for improving the form, return to Design and have fun making your changes.

USING A DATA ENTRY FORM

With a data entry form created, you can use it to view, edit, and add records.

VIEWING RECORDS

When you switched to View Data, the form appeared with the first record showing. There are four ways to move to other records:

- press Page Down to move down to the next record, Page Up to move up to the previous record, Ctrl+End to move to the last record, or Ctrl+Home to move to the first record

- choose Record, and then click Next, Previous, Last, or First

- press the function keys F12 (next), F11 (previous, Ctrl+F12 (last), or Ctrl+F11 (first)

- click the Speedbar buttons identified in Figure 3.19

FIGURE 3.19:

Speedbar buttons used to move among records.

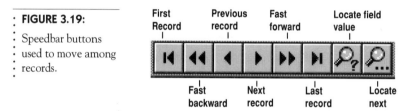

Try each of these ways of moving from one record to another for yourself.

VIEWING RECORDS IN SECONDARY-INDEX ORDER

When you went from one record to the next, records appeared in company-number order, because Co. No. is the key field in the Company table. You can change the order in which records appear by selecting a field designated as a secondary index (in this example, Name).

1. Choose Form ➤ Order/Range to display the Order/Range dialog box.
2. Click Name Order in the Index List, then OK.

Now you will find that records are displayed alphabetically by name.

LOCATING RECORDS

To search for records containing specific data, click a Speedbar button or access the Record menu.

To use the Speedbar to find a company in Maine:

1. Click the Locate Field Value button. The Locate Value dialog box (shown in Figure 3.20) appears.

2. Type **ME** (the abbreviation for Maine) in the Value text box.

3. In the Fields drop-down list box, click State and then OK. After a few seconds, the Bugfree Software record appears.

To search using the Record menu, choose Record ➤ Locate ➤ Value to display the Locate Value dialog box.

FIGURE 3.20:

The Locate Value dialog box.

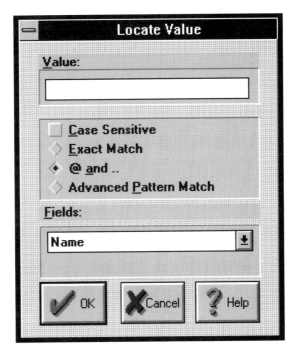

EDITING RECORDS

You can use a form to make changes to records. Suppose, for example, the CanDo-ItAll company changes its name to CanDoItAll Corporation.

1. Bring the CanDoItAll record up on your screen.

2. Press F9 to switch to Edit mode.

3. Click an insertion marker at the right of the company name.

4. Press the space bar, type **Corporation**, and then press Tab to move to the next field.

5. Press F9 to switch to Edit mode.

You can edit any field in any record this way.

ADDING A NEW RECORD

To add a new record to the Company table, you must be in Edit mode and have a blank record displayed.

1. Click the Last Record button in the Speedbar.

2. Choose Form ➤ Edit Data.

3. Click the Next Record button in the Speedbar. A blank form appears.

4. If necessary, click the Name field to highlight it.

5. Type **Compatible Software** as the company name. As soon as you type the first character, the default value CA appears in the State field. After you have typed the company name, press Tab.

6. Type **11** as the company number, then Tab.

7. Fill in the remaining fields as you wish.

8. Press F9 to turn off Edit mode.

That is all there is to adding a new record. You might like to choose Form ➤ Table View to see the new record in the Company table.

TIP

You may be wondering whether there is any way for Paradox to keep track of numbers in the Co. No. field for you. You can have Paradox automatically assign such numbers, but you'll need to use the ObjectPAL programming language to do so, and programming is beyond the scope of this book. Consult Paradox for Windows Programmer's Instant Reference, *by Loy Anderson and Cary Jensen (SYBEX, 1993), for information about ObjectPAL.*

FOR MORE INFORMATION

You will find more information about the topics covered in this lesson by referring to these Reference entries:

Color

Design Objects

Fields in a Table

Folders

Forms

Inspecting Objects

Properties of Objects

*L*INKING TABLES

Most databases consist of more than one table, because they contain several kinds of related information. So far, we've worked only with a single table, in which each record contains information about one software supplier. To demonstrate the ways database tables can be linked according to the relationships between data they contain, we will expand our database to include a table listing software products and another listing individual users. We will also see how to simplify data entry and reduce the chance of errors by using a lookup table.

To understand why the ability to link related tables is such an important database tool, you should first look briefly at some of the problems that arise when you try to include too much information in a single table.

LIMITATIONS OF SINGLE-TABLE DATABASES

Let's suppose that our company uses five software products made by Strong Software and we want to list these in our database. We could add three fields to the Company table so that each record would contain a product's name, version, and classification, in addition to information about the company. The disadvantage of this approach is that we would need five records for Strong Software, one for each of the products. Each record would have identical values in the nine fields that hold company information.

If we adopt this table structure:

♦ Someone has to enter identical values into nine fields of five records, wasting time and increasing the possibility of errors.

♦ If any of the information about the company changes, someone has to edit fields in all five records.

♦ The redundant information in the table occupies excessive disk space.

These problems would become significant in the case of a database containing information about hundreds of companies, each with many products. The solution is to use two tables, one for information about companies and the other for information about products, and to link the tables together.

MULTIPLE-TABLE DATABASES

Our second table, called Software, lists software packages. It has four fields, containing a package's name, version number, classification, and, in the fourth field, the supplier's company number (the number in the first field of the Company table).

The two tables can be linked in two ways, as shown in Figure 4.1.

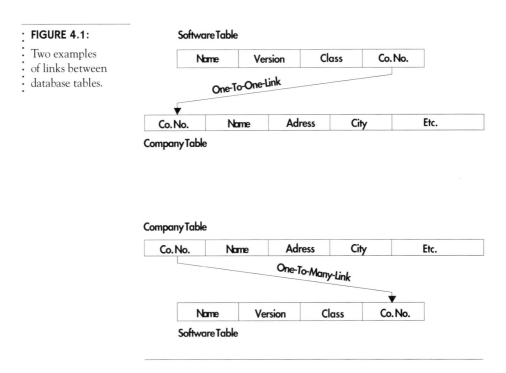

In the first case, the link originates in the company-number field in the Software table and extends to the company-number field in the Company table. Now each software package is associated with a company so that we can display or print a list of software with information about the company that supplies it. Each Software record is linked to only one company. Linked in this way, the Company and Software tables have a *one-to-one* relationship, because each software package is associated with only one company.

Alternatively, the link can extend from the company-number field in the Company table to the company-number field in the Software table. Now each company is associated with all the software packages it supplies, and we can get a list of companies together with the software each company supplies. This way, Company and Software have a *one-to-many* relationship because each company can be linked to many software packages.

By using different Paradox forms, we can link the tables in both ways.

With two tables, the Company table will contain just one record for each company, no matter how many products that company provides. The only penalty is the need to add a company number field to the Software table.

CREATING A SECOND TABLE

If you're working through the examples, you need to create the second table, Software, to be linked to the Company table. Use the techniques you learned in Lesson 3 to create the structure shown in Figure 4.2 and enter the data shown in Figure 4.3. (Fill in the Notes field as much or as little as you like.)

The first field, SW No., is necessary so that we can index the table without concern for duplicated software names. Later in this lesson, we will use this field to link this table to a third table. Make sure you mark the SW. No. field as a key.

The Name and Version fields contain software names and version numbers. In the Restructure dialog box, mark Name as Required, because we do not want to have any record in which a software package is not named.

FIGURE 4.2:

The structure of the Software table.

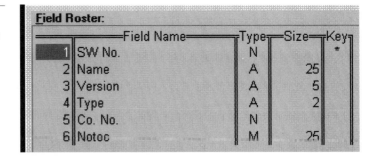

FIGURE 4.3:

The Software table with values added.

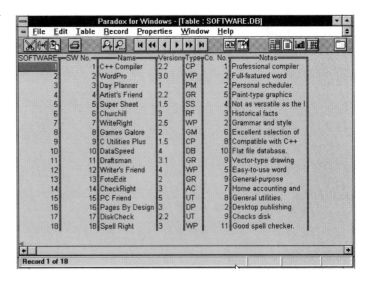

The field named Type is a two-letter field we'll use to indicate the category of each package, DB for database, SS for spreadsheet, WP for word processing, and so on.

The Co. No. field provides a link to the Co. No. field in the Company table. The fields that link two tables must have the same type and size, so this field's type is Number, the same as the field already in the Company table. In the Restructure dialog box, mark Co. No. as a secondary index because we shall be creating a link from the Company table to that field in the Software table. Name this under Company Number.

Fields that link two tables need not have the same name. However, using the same name for both fields simplifies the process of creating the link.

LINKING TWO TABLES

As you have already seen, you can link the two tables to form a one-to-one or a one-to-many relationship. First, let's create a one-to-one relationship that links each software package to information about its supplier.

CREATING A ONE-TO-ONE RELATIONSHIP

Paradox uses forms to link tables, so we will start by opening a new form and identifying the tables to be linked.

CREATING A FORM TO LINK TABLES

1. In the Desktop, choose File ➤ New ➤ Form. The Data Model dialog box opens, with Company and Software in the File Name list.

2. Click COMPANY.DB, and then click the arrow pointing right from the File Name list to incorporate that table into the data model.

3. Click SOFTWARE.DB, and then click the arrow pointing right from the File Name list to add a second table to the data model. At this point, your dialog box should look like the one in Figure 4.4.

FIGURE 4.4:

The Data Model dialog box identifying the two tables to be linked.

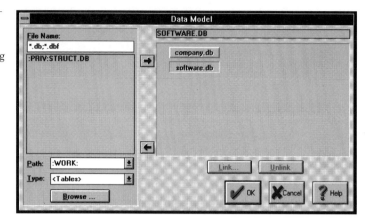

If you bring the wrong table into the data model, you can remove it by clicking it and then clicking the left-pointing arrow.

TIP

DEFINING THE LINK

We are going to link records in the Software table to records in the Company table; Software will be a *master* table and Company will be a *detail* table.

1. Move the cursor onto the software.db box in the data model so that the cursor changes to the shape shown in Figure 4.5.

2. Press and hold down the mouse button, and drag up until the tip of the arrow is within the company.db box. As you draw, a gray line extends from one box to the other.

3. Release the mouse button and the Define Link dialog box, shown in Figure 4.6, appears.

FIGURE 4.5:

The cursor placed
to define where a
link starts.

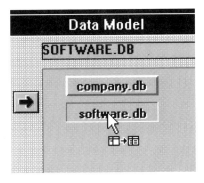

FIGURE 4.6:

The Define Link
dialog box suggesting
a possible link.

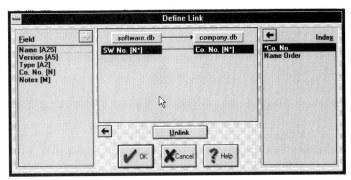

The Define Link dialog box has three sections. The center section shows a proposed link with an arrow indicating a link from the Software table to the Company table. Below this, Paradox shows the fields in the two tables that it proposes to link. These may or may not be the fields you have in mind.

The left section of the dialog box shows the names of those fields in the originating table that could possibly be used as linking fields. Notice that the originating field does not have to be a key or secondary index field.

The right section of the dialog box shows the indexes in the detail table (Company) to which the master table (Software) can be linked. These are the key or primary index (Co. No.) and the secondary index (Name Order).

Paradox tries to make a good guess about the fields that link the tables. It suggests only fields of the same type and size, and it gives preference to key fields. It has correctly chosen Co. No. as the receiving end of the link in the Company table, but incorrectly chosen SW No. as the originating field. To correct this error:

1. Click Co. No. in the list of fields at the left side of the dialog box, then click the right-pointing arrow. Now the linking fields are correct, as shown in Figure 4.7(a).

2. Click OK and the Data Model dialog box reappears with the link from the Software table to the Company table shown, as in Figure 4.7(b). Compare this representation with that of a one-to-many relationship, shown in Figure 4.10.

FIGURE 4.7:

A one-to-one relationship in the Define Link (a) and Data Model (b) dialog boxes.

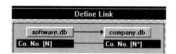

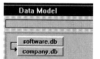

3. Click OK, and the Design Layout dialog box appears, showing all the fields in the two tables.

As you learned in Lesson 3, you can select from various form styles in the Design Layout dialog box. For the present, we will stay with the default Single-Record style.

Now we will see what the form looks like with linked tables.

1. Click OK in the Design Layout dialog box to see a Form Design window, then maximize the window.

2. Click the View Data button in the Speedbar to see the first record of the Software table together with information about its supplier, as shown in Figure 4.8.

The form initially shows only the first few characters of the memo fields in the two tables. To see as much of the memo field as will fit in the memo frame, click on the memo. To look at other software records and their associated company records, you can click the Next Record button in the Speedbar.

You have successfully created a one-to-one link between two tables. To save the form that establishes this link, go back to the Form Design window.

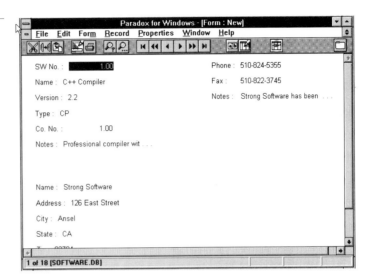

FIGURE 4.8:

A form displaying values from the linked Software and Company tables.

1. Click the Design button in the Speedbar.
2. Choose File ➤ Save.
3. In the Save File As dialog box, type **1TO1** as the file name, then click OK.
4. Double-click the Form Design window's Control-menu box to close the form and return to the Desktop.

CREATING A ONE-TO-MANY RELATIONSHIP

Let's create a one-to-many relationship that shows the software packages available from each company.

1. Open a new form.
2. Place the Software and Company tables in the data model.
3. Initiate a link from Company to Software by pointing onto the company.db box and then dragging to the software.db box (the reverse of what you previously did).

This time, the Design Link dialog box correctly shows the link starting at the Co. No. field in the Company table and terminating at the Co. No. field in the Software table, as shown in Figure 4.9. If you wanted to link from a field other than the one Paradox suggests, you would proceed to select the correct field in the Field list or the correct index in the Index list, as you did previously.

4. Click OK and the Data Model dialog box returns with the linked fields shown side by side with a double-headed arrow pointing from one to the other, as in Figure 4.10. Compare this representation of a one-to-many relationship with that of a one-to-one relationship shown in Figure 4.7.

Now we will look at the form design.

1. Click OK to get to the Design Layout dialog box shown in Figure 4.11.

This version of the dialog box is different from the one you used when creating a form based on a single table or a form that linked two tables with a one-to-one relationship. By default, it displays the master table as a column of individual fields and the detail table in table format. It places data from the master table before data from the detail table. Thus, you see a Company record as a vertical list of fields, and Software records as a table to accommodate multiple records.

FIGURE 4.9:

The Design Link dialog box with a link from company.db to software.db.

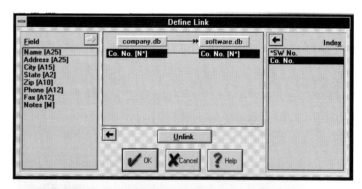

FIGURE 4.10:

The data model with a one-to-many relationship.

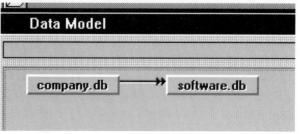

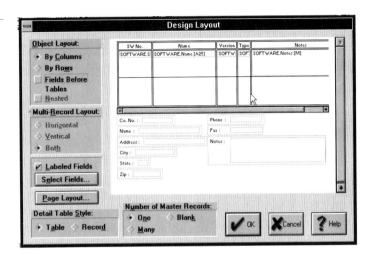

FIGURE 4.11:

The Design Layout dialog box for a one-to-many relationship.

You can click buttons in the dialog box to change the display:

- Click buttons in the Object Layout section to display master table fields in rows rather than columns, or to display the master table fields after the detail table.

- Click Record in the Detail Table Style section to display the detail table as individual fields, rather than in table format.

- Click Many in the Number of Master Records section to display data from the master table in table format.

In this example we'll accept the default layout.

2. Click OK to accept the default layout and display the Form Design.

3. Maximize the Form Design window, then click the View Data button in the Speedbar. The Form window shows the first record in the Company table, together with the names of all software packages the company provides.

4. Click the Next Record button in the Speedbar, to see the next company record and the names of the software packages the company provides, as shown in Figure 4.12.

That is all we will do with this form at present, so return to Design mode and save it as **1TOMANY**, then close the form.

FIGURE 4.12:

A form showing the
name of a software
company together
with its products.

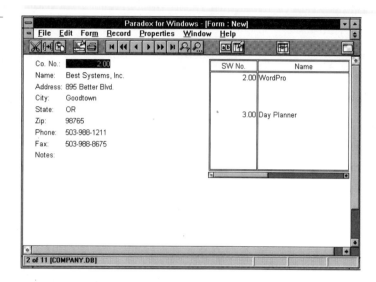

WORKING WITH LINKING FORMS

Practically all of the techniques you learned in Lesson 3 for working with single-table forms also work the same way with linking forms. For editing records within a form that links tables, however, there is an important difference: Paradox allows you to edit the master table in a one-to-one relationship, but refuses to let you edit the detail table. The reason for this restriction is that a record in the detail table is often linked to many records in the master table; and a change in a detail table record that is appropriate for one record in the master table may not be appropriate for other records in the master table.

Paradox enforces this restriction by making the detail table *read-only*, which simply means that the file can be read but not changed in any way. For those occasions when we do need to edit records in the detail table, we need to change the linking properties. To do so, we need to open the form.

OPENING A FORM IN DESIGN MODE

In Lesson 3 we did all our work with a single form, and we never needed to close one form and open another. With forms linking several tables, however, you will often need to open a form you've previously closed.

You can open a form in View Data mode or in Design mode. After you have opened it you can easily switch from one mode to the other by clicking a Speedbar button. We are going to look at changing the form's appearance, so let's open it in Design mode.

1. Choose File ➤ Open ➤ Form. The Open Document dialog box appears with a choice of forms in the File Name list, and a choice of View Data or Design modes.

2. Click 1TO1.FSL, click Design, and then click OK. The Form Design window appears showing the 1TO1 form.

3. Maximize the form.

EXAMINING AND CHANGING THE LINK

Whether or not you need to change a link, as we'll do next, it's often a good idea to examine the links in a form, to verify that they are correct.

1. Choose Form ➤ Data Model to see the Data Model dialog box that you had when you completed linking the tables.

2. Examine the Software table side of the link by pointing into the box containing software.db in the data model and clicking the right mouse button. The pop-up menu at the left of Figure 4.13 appears.

3. Examine the company.db table side of the link and look at the pop-up menu. It should be the same as the right side of Figure 4.13.

FIGURE 4.13:

The pop-up menus for the software.db (a) and the company.db (b) tables.

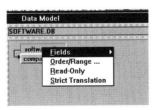
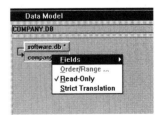

Notice that Read-Only is not checked for the Software table, but is checked for the Company table.

The read-only property affects the Software table only when it is linked by the 1TO1 form. It has no effect on editing the table directly or by way of other forms, in which the read-only property is not set.

Let's change the linking properties so that we can edit values in the Company table, using the 1TO1 form.

5. With the COMPANY.DB pop-up menu displayed, click Read-Only and the pop-up disappears.

6. Display the pop-up again and notice that Read-Only is now not checked.

7. Click an unoccupied part of the screen to make the pop-up disappear.

If you like, click OK to go back to the 1TO1 form, switch to the View Data mode, select Edit Data, and confirm that you can now edit fields in a Company record. After you have done that, go back to the Data Model dialog box.

Paradox turns on the read-only property for the detail field in one-to-one relationships. It does not do this in the case of one-to-many relationships.

VERIFYING FIELD LINKS

The Data Model dialog box shows which tables are linked, and whether the link is one-to-one or one-to-many, but it does not show which fields are linked. To verify that you've linked the correct fields, point onto the tip of the arrow that shows the link between the two tables and right-click. The Define Link dialog box appears, showing the Co. No. field in the Company table linked to the Co. No. field in the Software table.

If you had made a mistake when you previously created the link, you could change the linking fields at this time.

After you have looked at the Define Link dialog box, click Cancel to return to the Data Model dialog box. Then click OK to accept the change you made (turning off read-only status). This takes you back to the 1TO1 form in Design mode.

ADDING RECORDS VIA A LINKING FORM

With a linking form such as 1TO1, you can easily add records to both of the linked tables, as long as neither table has read-only set in the linking form. To try this out, let's suppose Strong Software introduces a word processor called Strongword.

1. Click the View Data button in the Speedbar.

2. Click the Last Record button in the Speedbar.

3. Click the Edit Data button in the Speedbar.

4. Click the Next Record button in the Speedbar, so that your screen displays a form with no values in the Software or Company sections.

5. In the Software section of the form add **19** to the SW No. field, **Strongword** to the Name field, **1.0** to the Version field, and **WP** to the Type field. Press ↵ to move from one field to the next.

6. When you get to the Co. No. field, type 1 (the company number for Strong Software) and then press ↵. The name, address, and telephone numbers for Strong Software are automatically added to the form.

7. Press Page Down to complete the new entry.

TIP *In step 5 you typed the next available software number. If you had typed a number already used, Paradox would have refused to accept the new record because the software-number field is a key and must contain a unique value for every record.*

Now let's see what happens if you enter information about a software package from a company not already in the Company table.

1. In the Software section of the form add **20** to the SW No. field, **WritePro** to the Name field, **2.1** to the Version field, and **WP** to the Type field.

2. When you get to the Co. No. field, type **12**, the next available company number. This time, nothing is added to the Company section because there is no company with the number 12 in the Company table.

3. Type **Watkins Company** for the company name, **559 Tall Oak Avenue** for the address, and **Marysville** for the city. Accept the default state abbreviation. Type **95301** for the zip code, **714-867-2211** for the phone number, and **714-867-6397** for the fax number.

4. Press Page Down to complete the entry. Click Edit data to leave Edit mode.

5. Double-click the form's Control-menu box to close the form. Click Yes in the dialog box that asks you to confirm the change you've made to the form.

TIP

The dialog box tells you that the design of the form has changed because you have changed the read-only status of the Company table as it is linked by the form.

If you like, you can open the Company table to verify that the Watkins company has been added, and you can open the Software table to confirm that the Strongword and WritePro software packages are there.

USING A LOOKUP TABLE

The Type field in our sample database gives us another way to look for information. (We can ask, for example, "What word processors do we have?") But the two-letter codes in this field may be difficult to remember, and they must be used consistently. Paradox allows us to simplify data entry by creating a *lookup* table listing the codes and their meanings.

CREATING A LOOKUP TABLE

First, create a table of software codes, just as you create any other table. The codes must be in the first field of the table. Other fields can have any additional information. In our case we will put a brief explanation of the code in the second field.

1. Create a new table with two fields. Name the first field **Abbreviation**; make it Alphanumeric type with a size of 2. Mark this field as a key.

2. Name the second field **Software Class**; make it Alphanumeric type with a size of 20. Make this field a secondary index and name it Class Order.

3. Save the table structure with the name **SWCLASS**.

4. Enter the values shown in Figure 4.14 into the table.

5. Choose Table ➤ Order/Range and index the table on Software Class.

6. Close the table.

FIGURE 4.14:

The table of software classes.

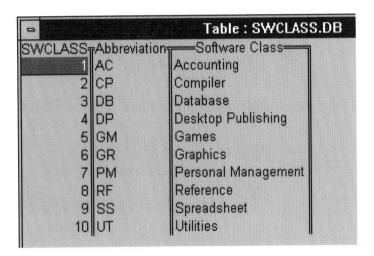

ATTACHING A LOOKUP TABLE TO A FIELD

Now we need to attach the lookup table to the Type field in the Software table.

1. Choose File ➤ Utilities ➤ Restructure.

2. Double-click SOFTWARE.DB to display the Restructure dialog box showing the Software table.

3. Drop down the Table Properties list box and click Table Lookup.

4. Click Define to display the Table Lookup dialog box shown in Figure 4.15.

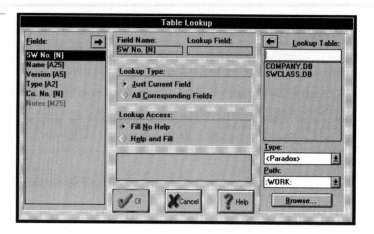

FIGURE 4.15:

The Table Lookup dialog box.

The left side of the dialog box shows the fields in the current table. You will use this list to select the field that refers to the lookup table. Notice that the Notes field is dimmed because it is Memo type and you cannot attach a lookup table to a field of that type.

The right side of the dialog box shows the tables available in your working directory. You will use this list to identify the lookup table.

The center of the box allows you to make some choices about how table lookup will work. See the Lookup Tables entry in Part II for information about these choices.

5. In the left side of the dialog box, click Type and then click the right-pointing arrow so that the field named Type is selected. This identifies the Type field as the one to which the lookup table applies.

6. In the right side of the dialog box, click SWCLASS.DB, and then click the left-pointing arrow to identify the lookup table. Notice that Abbreviation (the name of the first field in the lookup table) appears in the Lookup Field box.

7. In the center of the dialog box, click Just Current Field and click Help and Fill. At this stage, the dialog box on your screen should look like that in Figure 4.16.

8. Click OK and the Restructure dialog box reappears.

9. Click Save in the Restructure dialog box, and click OK in the Restructure Warning box.

FIGURE 4.16:

The Table Lookup
dialog box.

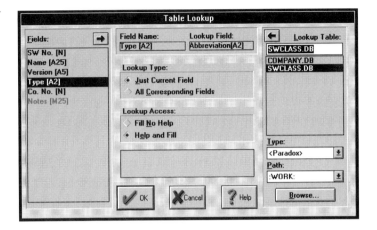

USING A LOOKUP TABLE

Let's see how the lookup table works by entering a new spreadsheet program into the database.

1. Open the 1TO1 form in View Data mode and maximize it.

2. Go to the last record, select Edit Data, and move to an empty record.

3. Start to enter a new record. Enter **21** into the SW No. field, **Number Magic** into the Name field, and **2.2** into the Version field, pressing ↵ to move from field to field.

4. When you are ready to enter an abbreviation into the Type field, press Ctrl+Space and the lookup table appears, superimposed on your form, as shown in Figure 4.17.

5. Scroll down the lookup table until you see Spreadsheet in the second column, click Spreadsheet, and then click OK. The lookup table disappears and SS appears in the Type field on the form.

6. Press ↵ to commit this value, then type **9** for the Co. No. field.

7. Close the form.

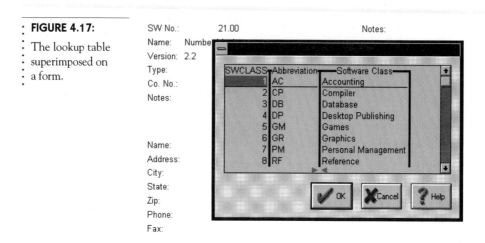

FIGURE 4.17:

The lookup table superimposed on a form.

You can attach lookup tables to as many fields in a table as you wish.

MANY-TO-MANY LINKS

Another important way of linking databases is through a many-to-many relationship. To see how this works, we will expand the database to include the names of the people in our company who use each software package.

DEVELOPING THE DATABASE STRUCTURE

We will need a table, which we will call People, containing people's names and perhaps other information such as their locations and phone numbers. But how do we identify the software that individual people use? Most people use several software packages, so we cannot have a single field in the People table for a software number. We certainly do not want to provide, say, ten fields for software numbers, on the assumption that nobody uses more than ten software packages.

When we linked the Company table to the Software table, each company could be associated with many software packages, but each package was associated with only one company. Here, each person can use many packages, and each package can be used by many people. There is "many" on both sides of the relationship, so this is known as a many-to-many relationship.

Using a Linking Table

To link the People table to the Software table in a many-to-many relationship, we create a table with two fields, one identifying a record in the People table, and the other identifying a record in the Software table. This table will have one record for each software package owned by the company. Notice that this database structure places no limit on the number of software packages used by any person, or on the number of copies of each package owned by the company.

Figure 4.18 shows how records in the People table are linked to records in the Software table by a table we will call Peopsoft. Each person in the People table is identified by a number in the key field, and each software package in the Software table is identified by a number in its key field. The Peopsoft table simply relates the two keys.

To see this structure at work, we have to create a People table and a Peopsoft table.

FIGURE 4.18:
The database structure that relates people to the software they use.

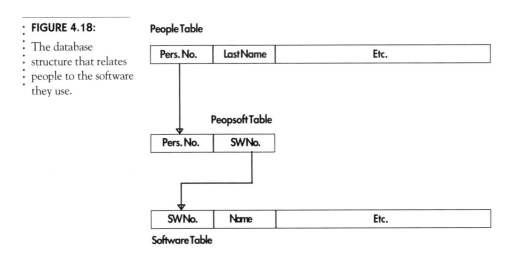

CREATING THE PEOPLE TABLE

To keep things simple and save a lot of typing, we will create a People table with just two fields, Pers. No. and Last Name.

1. Choose File ➤ New ➤ Table.

2. Create the first field with **Pers. No.** as its name. Make the field Number type and make it a key field.

3. Create the second field with **Last Name** as its name. Make it Alphanumeric with a size of **15**.

4. Save the table structure with the name **People**.

5. Add the values shown in Figure 4.19 to the table.

6. Close the table.

FIGURE 4.19:

Values entered into the People table.

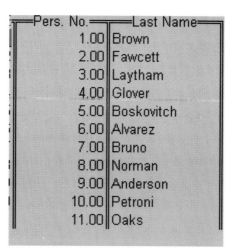

Pers. No.	Last Name
1.00	Brown
2.00	Fawcett
3.00	Laytham
4.00	Glover
5.00	Boskovitch
6.00	Alvarez
7.00	Bruno
8.00	Norman
9.00	Anderson
10.00	Petroni
11.00	Oaks

CREATING THE LINKING TABLE

The linking table, Peopsoft, will contain three fields: Pack. No., which identifies each individual copy of each program used in the company, so that every value in the field is unique; Pers. No., which links the Peopsoft table to the People table, and SW. No., which links Peopsoft to the Software table.

1. Choose File ➤ New ➤ Table.

2. Create the first field with **Pack. No.** as its name. Make the field Number type, and make it a key field.

3. Create the second field with **Pers. No.** as its name. Make it Number type.

4. Create the third field with **SW No.** as its name. Make it Number type.

5. Make the Pers. No. field a secondary index named **Person Number**.

6. Make the SW No. field a secondary index named **Software Number**.

7. Save the table structure with the name **Peopsoft**.

CREATING THE LINKING FORM

Now we will create a form we can use to enter the software packages each person uses. This form links the People table to the Software table through the Peopsoft table. First, we will link the People table to the Peopsoft table. The link will be one-to-many, because each person in the People table may have several software packages and, therefore, be linked to several records in the Peopsoft table.

1. Choose File ➤ New ➤ Form to display the Data Model dialog box.

2. Click PEOPLE.DB and then click the right-pointing arrow to bring the People table into the data model.

3. Click PEOPSOFT.DB and then click the right-pointing arrow to bring the Peopsoft table into the data model.

4. Point onto the people.db box in the data model. Press the mouse button, drag down into the peopsoft.db box, then release the mouse button. The Define Link dialog box appears.

5. Click Person Number in the list of possible Index fields and click the left-pointing arrow. The dialog box should now show a one-to-many link between people.db and peopsoft.db, as shown in Figure 4.20.

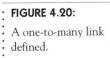

FIGURE 4.20:

A one-to-many link defined.

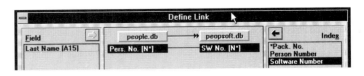

6. Click OK to return to the Data Model dialog box.

Now, we will add the Software table to the data model.

1. Click SOFTWARE.DB in the left part of the Data Model dialog box, then click the right-pointing arrow.

2. Point into the peopsoft.db box in the data model, press the mouse button, drag down and to the left into the software.db box, and release the mouse button.

3. In the left side of the Define Link dialog box, click SW No. and then click the right-pointing arrow to start the link with the SW No. field in the Peopsoft table.

4. In the right side of the Define Link dialog box, click SW No. and press the left-pointing arrow. Now the dialog box shows the SW No. field in the Peopsoft table linked to the SW No. field in the Software table. Click OK to return to the Data Model dialog box shown in Figure 4.21.

As you can see, there is a one-to-many link between people.db and peopsoft.db, and a one-to-one link between peopsoft.db and software.db.

After establishing links between the tables, our next task would be to design the layout of the form, but we will just accept the default layout for now.

5. Click OK in the Data Model dialog box to proceed to the Design Layout dialog box. The dialog box offers the same choices you saw when creating a one-to-many relationship.

6. Click OK to accept the default layout, which shows data from the master table in field format and data from the detail table in table format, and display the Form Design window.

: **FIGURE 4.21:**
: The Data Model
: dialog box showing
: how the three tables
: are linked.

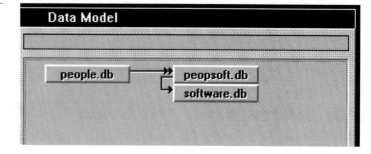

7. Click Save, and save the form with the name **PEOPSOFT**.

8. Click the View Data button in the Speedbar, then maximize the form so that your screen looks like the one in Figure 4.22.

Now you are ready to complete the link, so that the table will show which software packages each person uses.

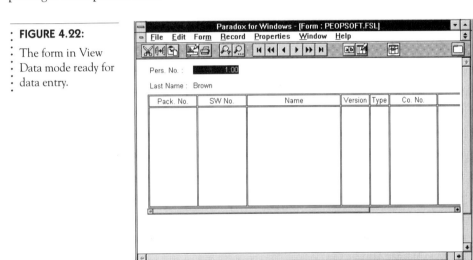

COMPLETING THE MANY-TO-MANY LINK

The top section of the form shows the name of the first person, Brown, in the People table. The lower section is an empty table in which you will identify the software that person uses. All you need to do is type in the software numbers, and Paradox fills in the details. Paradox uses the number in the SW. No. field to link to the detailed information in the Software table. Paradox uses the F4 key, called "super tab" in the User's Manual, to move between the two sections of the form.

Let's suppose that Brown uses software packages 1, 5, and 6.

> *If you like, you can create a lookup table that relates software numbers to their names. Then you do not have to remember software numbers.*

1. Click the Edit Data button in the Speedbar.

2. Press F4 (super tab) to highlight the first field in the lower section of the form.

3. Type **1** as the number of the first record in the Peopsoft table, and then press ↵ to move to the SW No. field.

4. Type **1** as the number of the first software package Brown uses, then press ↵. Paradox completes the remaining fields automatically, as shown in Figure 4.23.

> *You cannot edit the fields in the Software section of this form because the Software table is on the receiving end of a one-to-one relationship and is, therefore, read-only. This is a good example of why Paradox makes detail tables read-only, because you would not want anyone to use this form to alter the detailed information about software packages.*

5. Press ↓ to move to the next line, type **2** for Pack. No., **5** for SW No., and press ↵.

6. Press ↓, type **3** for Pack. No., **6** for SW No., and press ↵.

This completes entering the three software packages Brown uses. To satisfy yourself that everything is working correctly, open the Peopsoft table and you will

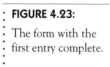

FIGURE 4.23:

The form with the first entry complete.

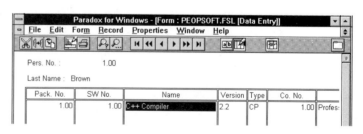

see three records there, each containing the correct person and software numbers. After you have done that, return to the form.

Now move to the next person in the People table and enter the software packages Fawcett uses.

1. Press F4 to highlight the top section of the form.

2. Click the Next Record button in the Speedbar.

3. Enter two or three software packages Fawcett uses. (Use your imagination.) Do not forget to enter a unique number in the Pack. No. field for each entry.

In order to have a reasonable amount of data to work with when we look at reports and queries in the next two lessons, enter a few software packages for each person in the People table.

Finally, close the form.

FOR MORE INFORMATION

You will find more information about the topics covered in this lesson by referring to these entries in Part II.

Design Objects

Forms

Tables

CREATING REPORTS

Lesson 3 described many of the techniques available in Paradox to create one type of document—data entry forms. In Lesson 4, you learned how to use forms to link tables. Now we will see how we can apply these techniques to creating reports, which are principally used to print information stored in a database.

As you progress through this lesson, you will learn some techniques you can also apply to data entry forms.

CREATING A REPORT

A report presents an output from one or more tables in a database, usually printed but sometimes displayed on a computer screen. The report we will consider in this lesson is intended to be printed.

 If all you want is a fast way to print the contents of a table, you can use a Paradox quick report. Just open a table, click the Quick Report button on the Speedbar, and the report is ready for printing. Usually, though, you will want to design a report to suit your specific needs. That is what you will learn in this lesson.

Paradox lets you prepare multipage reports consisting of:

- a report body consisting of data extracted from a database and formatted to suit specific requirements;

- optional summaries of specific groups of data;

- an optional report header (title) printed at the beginning of the report;

- an optional report footer (summary) printed at the end of the report;

- an optional page header printed at the top of every page;

- an optional page footer printed at the bottom of every page.

These elements of a report, shown in Figure 5.1, are created in regions of the report document known as bands.

DESIGNING A REPORT LAYOUT

There are two stages in designing a report: preparing the layout and placing objects on it.

FIGURE 5.1:

The general layout of
a Paradox report.

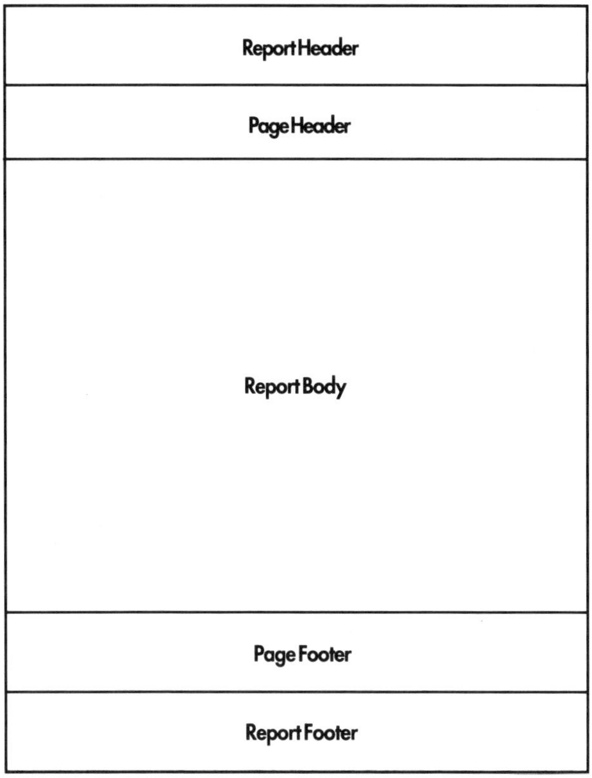

Report Header
Page Header
Report Body
Page Footer
Report Footer

PREPARING THE LAYOUT

We have to choose which fields to include in a report and where those fields will be placed.

The first step in preparing a report layout is to open a new report, which is similar to opening a new form. We shall start to design a report that lists the software our company uses, together with the name of each software supplier.

1. From the Paradox Desktop choose File ➤ New ➤ Report. The Data Model dialog box appears, the same as when we started to create a new form.

2. Click SOFTWARE.DB in the File Name list, and then click the right-pointing arrow, to place the Software table in the data model.

3. Click COMPANY.DB in the File Name list, and then click the right-pointing arrow, to place the Company table in the data model.

4. Link the Software table to the Company table, as you did in Lesson 4.

5. In the Define Link dialog box, select Co. No. to originate the link, then click OK. At this stage, the Data Model dialog box shows a one-to-one link. Click OK.

6. Click OK. The Design Layout dialog box appears with a suggested basic layout of the report, as shown in Figure 5.2.

This Design Layout dialog box has a significant difference from the one you saw when you designed a form. Dark horizontal bars, known as *band labels*, separate the header and footer bands from the report body band. You will soon see how to use these bands.

If the Band Labels property is turned off, you will not see the dark bands on your screen. To correct this, choose Properties ➤ Band Labels.

TIP

The dialog box offers a choice of four possible styles: Single-Record, Multi-Record, Tabular, and Blank (just the same as the one you saw when you were designing a form). You can see what these styles look like by clicking the buttons in the Style section of the dialog box one after the other.

FIGURE 5.2:

The Design Layout dialog box showing the preliminary report layout.

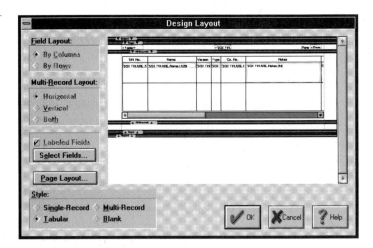

Instead of using the Single-Record style as we previously did in Lesson 3 when we were designing a data entry form, we will select the Blank style as the basis of the report because we want to choose which fields to include in the report.

When designing layouts for forms or reports, you can choose to let Paradox place fields and then move those fields to where you want them, or you can start with a blank layout and place the fields on the form or report. When you prepare your own forms and reports, use whichever method you prefer.

5. Click the Blank button. Now the dialog box shows a report layout with no fields.

6. Click Page Layout. The Page Layout dialog box appears, as shown in Figure 5.3.

The Page Layout dialog box allows you to choose to prepare a report to be printed or displayed on the screen. It also allows you to choose page size and orientation, and to set margins.

7. Click where appropriate in the Page Layout dialog box to suit your printer and the size of paper you will be using. Unless you have a specific reason for choosing otherwise, use the parameters shown in Figure 5.3.

FIGURE 5.3:

The Page Layout dialog box.

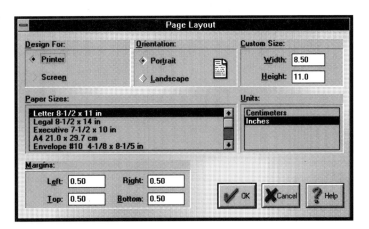

8. Click OK. The Design Layout dialog box reappears.

9. With the Blank style selected, click OK. The Report Design window appears.

10. Maximize the Report Design the window, as shown in Figure 5.4. Your window may look a little different from that in the figure until you have completed the following steps.

11. Choose Properties in the Menu bar. Click as necessary in the Properties menu so that only Band Labels, Horizontal Ruler, and Vertical Ruler are checked.

12. Choose Properties ➤ Report Options ➤ Save Defaults.

When you start to create a report, you should select whichever of the four styles—Single-Record, Multi-Record, Tabular, or Blank—is closest to what you want and then modify it to suit your requirements. Whichever style you choose, you can add and delete fields, and place them wherever you want.

The window in Figure 5.4 clearly shows the report's band structure. The region between the top band label, marked Report, and the second band label, marked Page, is for the report header. The region between the second band label and the third, marked Record, is for the page header.

FIGURE 5.4:

The Report Design window, showing a blank style of report.

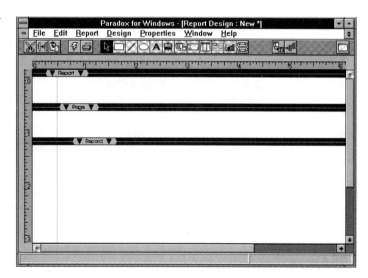

If you scroll down, you will see another band label, marked Record. The region between the two Record band labels is where the report data will appear in the body of the report.

Scroll down to the bottom of the window. Here, the region between the Record and Page band labels is for the page footer. The region between the Page and Report band labels is for the report footer.

The gray vertical line at the half-inch horizontal position indicates the left margin specified in the Page Layout dialog box. You can see the right margin at the eight-inch position if you scroll to the right.

The Design Report window's Menu bar and Speedbar are similar to those for the Form Design window. Notice, though, that the Menu bar now contains Report instead of Form. If you click Report you will see that its menu contains several commands related to preparing reports. With the exception of Properties, which contains one additional command, the other menus contain the same commands as they do when you work with forms.

The Speedbar has one additional button, the Add Band button labeled in Figure 5.4. The Design Report Speedbar omits the Button tool because buttons have no function on a printed report.

With the initial layout prepared, you are ready to place objects on it, but first, save your work. Choose File ➤ Save, and save the report with the name **SOFTLIST**. Paradox automatically adds RSL as the file-name extension.

Now, we are ready to start working on the details of the report layout. First, we will create the report header.

CREATING A REPORT HEADER

A report header is a title that will be printed at the beginning of the report. We will create the report header consisting of a logo, the words *Company Software Usage*, and the date the report is printed.

Making Space for the Report Header   When you place the logo into the header, you will find that Paradox automatically increases the depth of the report header band to allow as much space as is necessary. For the present, we shall increase the depth of the band to about one inch to allow plenty of space for the header text.

Be prepared to spend some time learning how to change band sizes. You need a steady hand on your mouse to position the cursor correctly. And it may seem somewhat strange to drag a band label outside the work area. However, if you follow the steps below, you will soon become comfortable with the technique.

1. Click the band label marked Report at the top of the layout. The label becomes highlighted to show it is selected, and the Status bar indicates that the report header band is selected.

2. Move the mouse until the cursor is just above the center line of the Report band label. When the cursor is in the correct position, it changes to a double-headed arrow.

3. Press and hold down the mouse button.

4. Drag up about half an inch, then release the mouse button. The Report Design window is redrawn with about an inch of space between the Report and Page band labels.

5. Repeat steps 2 through 4, dragging up or down, if you need to adjust the size of the report band. Now there is plenty of room for the report header, as shown in Figure 5.5.

You do not have to be concerned initially about setting band sizes exactly, because you can easily adjust them later.

FIGURE 5.5:

The Report Design window with increased space for a report header.

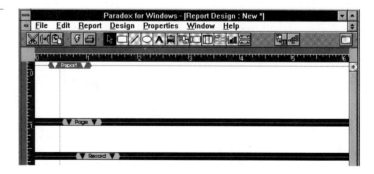

Adding Report Header Text Now that there is space in the report header, we can place the words *Company Software Usage* and center them.

1. Click the Text tool in the Speedbar.
2. Point with the text cursor to the 2½″ horizontal and ¼″ vertical position.
3. Press and hold down the mouse button, then drag to the 6″ horizontal and ¾″ vertical position to create a text frame. The Status bar indicates that a text object is selected.
4. Type **Company Software Usage**.
5. Click the Selection Arrow in the Speedbar and then click the text. Handles appear around the text box.
6. Right-click the text to inspect it.
7. Choose Alignment ➤ Center. The text becomes centered in the frame.

Now we shall make the text larger and bold.

1. Repeat steps 5 and 6 to inspect the text again.
2. Choose Font ➤ Size ➤ 14 to make the text larger.
3. Inspect the text again.
4. Choose Font ➤ Style ➤ Bold to make the text bold, as shown in Figure 5.6.

At any stage while preparing a report document, you can see an on-screen preview of your work by clicking the View Data button in the Speedbar. An information box appears temporarily to tell you that Paradox is preparing a report; then the first

FIGURE 5.6:

The Report Design window with text in the report header band.

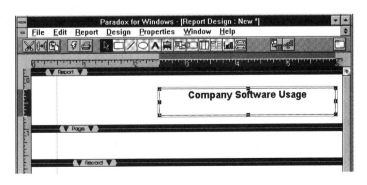

part of the report appears on the screen. At this time, you only see the report header. Click the Design button in the Speedbar to return to the Report Design window.

Before proceeding, save your report design.

Adding a Logo to the Report Header To show how you can add graphics to a report, we will use as a logo the SLASH.BMP bitmap graphic supplied with Windows. First, mark a position for the graphic.

1. Click the Graphic tool in the Speedbar.

2. Move the cursor into the workspace. The cursor changes to a cross with the graphics symbol below it.

3. Outline a graphics frame approximately one inch deep and 1½ inches wide at the left side of the report header. A graphics frame appears with the words *Undefined Graphic* inside it, as shown in Figure 5.7.

> *The size of the frame you create in step 3 does not matter because Paradox automatically changes the frame size to accommodate an imported graphic. A specific size is recommended here only to make sure your frame is large enough to show the words Undefined Graphic.*

The next step is to paste the graphic in position.

FIGURE 5.7:

The graphics frame ready for importing a bitmap.

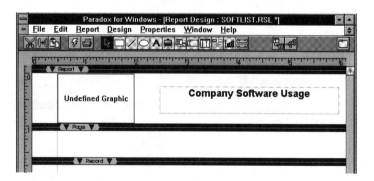

1. Right-click the graphic frame. The bitmap properties list, shown in Figure 5.8, appears.

2. Click Define Graphic.

3. Click Paste From. The Paste From Graphic File dialog box appears.

4. Click Browse. The Browser dialog box appears.

5. Use Browser to select your Windows (or other) directory that contains the sample bitmap files supplied with Windows. A list of bitmap files in the selected directory appears.

6. Double-click SLASH.BMP. After a few seconds, the bitmap appears in the report header, as shown in Figure 5.9.

· **FIGURE 5.8:**

· The bitmap
· properties list.

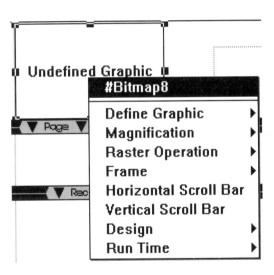

· **FIGURE 5.9:**

· The Report Design
· window with added
· graphics.

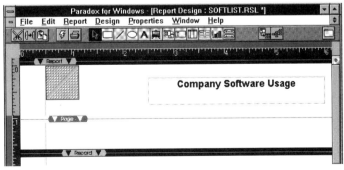

We are just using SLASH.BMP to represent a logo. If you don't have this file on your disk, choose any other bitmap.

Instead of using the steps described above to place a graphic into the report, you could have copied the graphic into the Clipboard, and then pasted it from the Clipboard into the report.

The report header band is larger than we need, so we will decrease its size.

1. Drag the logo down so that it is close to the page band label.

2. Drag the report band label close to the top of the logo.

3. Adjust the position of the report header text, as shown in Figure 5.10.

Adding the Printing Date The third object we want to place in the report header band is the date the report is printed. We do that by placing a field object in the band and defining it as a "Today" field. First place a field object in the band.

1. Click the right end of the horizontal scroll bar so that you can see the right side of the Report Design window.

2. Click the Field tool in the Speedbar.

· **FIGURE 5.10:**

· The report header
· with the logo and
· text correctly
· positioned.

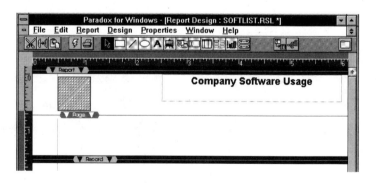

3. Move the field cursor to the 6¼″ position on the horizontal ruler and at the same vertical position as the existing text box. Press the mouse button, drag to the left margin and to the same vertical position as the bottom of the text box, then release the mouse button. At this stage, your window should be similar to the one shown in Figure 5.11.

Now define the field object.

1. Right-click the field object to inspect it. The properties pop-up menu appears.

2. Click Define Field in the properties pop-up menu. A list of available field names appears, as shown in Figure 5.12.

The list of fields shows the names of the fields in the data model. The bottom, checked line shows that the field is currently undefined. The top line of the list, which contains three dots (Paradox calls this item the list's *header*), provides access to other possibilities.

3. Click the top line of the list of field names (the header), and the Define Field Object dialog box appears, as shown in Figure 5.13.

4. Open the Special Field list at the right side of the dialog box. The list allows you to choose Today, Now, Page Number, or Number of Pages. Click Today, then click OK. The Report Design window reappears with the new field defined, as shown in Figure 5.14.

Click the View Data button in the Speedbar to look at a preview of the report. Scroll right to see the three objects in the report header band. The Today field you just added appears as *Today:* followed by today's date.

FIGURE 5.11:

The Report Design window with a new field object in position.

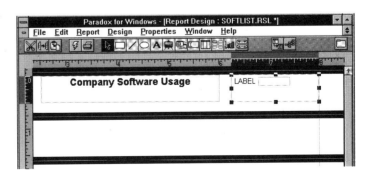

FIGURE 5.12:

The field object being inspected, with a list of possible fields to identify.

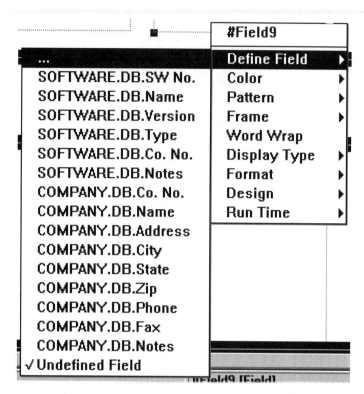

FIGURE 5.13:

The Define Field dialog box.

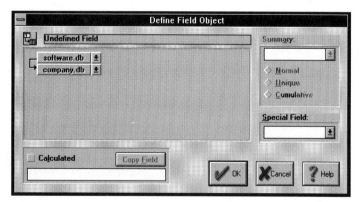

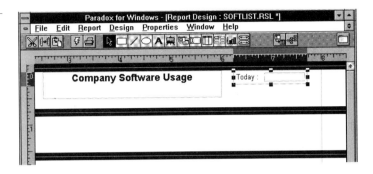

FIGURE 5.14:

The Report Design
dialog box with the
new field defined.

We do not want the field label *Today:* printed in our report, so let's eliminate it.

1. Click the Design button in the Speedbar.

2. Right-click the Today field to inspect it.

3. In the properties pop-up menu, click Display Type to see a list of display-type choices, as shown in Figure 5.15.

4. Click Unlabeled. The Report Design window reappears without the field label.

5. Click the View Data button in the Speedbar. When the report preview appears, scroll to the right to see the Today field. All you see is the date.

6. Click the Design button in the Speedbar.

7. Save the report design.

If you wish, you can do much more with the report header. For example, you can:

- change the font (typeface, size, style, and color) of the report title and the date;

- reposition the logo, title, and date;

- add more graphics, such as a box around the title;

- add text, such as "Date printed:" to the left of the date.

The more you experiment, the better you will be able to design the reports you need, so take some time to practice. When you have finished practicing, save your work with a different name so that you do not make changes to SOFTLIST.

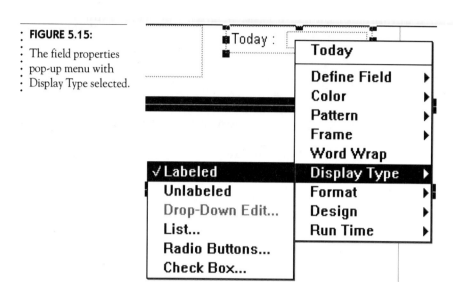

FIGURE 5.15:
The field properties
pop-up menu with
Display Type selected.

CREATING A PAGE HEADER

Whatever you place in the page header is printed at the top of every page of the report, although you can omit the header from the first page if you choose to do so. A typical page header consists of the title of the report and the page number.

If you base your report on any of the report styles except Blank, Paradox automatically places date, file name, and page number fields in the page header.

Reducing the Height of the Page Header First, reduce the height of the page header to allow just enough space for a single line.

1. If necessary, click the left end of the horizontal scroll bar so that you can see the left side of the Report Design window.

2. Move the cursor onto the Page band label, click to select the label, and then adjust the cursor position until it changes to a double-headed arrow.

3. Press and hold down the mouse button while you drag down to make the page header band about a quarter-inch deep.

Adding a Page Number and Title You can add a page number to the page header in the same way you added the date. Then you can add the text for a title.

1. Place the Page Number special field close to the right edge of the page header band.
2. Use the Text tool to create a frame at the left side of the page header.
3. Type **Company Software Usage**.

You will notice some vertical misalignment between the text you just typed and the text in the Page Number special field. Paradox does not offer any automatic way to correct this misalignment, so you have to make the correction manually. The following steps are an easy way to do this.

1. Select the text field and drag it to the right until part of it overlaps the Page Number field.
2. Move the text field vertically, so that the two fields are vertically aligned.
3. Inspect the text field and turn on the Pin Vertical design property.
4. Drag the text back to the left margin.

To complete the page header, we will draw a moderately thick, horizontal line to separate the header from the data.

1. Click the Line tool in the Speedbar.
2. Choose Properties ➤ Zoom FR 50%.
3. Place the cross-shaped cursor anywhere on the left margin, press the mouse button and drag to the right margin, making sure the line is exactly horizontal.
4. Right-click the line to inspect it.
5. Choose Thickness ➤ 2 Points.
6. Choose Properties ➤ Zoom ➤ 100%.
7. Drag the horizontal line up or down as needed so that it is slightly below the text in the page header.

8. Click the View Data button in the Speedbar to see what the report looks like with the page header completed. It should be similar to that in Figure 5.16.

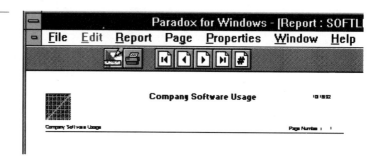

FIGURE 5.16:

The report with the report header and page header completed.

You will find it easy to draw a line that is exactly horizontal if you turn on Snap to Grid before step 3. If you do, turn Snap to Grid off before step 5 so that you can position the line exactly where you want it.

Return to the Design view of the report and save the partially completed design.

CREATING THE REPORT AND PAGE FOOTERS

You can add text, fields, graphics, and so on to the report footer and to the page footer bands in the same way that we added them to the header bands. For this report, we shall leave the footer bands empty.

FORMATTING REPORT DATA

So far, we have been working with the report and page headers, which is necessary unless you are preparing a very simple report and are willing to accept the Paradox defaults. Now we turn to the body of the report, which contains values from tables and, perhaps, data calculated from those values.

Formatting report data is simply a matter of placing fields where you want them in the space between the two Record bars in the Report Design window. We shall place the fields that contain the name, version number, and type of each software package, together with the fields that contain the name, address, and phone number of the supplier.

Placing Fields If you had selected the Single-Record style for your report, all the fields in the Software and Company tables would already be in the table. You would delete those fields you do not want in the report, and move the remaining fields to create a satisfactory format. However, we are using the Blank style, so we shall proceed as follows:

1. Use the Field tool to draw a frame with its top left corner on the left margin and at the 1½″ position on the vertical ruler. The width and depth of the frame are unimportant.

2. Right-click anywhere inside the frame to inspect it. The field properties list appears.

3. Choose Define Field and click the header (…) to display the Define Field Object dialog box.

Now you are ready to construct the first line of each record as it will be printed. This line will consist of the name, version number, and category of a software package.

1. Click the Calculated button in the dialog box. A check mark appears in the button.

2. Open the software.db list. A list of fields in the Software table appears.

3. Click Name in the list of fields, then click the Copy Field button. [SOFTWARE.Name] appears in the box under the Calculated button, as shown in Figure 5.17.

So far we have placed one alphanumeric field from a table into the calculated field. We want the printed report to contain the value in that field followed by a comma, a space, the word *Version*, a space, and then the value in another field.

Paradox uses the + operator to concatenate (join) components of a calculated alphanumeric field. Those components can be field names and constants. Constants are any keyboard characters placed within double quotation marks. The next step shows how to add constants to the calculated field, and step 6 shows how to add another named field.

FIGURE 5.17:

The Define Field Object dialog box with one object placed in a calculated field.

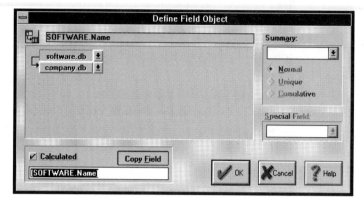

5. Click to the right of [SOFTWARE.Name] in the calculated field box, then type a plus sign, a double quotation mark, a comma, a space, the word **Version**, a space, another double quotation mark, and another plus sign.

6. Open the software.db list box again, click Version, and then click Copy Field. The calculated field should now look like that in Figure 5.18.

7. Click to the right of [SOFTWARE.Version] in the calculated field box, then type a plus sign, a double quotation mark, a comma, a space, the word **Type**, a space, another double quotation mark, and another plus sign.

8. Open the software.db list box one more time, click Type, and then click Copy Field.

9. Click OK. The Report Design window reappears, as shown in Figure 5.19.

We do not want a label at the left of the software name.

1. Right-click the field you just placed in the report to inspect it.

2. In the properties pop-up menu, choose Display Type ➤ Unlabeled.

Click the View Data button in the Speedbar to preview the report with some data. The top part of your report should be similar to the one in Figure 5.20.

FIGURE 5.18:

The calculated field with two fields from the Software table.

FIGURE 5.19:

The Report Design
window with the
calculated field in
position.

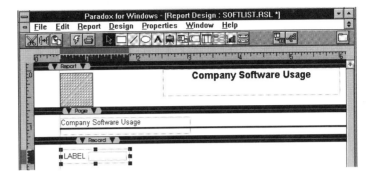

FIGURE 5.20:

The report with
information about the
first software package
in the Software table.

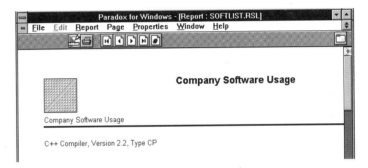

Notice that Paradox automatically removes unneeded spaces when fields are combined in a calculated field.

Now we shall add information about the software supplier.

1. Return to the Report Design window, then use the Field tool to draw a field box with its top-left corner at the $1\frac{3}{4}''$ vertical position and the $\frac{3}{4}''$ horizontal position.

2. Inspect the field and choose Define Field. From the list, choose COMPANY.DB.Name. The Name field appears in the report design. Click outside the field to deselect it.

3. Draw another field box with its top-left corner on top of the bottom left corner of the Name field box.

4. Inspect the field, Choose Define Field, and click the header (…).

5. In the Define Field Object dialog box, click Calculated.

6. Using fields from company.db, create a calculated field consisting of [COMPANY.Address]+", "+[COMPANY.City]+", "+[COMPANY.State]-+" "+[COMPANY.Zip]. Click OK to place the calculated field in the report design.

7. Draw another field box with its top-left corner at the bottom-left corner of the calculated field box.

8. Inspect the field and Choose Define Field. From the list, select COM-PANY.DB.Phone to place the Phone field in the report design.

9. Separately inspect each of the three objects you just created, and change their Display Type properties to Unlabeled.

Now, click View Data to preview the report. It should be similar to that in Figure 5.21.

Adjusting Spacing The report is almost complete, but we still need to give some attention to spacing, something you will almost always need to do if you are concerned about the appearance of your reports.

While you are looking at the report in View Data mode, scroll down to see the second record. As you see, there is too much empty space between one record and the next. There is also too much space between the three lines of company information.

FIGURE 5.21:

The report with one complete record.

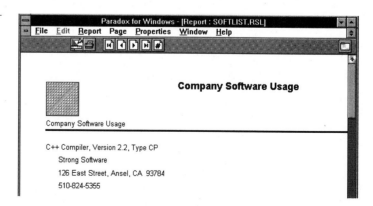

In the next few steps, we shall reduce the spacing between the company information fields, making the line spacing approximately equal, then we shall use Paradox's Adjust Spacing command to make the spacing exactly uniform.

1. Click the Design button.

2. In the Design Report window, drag the second line of company information up to reduce the space between the first and second lines. Do not be concerned if you move the line horizontally; we shall correct that later.

3. Drag the third line up so that is close to the second line.

4. Select all three lines of company information.

5. Choose Design ➤ Adjust Spacing ➤ Vertical.

If there was any difference in spacing, the middle line moved up or down so that it is now centrally spaced between the first and third lines.

While we have all three lines of company information selected, let's make sure they are aligned vertically.

1. Choose Design ➤ Align ➤ Align Left.

2. Click on an unoccupied part of the screen to deselect the three lines.

That corrects any vertical spacing and alignment problems. Now we can tackle the problem of space between records.

1. Scroll down, if necessary, until you can see the top and bottom record band labels. Both labels are selected because you are working in the record band.

2. Point onto the lower record band label, adjust the cursor position until it changes to a double-headed arrow, then press the mouse button and drag the label up to the 2½″ position on the vertical ruler.

We have not placed anything in the page and report footer bands, so let's eliminate the space in those bands.

1. Select the lower page band label and drag it up to the lower record band label.

2. Select the lower report band label and drag it up to the lower page band label. Your completed report design should be similar to the one in Figure 5.22.

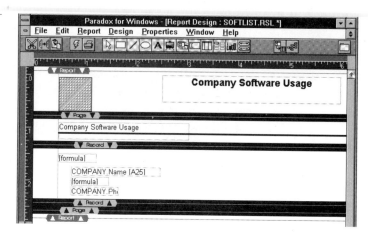

FIGURE 5.22:

The completed report design

3. Save the report design.

Preview the report to check your work. You might want to go back to Design mode to make some final adjustments to spacing or alignment. When you are satisfied, you are ready to make a printed copy of the report.

PRINTING THE REPORT

To print the report, start by previewing the report in View Data mode, then do the following:

1. Choose File ➤ Printer Setup and, in the Printer Setup dialog box, make sure the right printer is selected and is set up correctly.

2. Choose Print and then click OK in the Print File dialog box.

You will probably find that page breaks in the printed report occur within a record. For example, the name of a software package might be at the bottom of one page and information about the supplier at the top of the next page. Paradox allows you to correct this problem.

CONTROLLING PAGE BREAKS

Paradox prints a report page by page. Neither you nor Paradox knows where page breaks will occur until the report is printed. Controlling page breaks, therefore, is something that has to happen as report generation occurs. In Paradox terminology, page breaks occur at *run-time*. As you have already seen, Paradox objects have many properties. Some of those are run-time properties, things that can be controlled at the time an event happens.

You can control page breaks by inspecting the record band label and setting a run-time property.

1. Return to the Report Design window and right-click one of the record band labels. The properties list contains just one item—Run Time.

2. Click Run Time. Two run-time properties are displayed, as shown in Figure 5.23.

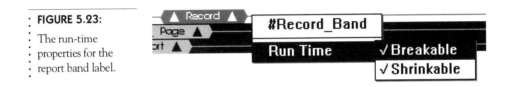

The two run-time properties, Breakable and Shrinkable, are checked by default. When Breakable is checked, Paradox allows a page break within a record. When Shrinkable is checked, any blank lines at the end of the last record on a page are ignored in an attempt to fit the record onto the page.

To ensure that all records start and end on the same page, unless a record is too long to fit on one page, click Breakable to turn it off. Then return to View Data and print the record to confirm that the problem is solved.

PLACING RECORDS IN ORDER

Whether you look at a report on the screen or print it, the report shows the records in the order they exist in the underlying table. Even if you use a secondary index to display records in a different order when you look at the table, this does not affect the order in which they appear in a report.

To change the order of records in a report, you must add a group band to the report. We shall see how this works as we modify the report design so that software packages are grouped according to their type.

PREPARING AN ALPHABETIZED REPORT

You will probably often want to prepare a report in which items are listed in alphabetical order. The following steps show how this can be done, in this case alphabetizing by software type.

1. Display the Report Design window.

2. Choose Report ➤ Add Band. The Define Group dialog box, shown in Figure 5.24, appears.

3. With SOFTWARE.DB selected in the list of tables, click Type in the Field list, then click OK. The Report Design window reappears with a group band inserted, as shown in Figure 5.25.

FIGURE 5.24:

The Define Group dialog box.

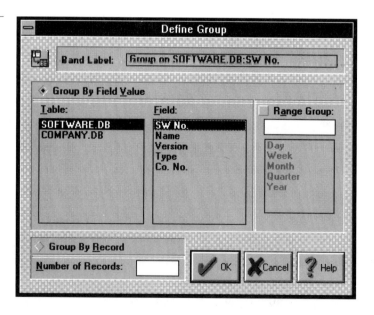

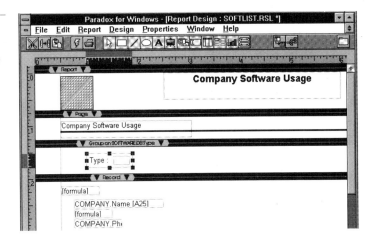

· **FIGURE 5.25:**
· The Report Design
· window with a group
· band.

The field frame in the group band has Type as a label. The presence of this frame has the effect of printing groups of records in alphabetical order of software types, with a header before each group. Preview the report to confirm this.

To improve the appearance of the report, draw a horizontal line under the group header and reduce the group's height, just as you did for the page header. The first part of the resulting report is shown in Figure 5.26.

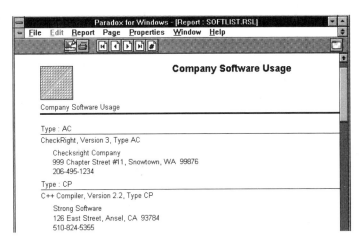

· **FIGURE 5.26:**
· The grouped software
· report.

GROUPING WITHIN GROUPS

Paradox allows you to design reports that contain groups within groups. This allows you to show groups of items sorted by a major category and, within each group, sorted by a secondary category.

We will see how to use groups within groups by preparing a report in which records are grouped in order of software type, and alphabetized by software name within each group. This time, however, we do not want to print the software name as a header before each software record.

1. Display the Report Design window.

2. Choose Report ➤ Add Band.

3. Click Name in the Field list, and then click OK. The Report Design window reappears with two group bands, as shown in Figure 5.27.

4. Delete the frame in the new group band by selecting it and then pressing Delete.

5. Remove the space for the new group by selecting the new group band header label and dragging it down to the record band label.

6. Delete the space for the new group band footer. The Report Design window is now similar to that in Figure 5.28.

7. Save the design and then preview it. Scroll through the preview to confirm that the software is grouped alphabetically by type and alphabetically by name within each group.

FIGURE 5.27:

The Report Design window with two group bands.

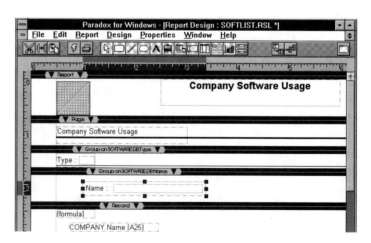

FIGURE 5.28:

The Report Design window finalized for grouping within a group.

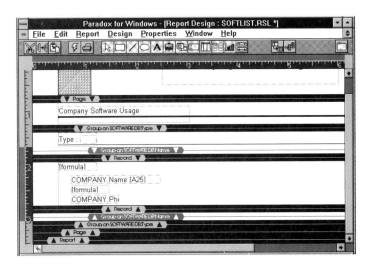

The order in which you create group bands is important. Start with the outermost group, then the next to outermost, and so on. The indentation of the group band labels in the Report Design window indicates how groups are nested in the report.

CHANGING GROUP PROPERTIES

There are several ways in which you can change group properties. For example, you can change the sort order from the default ascending to descending. For information about this, refer to Reports in Part II of this book.

CREATING A REPORT TO PRINT ADDRESS LABELS

Paradox can print reports in many formats. As an example, here is how you create a report that prints address labels using data in the Company table.

To be realistic, we will create a report that will print labels on 8½″ by 11″ sheets that you can use in your laser printer. The labels we will use are 1″ by 4″ in size.

DESIGNING THE LAYOUT

First, we shall open a new report and create the overall page layout. The steps here are described only briefly. Refer to the earlier parts of this lesson if you need more information. Before you begin, close the SOFTLIST report design.

1. Choose File ➤ New ➤ Report.

2. Select COMPANY.DB in the Data Model dialog box and select Blank in the Design Layout dialog box.

3. Maximize the Report Design window.

4. We don't need headers and footers, so close up the band bars to eliminate space for report and page headers and footers.

5. Choose Report ➤ Page Layout, and then choose Printer, Portrait, and Letter size.

6. Set the top and bottom margins to 0.5 inch to correspond to the position of the labels on the sheets.

7. Set the left and right margins to 0.4 inch to allow for the fact that the laser printer cannot print right to the edge of the paper.

8. Use the Multi-Record tool to draw a rectangle at the top of the report, starting at the left margin and extending to a depth of 1″ and to the right edge of the visible part of the window.

9. Scroll to the right edge of the window, then drag the handle on the right edge of the rectangle to the right margin.

You now have a rectangular frame which contains two smaller rectangles. The inner rectangles are the areas in which there will be two side-by-side labels. The rectangle on the left is where you design the label. The one on the right is a dummy that shows the placement of a second label that has the same size and design as the first.

To adjust the size of the labels:

1. Scroll to the left edge of the window.

2. With the outer frame already selected, click the left inner frame to select it, then drag the right edge of the frame to the right until it is just to the left of the $4\frac{1}{4}''$ position on the horizontal ruler.

3. Choose Properties ➤ Zoom ➤ 50% to verify that you have equal-size label frames.

4. Choose Properties ➤ Zoom ➤ 100% to return to normal size.

5. Select the upper Record bar and pull it down to eliminate space between it and the top of the label frame.

6. Select the lower Record bar and pull it down to eliminate space between it and the bottom of the label frame.

7. Choose Properties ➤ Band Labels to remove band labels from the screen.

8. Save the report with the name **Labels**.

Now you are ready to place objects in the left of the two frames. When you preview or print the report, whatever you place in the left frame will be replaced by field data in the remaining frames.

PLACING OBJECTS IN THE LABEL

Use the same techniques as you did earlier in this chapter to place three objects in the label: the company name in one line, the street address in the second line, and a calculated field consisting of the city, state, and ZIP code in the third line. Save the report again, then preview it. The address labels should be arranged as you see in Figure 5.29.

•
•
•
•
•
• **FIGURE 5.29:**

A preview of the
address labels.

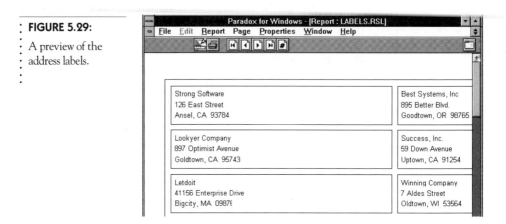

FOR MORE INFORMATION

You will find more information about the topics covered in this section by referring
to these entries in Part II of this book:

Browser

Data Models

Design Objects

Documents

Fields in a Document

Inspecting Objects

Printing

Reports

Spacing Objects in a Document

6

USING QUERY BY EXAMPLE

A database exists to provide information. Sometimes you need a printed version of some or all of the information in the database—a report. At other times you want an answer to a specific question—in database language, an answer to a query. This lesson is about queries.

This book's underlying example is a set of tables that contain information about software used by people in a company. In that context, you might want to ask such questions as these:

- What software is the company using?

- What software do specific companies provide?

- What software is each employee using?

This lesson shows you how to get answers to these types of questions. If you have a suitably structured database, you can easily get answers to these questions without having to use reports. Just use Query By Example (QBE). As the name implies, Query By Example simply means that you provide Paradox with an example of the kind of information you want.

USING QUERY BY EXAMPLE

We will start by looking at a simple example of QBE—getting an answer to the question: what software packages does our company use?

ASKING A QUESTION

To ask a question, you select the table you want to use, state what information you want from that table, and then run the query. Here is an example.

1. From the Paradox Desktop, choose File ➤ New ➤ Query. The Select File dialog box appears.

2. Double-click SOFTWARE.DB, and the Query window appears, as shown in Figure 6.1.

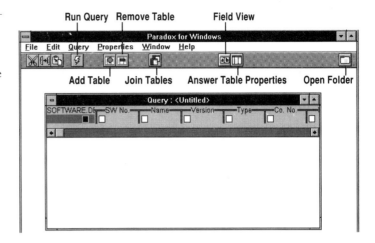

FIGURE 6.1:

The Query window, showing the first few fields in the Software table.

Notice the buttons in the Speedbar, some of which are different from what you have seen previously.

The Query window shows some of the fields in the table you selected, with the name of the table at the extreme left. You can scroll to the right to see additional fields.

You use this window to select the field values you want to see in the answer to your query. Notice that there is a small check box in each field. Click a field's check box to select that field. You can select as many fields as you wish. First, we shall select just one.

3. Click the check box under Name and a check mark appears there.

4. Click the Run Query button in the Speedbar. After a short delay, you see a table containing the names of the software in the Software table, as in Figure 6.2. This table, named ANSWER.DB, is written into your Private directory. The figure also shows the Query window with the Name field selected.

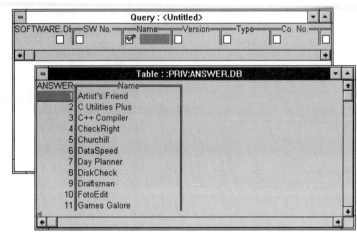

FIGURE 6.2:

The Answer table containing the names of the software packages in the Software table.

If you select a field and then want to deselect it, click its check box a second time. To select all the fields in a table, click the check box under the table name.

SAVING THE ANSWER

As you just saw, Paradox answers your query by creating a table. In most aspects, this table is identical to other Paradox tables. You can format the table in any way you wish, you can use it as the basis of a report, and you can use QBE to make a query about its contents.

The difference between this table and those you create yourself is that this one has a special name—ANSWER.DB. Whenever you make a query, Paradox presents the answer in a table with this name. Each time you make a query, the new answer replaces the information that was previously in ANSWER.DB. Also, whenever you exit from Paradox, ANSWER.DB is automatically deleted.

Do not use the name Answer for any table you create yourself. If you do, your table will be deleted the first time you run a query or when you exit Paradox.

You must rename ANSWER.DB to keep the answer to your query. To keep the list of software packages, change the name of ANSWER.DB to a name such as SW.DB.

1. Choose Table ➤ Rename. The Rename Table dialog box appears with a flashing insertion marker in the New Name text box.

2. Type **SW** and click OK. The table reappears with its new name in the title bar.

If you already have a table named SW.DB, you will get an error message when you click Rename in step 2. In this case, either try again with a different name, or delete the existing SW.DB table and then try again.

SAVING A QUERY

Suppose you often purchase new software and update your Software table regularly, and you frequently want to get a list of the software currently in use. It would not be too difficult to recreate the query each time but, as you will see later in this lesson, queries can be much more complex than the one we currently have. Paradox allows you to simplify your work by saving a query so that you can rerun it another time. To see how this works, do the following to save the query, and then rerun it:

1. Double-click the Control-menu box in the SW.DB title bar. The SW.DB table disappears, leaving the Query window on the screen.

2. Choose File ➤ Save. In the Save File As dialog box, notice that Paradox proposes to save the file with the extension .QBE.

3. Type **SW** and click OK. The Query window's title bar now shows the name of the query as SW.QBE.

4. Double-click the Control-menu box in the SW.QBE title bar to close the query.

RERUNNING A QUERY

To repeat a saved query, just open the query file and run it.

1. From the Desktop, choose File ➤ Open ➤ Query, and a dialog box appears containing the names of existing query files.

2. Double-click SW.QBE and the Query window opens.

3. Click the Run Query button in the Speedbar. An ANSWER.DB table appears, showing the list of software.

MODIFYING A QUERY

You can modify a saved query before you run it. Suppose you want to create a list of software the company uses, but this time include version numbers and two-letter type codes. Do this:

1. Display the Query window.

2. Click the check boxes under Version and Type so that check marks appear in both.

3. Click the Run Query button in the Speedbar. After a few moments of delay, an ANSWER.DB table appears showing the list of software, this time with version numbers and type codes.

CHANGING THE ANSWER FORMAT

You can control the format of an answer to a query by modifying the format of the ANSWER.DB table, by changing the format of the query, or both.

MODIFYING THE ANSWER TABLE

You can change the format of the data in an ANSWER.DB table in the same ways you can reformat the data in any other table. You can change the order of fields, change spacing, alignment, fonts, type size, color, and so on. The changes you make in this way apply only to the current Answer table; they do not affect Answer tables the query subsequently produces.

FORMATTING THE ANSWER TO A QUERY

To control the format of all Answer tables a query produces, you must change the Answer table properties. This allows you to choose a name other than Answer.db for the Answer table and to control the appearance of the Answer table. Let's see how this works.

1. Click the SW.QBE table to make it active.

2. Click the Answer Table Properties button in the Speedbar. The Answer Table Properties dialog box appears, as shown in Figure 6.3.

To change the name of the Answer table, simply replace the name in the Answer Name text box. Click the dBASE button in the Answer Table Type section of the dialog box if you want the Answer table in dBASE format.

The Image of Answer Table section of the dialog box allows you to change the table's format. You can change the order of fields in the table and change various properties of objects in the table.

Suppose you want to place the Type field before the Version field.

1. Place the cursor on the word Type and press the mouse button.

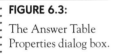

FIGURE 6.3:
The Answer Table Properties dialog box.

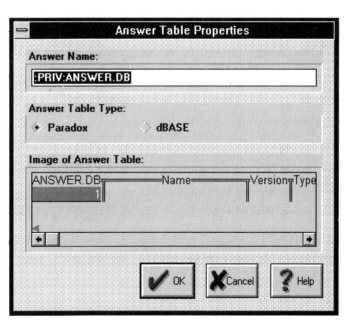

2. Drag to the left to a position on top of the word Version, then release the mouse button. The table image is redrawn with the fields in the new order.

3. Click OK, then run the query. The Answer table now displays the fields in the new order.

4. Click the Query window, and display an Answer Table Properties dialog box again.

To change the properties of a field title, right-click the field to display a properties pop-up menu. Similarly, to change the properties of field values, right-click the space under a field title. In both cases, you can choose Alignment, Color, or Font properties. For field values you can also choose the Data Dependent property, with which you can make the Answer table display fields differently according to their value. See Queries in Part II of this book for information about properties in Answer tables.

Click Cancel in the Answer Table Properties box to remove it from your screen.

CONTROLLING INFORMATION IN AN ANSWER

Earlier in this lesson, you clicked the check boxes under field names in the Query window to select the fields to be included in the Answer table. When you clicked a check box, a check mark appeared in it. You have more choices than this as you will see now.

1. With the SW.QBE Query window displayed, click all check boxes that contain check marks so that all are unchecked.

2. Point onto the check box under Type in the Query window, then press and hold down the mouse button. A menu of five field-selection icons appears, as shown in Figure 6.4.

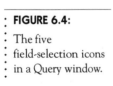

FIGURE 6.4:

The five
field-selection icons
in a Query window.

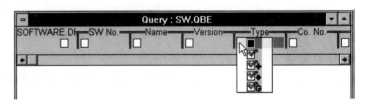

In order from top to bottom, names and functions of the five check icons in the menu are:

- Checkmark—include only unique values, sorted in ascending order, in the Answer table;
- Checkplus—include all values, in table order, in the Answer table;
- Checkdescending—include only unique values, sorted in descending order, in the Answer table;
- Checkgroup—specify a group of records;
- Uncheck—do not include field in the Answer table.

The first of these, check mark, is what you get when you click the box under a field name. To select any of the others, point onto a check box, press the mouse button, drag down to highlight the icon you want, then release the mouse button.

Let's see how three of these methods of selecting a field work, using the Type field as an example.

1. With the Query window displayed and no check boxes checked, click the Type check box so that a check mark appears in it.

2. Run the query. The Answer table contains the two-character type codes in alphabetical order. Although some type codes appear in more than one record, each code appears only once because the check mark places only unique values in the Answer table.

3. Close the Answer table, display the Query window, point onto the Type check box, and select the Checkplus icon.

4. Run the query. The Answer table now contains all the type codes, including duplicates, in the order they are in the Software table.

5. Close the Answer table, display the Query window, point onto the Type check box, and select the Checkdescending icon.

6. Run the query. The Answer table contains only unique type codes, this time in reverse alphabetical order.

The Checkgroup option is used when you have defined *sets* of records, a topic that is beyond the scope of this tutorial.

This way of controlling the order of records in an Answer table is mainly used when only one field is selected in a Query window. But what about when two or more fields are selected with different check types? Clearly, an Answer table cannot have some fields in alphabetical order and others in reverse alphabetical order. When you select two or more fields, the sort order is controlled by the check type of the leftmost selected field.

Let's look at another way of controlling sort order in an Answer table.

SORTING ON MULTIPLE FIELDS

Suppose we want to generate a list of software sorted in alphabetical order of type and, within each type, sorted alphabetically by software name. We can do this by using Answer table properties. Here's how.

1. With the SW.QBE Query window displayed, point to the check box in the first column headed SOFTWARE.DB. Press the mouse button, drag down to the Uncheck icon and release the mouse button. This removes check marks from all fields.

2. Click the Name, Version, and Type check boxes.

3. Choose Properties ➤ Answer Table ➤ Sort, to display the Sort Answer dialog box shown in Figure 6.5.

FIGURE 6.5:
The Sort Answer
dialog box.

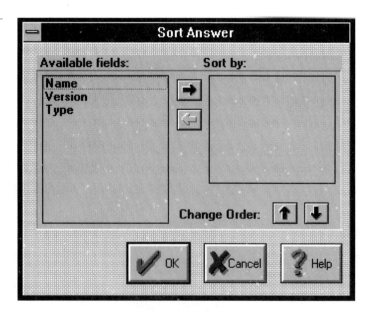

To select first- and second-level sort fields:

1. Click Type in the Available Fields list, then click the right-pointing arrow. The field name Type moves into the Sort By list.

2. Click Name in the Available Fields list, then click the right-pointing arrow. The field name Name moves into the Sort By list box below Type.

3. Click OK.

4. Run the query. The Answer table contains the Software records arranged in the order you specified.

With the Sort Answer dialog box open, you can move field names between the Available Fields and Sort By lists by clicking the right- and left-pointing arrows. You can change the sort priority by highlighting a field name in the Sort By list and clicking the up- and down-pointing arrows.

SELECTING RECORDS TO BE INCLUDED IN THE ANSWER

Our work so far has assumed that all records in the Software table should be included in the Answer table. But what if we want to list software packages only in certain categories? With Paradox, we can select which records are to be included in an answer by an exact match, an inexact match, or a range of matching values. First, we shall look at exact matches.

Exact Matches

An exact match is a record in which the values of specific fields exactly match an example. Suppose we want to list only software packages with the code WP in the Type field. Here is what we do.

1. Display the SW.QBE Query window with check marks in the Name, Version, and Type check boxes.

2. Click to the right of the Type check box to create an insertion marker, then type **WP**.

3. Run the query. The Answer table contains only those records that have WP in the Type field.

TIP

*When you specify an exact match, you must type the example exactly as values appear in fields, including matching capitalization. If you type the example as **wp**, rather than **WP**, Paradox will not find any matching records if all records in the Software table contain capitalized type codes.*

You do not need to check the field for which you specify an example. Here, for instance, you already know you are looking for a match with WP in the Type field, so that information does not need to appear in the Answer table. If a field is not checked, the matching records will still appear in the Answer table, just showing the checked fields.

You can specify an exact match in more than one field. For example, suppose you want to find all software packages of type WP that have a version number of 1.0.

1. Display the Query window.

2. Click to the right of the Version check box, then type **1.0**.

3. Run the query. Now the Answer table contains the one record that matches your specification.

INEXACT MATCHES

An inexact match is a record in which the values of specific fields closely, but not exactly, match an example you have specified. One type of inexact match, for instance, is an example in which capitalization does not match that in the records.

Paradox provides the LIKE operator as a means of specifying inexactly matching examples. Suppose some of the two-letter type codes in the Software table are capitalized and others are not. In this case, you could specify an inexact match as **LIKE WP** or **LIKE wp**.

The LIKE operator is particularly useful when you are not sure about the spelling of a value you want to match. Suppose you want to see information about a spell check program and you think its name is something like SpelRight. All you do is to type **LIKE spelright** as the example and run the query. If you do that, you will see that the Answer table contains the program name Spell Right.

For the LIKE operator to find a match, the example must meet two conditions:

- The first character of the example you type must match the first character in the table fields, although case is ignored.

- The example you type must contain at least half of the characters in the field, and these characters must be in the correct order.

Paradox provides two other operators—NOT and BLANK—which it includes in the inexact group. The NOT operator allows you to find all records in which a certain value is not in a specific field. To list all software not in the word-processing category, you would type **NOT WP** as the example in the Type field of the query table.

The example you type after the NOT operator must match the case of the value to be excluded from the Answer table.

The BLANK operator selects only those records in which a field is empty. You could use this to see if the Software table contains any records for which no software type is assigned. Just type the word **BLANK** in the Type field of the Query window and run the query. The Answer table will show just those records for which the Type field is empty.

You can also use the NOT and BLANK operators together. If you type **NOT BLANK** into a field in the Query window, the Answer table will contain only those records that contain any value in that field.

Occasionally, an example you want to use in a Query window field is exactly the same as the name of an operator. To identify the typed characters as an example rather than an operator, enclose them in double quotation marks. Paradox understands BLANK to be an operator; it understands "BLANK" to be an example value.

MATCHING RANGES

Ranges of records are those that contain fields with something in common. These may be specified in several ways, such as:

- Number fields having a range of numeric values;
- Alphanumeric fields having certain characters in common;
- Date fields having a range of dates.

Number Fields Ranges of number fields are normally expressed by using the five comparison operators:

OPERATOR	MEANING
=	equal to
>	greater than
<	less than
>=	greater than or equal to
<=	less than or equal to

If you have worked through the exercises in the preceding lessons of this book, your Software table has 21 records with values in the SW No. field numbered from 1 to 21. To get an Answer table containing only the last two records, you would type **>19** (or alternatively **>=20**) in the Query window's SW No. field.

But what if you want to list records with numbers 10 through 15? To do this, you type both conditions, separating them with a comma. You would type **>9,<16** or **>=10,<=15**.

Alphanumeric Fields Ranges of values in Alphanumeric fields are usually specified by using the wildcard operators @ and .. (two consecutive periods). The @ operator represents any one character; the .. operator represents any number of characters. In both cases, spaces and punctuation marks count as characters.

Suppose you want to search for all software packages with a name starting with Write. To do this, type **Write..** in the Query window's Name field. If you want to search for all software packages that include the word Friend, you would type **..Friend..** in the name field to include fields with any characters before or after Friend.

*Notice how the Paradox .. wildcard differs from the DOS * wildcard. DOS ignores all characters after *, whereas Paradox matches the characters after the .. string.*

You can use the @ operator to take care of the possibility that words may have been misspelled in a table. Suppose you suspect that the person who entered information into the Software table may have spelled Friend as Freind in some cases. You could take this into account by typing **..Fr@@nd..** in the Name field.

As we have already seen, you can use a word (such as Not) that is a Paradox operator within an example by enclosing it in double quotation marks. You can do the same with all other operators, including the comparison operators, and wildcard operators.

Date Fields If you are working with a table that contains dates, you can specify dates in much the same way as numbers. For example, to list records with Date values of January 1, 1993 or later, you would type **>=1/1/93** in the Query window's Date field.

The TODAY operator is particularly useful when you are working with Date fields. This operator represents the current date as set in your computer's internal calendar. To list all records with a date during the last 30 days, you would type **>=TODAY-30** as the matching condition.

If you want to experiment with queries involving dates, you can use the sample file ORDERS.DB which is supplied with Paradox. If you accepted the default installation procedure, this file is in your PDOXWIN\SAMPLE directory.

MULTIPLE MATCHING CONDITIONS

There are several ways in which we can specify more than one matching condition, either within a single field or among several fields.

COMBINING EXAMPLES WITH THE AND OPERATOR

When we specified a range of numeric values by expressing the example as **>9,<16**, we were using the AND operator, which is written as a comma. This example selected values that were greater than 9 *and* less than 16. The AND operator allows you to define separate conditions within a field, all of which must be true for a record to be in the Answer table.

COMBINING EXAMPLES WITH THE OR OPERATOR

The OR operator (written as OR) states alternative conditions; if any condition is met, the record will be included in the Answer table. Suppose we want to have a list of software that includes records of type WP or of type GR. For this example, you would type **WP OR GR**.

Let's look at another example of using the OR operator, this time querying the Company table to find software suppliers in California and Oregon. Doing so will demonstrate how to use the characters that represent an operator (OR in this case) as an example by enclosing them in double quotation marks.

1. Choose File ➤ New ➤ Query and select COMPANY.DB from the Select File dialog box.

2. In the new Query window, click the check boxes in the Name, Address, City, and State fields.

3. In the State field, type the example **CA OR "OR"**.

4. Run the query. The Answer table contains companies in California and Oregon.

EXAMPLES IN SEVERAL FIELDS

We can place examples in several fields of the Query window, in which case the values in corresponding record fields must match all the examples for a record to be included in the answer.

Suppose you want a list of all word processing software (type WP) together with all software that has a name starting with G. There is no way that you can define these two conditions in a single line of the Query window. In this case, you need to create a two-line query that expresses the two conditions. Do the following:

1. With the SW.QBE Query window open, click the Name, Version, and Type check boxes.

2. Type **WP** in the Type field.

3. Press ↓ to display a second line of fields in the Query window.

4. In the second line, click the Name, Version, and Type check boxes.

5. Also in the second line, type **G..** in the Name field. The Query window should now look like that in Figure 6.6.

6. Run the query. The Answer table includes all type WP software together with other software that has a name starting with G, as is also shown in Figure 6.6.

FIGURE 6.6:

The Query window with two sets of examples, together with the resulting Answer table.

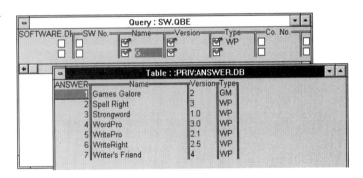

You can have many lines in a query as you wish, and each acts almost as if it were a separate query. However, all lines must have the same check boxes checked; otherwise, an error message will occur when you run the query.

RENAMING FIELDS IN THE ANSWER TABLE

Normally, fields in the Answer table have the same names as the fields in the source table. However, you can use the AS operator to rename fields in the Answer table. As you will see later in this lesson, this capability is useful when you query linked tables that have fields with the same name and also when you use calculated fields in queries.

Perhaps you want the Answer table to list software with the Name field titled Software Title. To do this, type **AS Software Title** under Name in the Query window. When you subsequently run the query, the Answer table shows the new heading for the list of software names.

QUERYING TWO OR MORE TABLES

We have already seen how forms and reports can use fields from two or more tables, and we have seen how tables can be linked. Now we'll see how queries can be used to obtain answers that include information from two or more tables. You can link tables within a Query window, or you can you can use table links that you have already established by a form.

First, we shall use the Query window to link two tables.

LINKING TABLES IN A QUERY

To illustrate how tables may be linked in a query, we shall produce an Answer table that shows the names and phone numbers of software suppliers, together with their products our company uses. The supplier information is obtained from the Company table, and the software information from the Software table.

First, we shall create a new Query window showing the fields in the Software and Company tables.

1. Choose Window ➤ Close All to close all open windows.
2. Choose File ➤ New ➤ Query.
3. Click COMPANY.DB in the Select File dialog box, then hold down Ctrl while you click SOFTWARE.DB. With both table names highlighted, click OK.
4. Maximize the Query window, and the top part of your screen should look like that in Figure 6.7.

FIGURE 6.7:

The Query window showing the fields in the Company and Software tables.

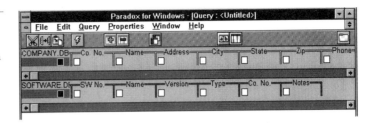

Next, link the two tables by way of the Co. No. field in each of them. Just as when we linked tables in Lesson 4, the two fields used to link the tables must be the same size and type. Also, the field we are linking to must be a primary or secondary index.

1. Click the Join Tables button in the Speedbar. When you move the cursor into either of the two table regions, the cursor changes to an arrow with EG below it, as in Figure 6.8.

FIGURE 6.8:

The Query window with Join Tables selected.

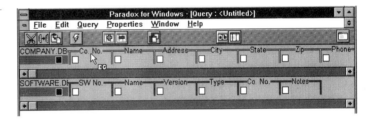

2. Click the example space in the Co. No. field of the Company table, and then click the example space in the Co. No. field of the Software table. In both cases, the text EG01, known as an *example element*, appears in the fields, as shown in Figure 6.9. The example element appears in red on a color monitor or is highlighted on a monochrome monitor.

FIGURE 6.9:

The Query window with the tables joined by example elements.

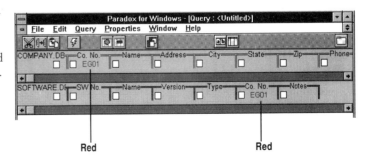

Red   Red

151

Pairs of example elements are numbered automatically, the first pair being EG01, the second EG02, and so on.

The fields to be included in the Answer table are identified by clicking the check boxes in the two tables, as before. Selection criteria are specified by typing examples in the tables.

1. Check Name and Phone in the Company table, and Name, Version, and Type in the Software table.

2. Run the query. The maximized Answer table appears showing the values for the checked fields, as in Figure 6.10.

Notice that the Answer table is alphabetized on the first checked field (Name) in the top table (Company) in the Query window. If you want the Answer table to contain an alphabetized list of software, you would have to place the Software table above the Company table in the Query window. One way to do this is to open the new Query window with just the Software table and then choose Query ➤ Add Table to add the Company table.

As before, you can save this query if you expect to use it again.

FIGURE 6.10:

The maximized Answer table showing field values from two tables.

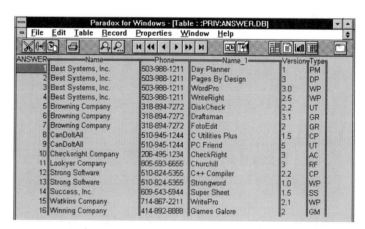

USING TABLES ALREADY LINKED BY A FORM

In Lesson 4, we designed a form that linked the People, Peopsoft, and Software tables, and we used that form to show which software various people use. We can use the table links in this form to get the same information by way of a query.

1. Choose File ➤ New ➤ Query. The Select file dialog box appears, initially listing tables.

2. Open the Type list box and click Forms. The dialog box now lists forms instead of tables.

3. Double-click PEOPSOFT.FSL. The Query window appears, showing the People, Peopsoft, and Software tables linked by example elements, as shown maximized in Figure 6.11.

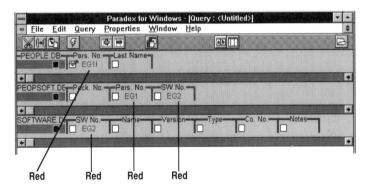

The red example elements show the links between tables. In this case, Paradox uses EG1 and EG2 as example elements.

Finally, click the appropriate check boxes in the three tables to identify the field values you want to see in the Answer table, then run the query.

Using Queries to Perform Calculations

Sometimes the information we want to extract from a database requires Paradox to perform calculations for us. Perhaps we want to get answers to queries such as:

- How many different software packages are we using?
- How many different software packages of each type are we using?

Paradox queries can provide answers to these, as well as much more complex queries, by using the CALC reserved word.

CALC precedes an expression in a Query window. Expressions allow you to:

- perform arithmetic calculations;
- combine alphanumeric values and constants.

Let's look at a few examples of using CALC.

CALCULATING AN ANSWER

In the work we have done with queries so far, we have created an Answer table that contains specific fields from certain records in one or more tables. Now we will consider how we can obtain an answer that is calculated from several fields.

The People table does not contain any fields on which meaningful calculations can be made, so we will use the Lineitem table. This table is in your PDOX-WIN\SAMPLE directory if you followed the default procedure to install Paradox.

Preparing the Lineitem Table

First copy the Lineitem table into your working directory. (By doing this, you will keep all the files you use while working with this book in one directory, and you will avoid making changes to the Paradox sample files.)

> *Always use the Paradox Copy command, rather than the DOS Copy command, to copy Paradox files. The Paradox Copy command copies the file you specify and all associated files, whereas the DOS command copies only the file you specify.*

1. From the Paradox Desktop, choose File ➤ Table Utilities ➤ Copy. The Table Copy dialog box appears.

2. In the Source Table text box, type **C:\PDOXWIN\SAMPLE\ LINEITEM.DB** and press Tab. You must include the file-name extension.

3. In the Copied Table Name text box, type **LINEITEM.DB**. Again, you must include the file-name extension.

4. Click Copy. Paradox copies the file together with any associated files into your working directory.

Look at the structure of the Lineitem table. (To display the structure of any table, use File ➤ Table Utilities ➤ Info Structure and select the file you want.) As you can see, the Lineitem table contains number and currency fields we can use to gain experience with calculated answers in queries. The Total field contains the product of the Selling Price and Qty fields. Let's delete this field from the table and, instead, use QBE to calculate values for the Total field.

1. Choose File ➤ Table Utilities ➤ Restructure. Select LINEITEM.DB and then click OK.

2. Click the 5 in the field-number column.

3. Press Ctrl+Delete. The Total field disappears.

4. Click Save and then click Yes in the Restructure Warning box. The Lineitem table reappears without the Total field.

5. Close the Lineitem table.

CREATING A CALCULATION IN A QUERY

Now we are ready to create a query that calculates the product of the Selling Price and Qty fields. To do this, we must assign names to the values in these fields. Most applications refer to these names as *variables*, but Paradox calls them *example elements*. We have already seen how Paradox uses example elements to link tables in a query. You can use any combination of characters for an example element, providing there is no conflict with a word Paradox uses for another purpose.

To assign an example element to a field value, click the field, press F5 and then type the example element characters. The example element appears in red within the field.

To use an example element in a calculation, press F5, then type the example element characters. As before, the characters appear in red on the screen.

> *Calculations can only be done on example elements, not on field names. You know that Paradox recognizes text as an example element when the text appears in red on your screen (or highlighted if you have a monochrome monitor). To assign or use an example element, press F5 before you type the example element's characters.*

Use the following steps to calculate the product of the values in the Selling Price and Qty fields. First, we shall open a new query and assign SP as the example element for Selling Price, and Quant as the example element for Qty.

1. Open a new query based on the Lineitem table.
2. Click the check box under LINEITEM, so that all fields will be included in the answer.
3. To assign an example element to Selling Price, click an insertion point under Selling Price, press F5, and type **SP**. SP appears in red.
4. To assign an example element to Qty, click an insertion point under Qty, press F5, and type **Quant**. Quant appears in red.

Now we are ready to define a new field that will contain the calculated product of the Selling Price and Qty fields. We can create this field within the space provided for any other field. If there is already text within that field's space, type a comma to start the new field.

We shall define the new field within the space provided for the Qty field. A flashing insertion marker is currently in that field after Quant.

1. Type a comma and a space.
2. Type **CALC** and a space.
3. Press F5 and type **SP**.

4. Type an asterisk (the multiplication operator).

5. Press F5 and type **Quant**. The top of your Query window should now look like that in Figure 6.12.

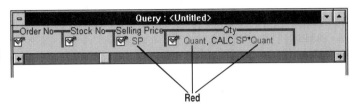

When you run the query you will get an Answer table similar to that shown maximized in Figure 6.13. Notice that the calculated field is included automatically in the Answer table.

*If you want the title of the calculated field to be Total instead of SP*Quant, use the AS operator.*

Paradox for Windows - [Table : C:\PDOXWIN\ANSWER.DB]

File   Edit   Table   Record   Properties   Window   Help

ANSWER	Order No	Stock No	Selling Price	Qty	Selling Price * Qty
1	1,001.00	1,313.00	$250.00	4.00	$1,000.00
2	1,001.00	3,340.00	$395.00	16.00	$6,320.00
3	1,002.00	1,314.00	$365.00	7.00	$2,555.00
4	1,002.00	1,316.00	$341.00	9.00	$3,069.00
5	1,002.00	1,320.00	$171.00	5.00	$855.00
6	1,002.00	2,341.00	$105.00	35.00	$3,675.00
7	1,003.00	1,314.00	$365.00	5.00	$1,825.00
8	1,003.00	2,390.00	$420.00	12.00	$5,040.00
9	1,004.00	1,364.00	$270.00	2.00	$540.00
10	1,004.00	1,390.00	$170.00	8.00	$1,360.00
11	1,004.00	9,316.00	$325.00	5.00	$1,625.00
12	1,005.00	1,320.00	$171.00	1.00	$171.00
13	1,005.00	1,330.00	$260.00	2.00	$520.00
14	1,005.00	1,364.00	$270.00	5.00	$1,350.00
15	1,005.00	1,390.00	$170.00	9.00	$1,530.00
16	1,005.00	1,946.00	$309.00	4.00	$1,236.00
17	1,006.00	11,564.00	$3,299.00	2.00	$6,598.00
18	1,006.00	12,301.00	$599.00	1.00	$599.00

COUNTING VALUES IN A FIELD

Let's look at another example of using CALC. Suppose we want to find out how many different software packages our company is using. All we have to do is to count the number of software names in the Names field of the Software table. To do this, we use the COUNT operator:

1. Open a new query window showing the Software table.

2. In the Name field, type **CALC COUNT**. Do not click the check box in the Name field or any other field.

3. Run the query. Paradox automatically creates the Count of Name column in the Answer table. This column shows the number of different values in the Name field, as shown in Figure 6.14.

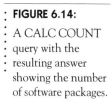

FIGURE 6.14:

A CALC COUNT query with the resulting answer showing the number of software packages.

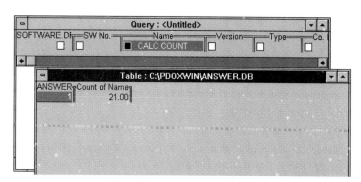

COUNT normally returns the number of unique values in the specified field. In the Name field, every value is unique, so the total number of names is the same as the number of different names. If you try the example using the Type field, where several records have the same value, you'll see the result shown in Figure 6.15. To get the total number of values where some may be duplicated, you would type CALC COUNT ALL in the Type field. See the Queries entry in Part II for a list of all the calculations you can perform.

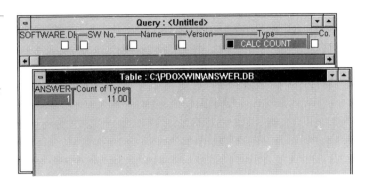

COMBINING ALPHANUMERIC VALUES AND CONSTANTS

Another important use of calculated fields is to combine alphanumeric values and constants. When we worked with reports, we saw how to combine values from several fields into a single field. We did this, for example, when we created one line in a mailing label which combined City, State, and Zip fields. We can do the same type of thing within queries.

Let's create a query that displays the name and address of companies in the Company table, with the city, state, and ZIP code in a single column. This new column will also contain punctuation marks and spaces, which are constants.

First, open a new query and assign example elements to City, State, and Zip, the fields we shall be using in the calculated field.

1. Open a new query based on the Company table and maximize the Query window.
2. Click the City field, press F5, and type **Cty**.
3. Click the State field, press F5, and type **St**.
4. Click the Zip field, press F5, and type **Zp**.

If you do this correctly, all the example elements are displayed in red on your screen.
Now, construct the calculated field within the ZIP field space.

1. Type a comma, a space, **CALC**, and a space.
2. Press F5 and then type **Cty**. Cty appears in red.

3. Type **+", "+**.

4. Press F5 and then type **St**. St appears in red.

5. Type **+" "+**.

6. Press F5 and then type **Zp**. Zp appears in red.

At this stage, the top part of your Query window should look like that in Figure 6.16.

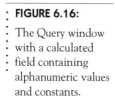

FIGURE 6.16:

The Query window with a calculated field containing alphanumeric values and constants.

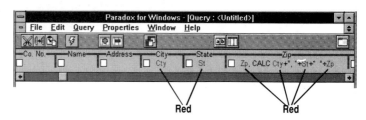

Do not forget to click the check boxes of the fields you want to appear in the Answer table before you run the query. The calculated field is always displayed, so you do not have to click anywhere to see that in the Answer table.

1. Click the check boxes in the Name and Address fields. Do not click any other check boxes.

2. Run the query.

3. Maximize the Answer table. It should look like that in Figure 6.17.

FIGURE 6.17:

The Answer table showing the calculated field.

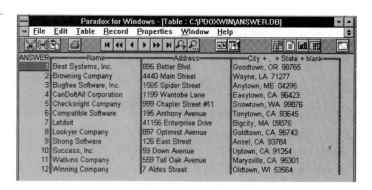

EXPERIMENTING WITH QUERIES

This lesson has introduced you to some of the important concepts behind queries, but it has by no means shown everything Paradox has to offer. After you have become familiar with these examples, experiment for yourself. You will find that by using queries to construct new tables from existing tables, you can easily present data in the format you need.

Throw problems at Paradox queries. You will be amazed at how quickly queries become intuitive.

IN CONCLUSION

This completes the Step-by-Step Tutorial section of this book. We hope we have been successful in giving you a quick start in understanding the most important basics of Paradox for Windows.

Part II, the Alphabetical Reference, contains a wealth of information you can use to develop your skills further, and to answer questions that arise as you use Paradox in more sophisticated ways.

FOR MORE INFORMATION

You will find more information about the topics covered in this lesson by referring to these entries in Part II of this book:

Fields

Queries

Tables

ALPHABETICAL REFERENCE

ALIASES

PURPOSE Aliases, names that replace the full path names of directories, simplify identification of directories. All aliases start and end with a colon. Paradox assigns :PRIV: as the alias for your private directory and :WORK: as the alias for your current working directory. You can create aliases for any number of additional directories.

Paradox maintains a list of aliases in the Object Database Application Programming Interface configuration file ODAPI.CFG.

TO GIVE A DIRECTORY AN ALIAS

1. Choose File ➤ Aliases ➤ New.
2. Enter the alias name into the Database Alias text box.
3. Enter the full path name of the directory into the Path text box.
4. Click Keep New.
5. If the new alias is for use in the current Paradox session only, click OK. To keep the alias for use in future Paradox sessions, go to step 6.
6. Click Save As to display the Save File As dialog box.
7. Click OK to save the new alias in the default ODAPI.CFG directory.
8. Click OK to overwrite the existing ODAPI.CFG directory.
9. Click Cancel to return to the Desktop.

TO REMOVE AN ALIAS

You can remove aliases that you have created, but you cannot remove the PRIV or WORK aliases.

1. Choose File ➤ Aliases.
2. Open the Database Alias list box.
3. Click the alias you want to remove, click Remove, and then click OK.

See Also Directories

A

ALIGNING OBJECTS

PURPOSE To align objects horizontally or vertically in a document.

TO ALIGN OBJECTS HORIZONTALLY OR VERTICALLY

You can vertically align objects on their centers, left edges, or right edges. You can horizontally align objects on their centers, top edges, or bottom edges.

1. Display a document in Design mode.

2. Select two or more objects in a document.

3. Choose Design ➤ Align.

4. Choose one of the six alignment options.

ARROWHEADS

PURPOSE You can place arrowheads at the ends of lines to draw attention to objects in a document.

TO ADD ARROWHEADS TO THE ENDS OF LINES

1. Select one or more lines.

2. Right-click a selected line to inspect all the selected lines.

3. Choose Line Ends.

4. Choose one of the three options: No Arrow, On One End, or On Both Ends.

NOTE If you choose On One End, the arrowhead appears at the end (as opposed to the beginning) of the line; that is, the end you drew last. If you want the arrowhead to appear at the beginning of an existing line, you must redraw the line starting from the other end.

See Also Objects

BROWSER

PURPOSE Browser is a built-in utility that simplifies finding and selecting files. When you choose an action that involves selecting a directory or file, Paradox displays a dialog box containing a Browse button. You can click this button to display the directory structure of your disks, and to select a directory or file.

TO USE BROWSER TO FIND AND SELECT A FILE

The following steps describe how to use Browser to select a Table file; you can use similar steps to select other types of Paradox files.

1. Choose File ➤ Open ➤ Table to open the Open a Table dialog box.

2. Click Browse.

3. Open the Aliases list box and do one of the following:

   ◆ select the alias (if one exists) for the directory you want to see, then proceed to step 7.

   ◆ select the disk drive that contains the file you want to find, then proceed to step 4.

4. Click the name of the highest-level directory you want to use. This displays the names of all table files in that directory.

5. If you want to see files in a subdirectory, double-click the top-level directory name, then click the subdirectory name.

6. Repeat step 5 as many times as necessary to go to lower-level subdirectories.

7. Double-click the name of the file you want to select. The Open a Table dialog box returns, displaying the new directory with the chosen file selected.

8. Double-click the table name to open that table.

See Also Aliases, Directories

COLOR

PURPOSE Paradox provides default colors for all objects. You can inspect an object and change its color to one of the standard colors or to a custom color.

TO CHANGE AN OBJECT'S COLOR

Use this procedure to apply a color from the color palette to an object. This procedure uses a color palette that disappears as soon as you use it and is, therefore, known as a *temporary* color palette.

1. Display a design object and select it.
2. Right-click the object to display its pop-up properties menu.
3. Click Color to display the temporary color palette.
4. Click the color you want to use, or click the rectangle at the bottom right of the palette to make the object transparent. The object is redrawn in the selected color.

TO CREATE CUSTOM COLORS

You can create custom colors and also modify existing custom colors.

1. Display the floating color palette, as described in *To Snap the Color Palette*.
2. Click one of the blank spaces in the right column of the color palette, then click the Custom Color button to display the Custom color dialog box.
3. Click a button to select the RGB (red, green, blue), HSV (hue, saturation, value), or CMY (cyan, magenta, yellow) color model.
4. Either enter color values into the three text boxes, or drag in the slider boxes to create the custom color. As you work, the large rectangle in the dialog box shows the color.
5. Click OK to accept the color. The new color appears in the color palette and also in the selected object.

TO MAKE AN OBJECT TRANSPARENT OR TRANSLUCENT

To make an object transparent (like clear glass), use the procedure *To Change an Object's Color* and select the transparent sample at the bottom right of the temporary color palette. To make an object translucent (like colored glass), use this procedure, which allows you to mix colors on screen.

1. Select an object, inspect it, and click Color to display the temporary color palette.
2. Click the circle at the top of the temporary color palette to convert it to a floating color palette.
3. Click a color in the floating color palette to apply an opaque color to the object.
4. Click the Transparent button to make the object translucent.

TO SNAP THE COLOR PALETTE

By default, when you click a color in the color palette, the color palette disappears and the selected object is redrawn in the selected color. You can keep the color palette on the screen by *snapping* it. This simplifies the process of selecting colors for several objects. The color palette used in this way is known as the *floating* color palette. Unlike the temporary color palette, the floating palette allows you to apply a color to an object, to its fill pattern, or to its frame.

1. Select an object, inspect it, and click Color to display the temporary color palette.
2. Click the circle at the top of the temporary color palette. This snaps the color palette so that it remains displayed after you select colors.
3. Drag the color palette to a convenient place on the screen.
4. When you have finished using the palette, click the circle in its title bar to remove the palette from the screen.

See Also Desktop, Properties of Objects

CONTAINERS

PURPOSE When Paradox objects are completely within another object, by default the outer object contains the inner objects. The outer object is a container; the inner objects are contained. As a result:

- when you move the container, the contained objects move with it;
- when you delete the container, the contained objects are deleted;
- when you cut or copy the container to the Clipboard, the contained objects are also cut or copied.

Object trees clearly show which objects are contained by others (see *Object Trees*).

TO BREAK A CONTAINMENT RELATIONSHIP

Use this procedure when you want an object to appear within another, but not to be functionally contained by it.

1. Right-click the containing object to display its pop-up properties menu.
2. Choose Design to display the design pop-up menu in which Contain Objects is checked.
3. Click Contain Objects to clear it.
4. Optionally, click the Object Tree button on the Speedbar to display the object tree and confirm that the objects within the selected object are no longer contained by it.

TO PLACE AN OBJECT WITHIN ANOTHER OBJECT

When one object is completely inside another, the former is contained by the latter. Use any of these methods to place an object inside another:

- create a new object within an existing object;
- move an existing object within another object;

- resize or move an existing object so that it contains another object;
- paste an object into an existing object.

See Also Object Trees

CROSSTABS

PURPOSE Crosstabs (cross-tabulations) present data in rows and columns in a spreadsheet-like structure. You can use crosstabs as an easy way of summarizing data.

TO CREATE A CUSTOM CROSSTAB

1. Open a new, blank form with the table (or tables) from which the Crosstab is to be created in the data model.
2. In Design mode, click the Crosstab tool.
3. Use the Crosstab cursor to draw a large rectangle.
4. Inspect the three Undefined Field labels separately and define a field for each of them.
5. Click the View Data button on the Speedbar to display the Crosstab in a new form.

TO CREATE A ONE-DIMENSIONAL QUICK CROSSTAB

A one-dimensional crosstab is a table showing a single row or column of values.

1. Open the table that contains the data you want to display as a crosstab.
2. Click the Quick Crosstab button on the Speedbar to display the Define Crosstab dialog box.
3. With Column selected (for a horizontal crosstab) or Categories selected (for a vertical crosstab), open the list of fields in the table.

4. Click the field to be tabulated.

5. Click Summaries.

6. Open the list of fields in the table.

7. Click the field to be summarized.

8. Open the Summary list box.

9. Choose the summary method according to the way you want to calculate values for the crosstab cells:

   ◆ Sum, for the sum of values in the selected summary field;

   ◆ Count, for the number of values in the selected summary field;

   ◆ Min, for the minimum value in the selected summary field;

   ◆ Max, for the maximum value in the selected summary field;

   ◆ Avg, for the average value in the selected summary field.

10. Click OK to display the crosstab as an object in a new form.

TO CREATE A TWO-DIMENSIONAL QUICK CROSSTAB

A two-dimensional crosstab is a table with more than one column, or more than one row, of values.

1. Open the table that contains the data you want to display as a crosstab.

2. Click the Quick Crosstab button on the Speedbar to display the Define Crosstab dialog box.

3. With Column selected, open the list of fields in the table and click the field to use as columns in the crosstab.

4. Click Categories.

5. Open the list of fields in the table and click the fields to use as rows in the crosstab.

6. Follow steps 5 through 10 in *To Create a One-Dimensional Quick Crosstab*.

NOTE To create a crosstab with data from two or more tables, open or create a form that links the tables with a one-to-one relationship. With the form in Design mode, click the Crosstab button on the Speedbar and follow the steps listed under *To Create a Custom Crosstab*. You cannot create a crosstab from tables linked in a one-to-many relationship.

See Also Data Model, Documents (Forms and Reports), Forms, Linking Tables, Tables

ATA MODELS

Dᴀᴛᴀ MODELS

PURPOSE Data models name the tables on which a document is based. When a document is based on two or more tables, the data model also defines any links between those tables.

TO ADD A TABLE TO A DATA MODEL

Use this procedure to add a table to a document's data model and, if necessary, to link the new table to an existing table.

1. Display a document in Design mode.
2. Click the Data Model button on the Speedbar to display the Data Model dialog box.
3. Click the name of the table to be added, then click the right-pointing arrow.
4. Indicate the two tables to be linked by pointing onto the table from which a link originates, then dragging to the table at which the link terminates. Release the mouse button to display the Define Link dialog box, showing the fields Paradox proposes to link.
5. If the originating field proposed by Paradox is not correct, click on the correct field in the Field list, then click the right-pointing arrow.
6. If the terminating key or secondary index proposed by Paradox is not correct, click on the correct name in the Index list, then click the left-pointing arrow.
7. Click OK to return to the Data Model dialog box with the link displayed.
8. Click OK to save data model with the added table.

TO CHANGE LINKS BETWEEN TABLES

Use this procedure to show which tables are linked in a document, to see which fields link pairs of tables and, if necessary, to make changes.

1. Display a document in Design mode.

2. Click the Data Model button on the Speedbar to display the Data Model dialog box, showing the tables used in the form and any links between them.

3. If any tables are linked and you want to examine the links in detail, right-click the arrowhead at the end of the line that indicates the link between two tables. The Define Link dialog box appears, showing the fields that link the two tables.

4. If you want to unlink the two tables, click the Unlink button.

5. If you want to change the field that originates the link, click that field in the Field list, then click the right-pointing arrow.

6. If you want to change the key or secondary index at the terminating end of the link, click the new name and then click the left-pointing arrow.

7. To accept changes in the Define Link dialog box, click OK to return to the Data Model dialog box. Alternatively, click Cancel to return without accepting changes.

8. Click OK to accept any changes made to the Data Model dialog box.

TO CHANGE THE ORDER OF FIELDS

By default, fields are displayed in the order in which they exist in a table. Use this procedure to change the order of fields in a document.

1. Follow steps 1 through 5 in *To Design a Page Layout*.

2. Click Select Fields. In the Select Fields dialog box, select a field that you want to move and click the up- or down-pointing arrow to move it to a new position in the list of fields.

3. Repeat step 2 as needed to move additional fields.

4. Click OK to return to the Design Layout dialog box.

5. Click OK to accept the design.

TO CREATE A DATA MODEL WITH A SINGLE TABLE

1. Choose File ➤ New ➤ Form.
2. Place a table into the data model by clicking its name and then clicking the right-pointing arrow.
3. Click OK to start the design layout.

TO CREATE A DATA MODEL WITH TWO OR MORE TABLES

1. Follow steps 1 and 2 in *To Create a Data Model with a Single Table*.
2. Repeat step 2 in that procedure to place additional tables into the data model. If any of the tables are to be linked, proceed to step 3, otherwise skip to step 8.
3. Indicate two tables to be linked by pointing onto the table from which a link originates, and then dragging to the table at which the link terminates. Release the mouse button to display the Define Link dialog box showing the fields Paradox proposes to link.
4. If the proposed originating field is not correct, click on the correct field in the Field list, then click the right-pointing arrow.
5. If the proposed terminating key or secondary index is not correct, click on the correct name in the Index list, then click the left-pointing arrow.
6. Click OK to return to the data model with the link displayed.
7. Repeat steps 3 through 6 as many times as required to establish links between additional pairs of tables.
8. Click OK to start the design layout.

TO DELETE A TABLE FROM A DATA MODEL

You must unlink a table before you can delete it from the data model.

1. In Design mode, display the form that contains the data model.

2. Click the Data Model button on the Speedbar to see the tables in the data model.

3. If the table is not linked to any other tables, go to step 7. Otherwise, right-click the arrowhead in the line that indicates a link between the table to be deleted and any other table.

4. Click Unlink in the Define Link dialog box.

5. Click OK to return to the Data Model dialog box.

6. If the table to be deleted is linked to another table, repeat steps 3 through 5 as many times as necessary for the table to have no links.

7. Click the table to be deleted, and then click the left-pointing arrow.

TO DESIGN A PAGE LAYOUT

A design layout determines how fields from a table initially appear in a document.

1. Display a document in Design mode.

2. Choose Design ➤ Design Layout.

3. In the Design Layout dialog box select a layout Style.

4. Click Field Layout and Multi-Record choices (if available in the selected style).

5. Click the Labeled Fields button to remove the check mark if you do not want fields labeled (not available in Blank style).

6. Click Select Fields if you want only certain fields initially displayed in the page layout. Then, in the Select Fields dialog box, select fields that are not to be displayed and click Remove Field. Click OK to return to the Page Layout dialog box.

7. Click OK to accept the design.

TO EXAMINE A DATA MODEL

Use this procedure to verify which tables are linked in a document, and also to see which fields link pairs of tables.

177

1. Display a form in Design mode.

2. Click the Data Model button on the Speedbar to see the tables in the data model and any links between them.

3. If any tables are linked and you want to examine the links in detail, right-click the arrowhead at the end of the line that indicates the link between two tables. The Define Link dialog box is displayed.

4. Click Cancel in the Define Link dialog box and again in the Data Model dialog box to return to the form.

NOTES The data model shows one field above the other for a one-to-one relationship. It shows two fields side-by-side for a one-to-many relationship.

See Also Documents (Forms and Reports), Forms

DATABASES

PURPOSE A database is an organized collection of data stored in tables. A Paradox database also includes information about how the tables are displayed (forms), how tables are related (forms), how data in the tables is printed (reports), and how operations on the data are automated (scripts).

All the files relating to a database are normally stored in a single directory which, when it is active, is the :WORK: directory. The major files in this directory are shown in the Folder.

TO CREATE A DATABASE

There are ten major steps involved in creating a database. These steps provide a general procedure which you may have to modify to suite specific requirements. Requirements usually change or become more completely defined during the process, so be prepared to work through the steps several times.

1. Write a detailed list of all the requirements for the database.

2. Plan the tables necessary to satisfy the requirements listed in step 1, including the key and secondary index fields needed to link the tables.

3. Create the tables planned in step 2. See *Tables*.

4. Define table properties to take advantage of such features as default field values, field pictures, minimum and maximum values, lookup tables, and referential integrity. See *Tables*.

5. Create forms to provide links between tables and to provide a means of data input. See *Data Models* and *Forms*.

6. Use the data entry forms created in step 5 to enter typical data into the database. See *Forms*.

7. Create reports to provide formatted data output. See *Reports*.

8. Use the reports to print data. See *Printing*.

9. Add password protection to tables and individual fields as required. See *Password Protection*.

10. Verify the database by having a small number of other people use it.

See Also Data Models, Documents (Forms and Reports), Folders, Forms, Printing, Reports, Scripts, Tables

DESIGN OBJECTS

PURPOSE Design objects can be created in documents by using Speedbar tools. The Paradox design objects are:

OBJECT TYPE	DESCRIPTION
Box	Boxes are rectangles that can be placed in a document.

OBJECT TYPE	DESCRIPTION
Button	Buttons are objects that can be placed on a form (but not in a report) to initiate actions. When you attach an ObjectPAL method to a button, that method is executed when you click the button.
Crosstab	Crosstabs present information derived from tables in a spreadsheet-like format in a document.
Ellipse	Ellipses may be used to draw attention to other objects in a document; the effect is as if you had circled the object in pencil.
Field	Fields contain values derived from one or more tables, or special values that show the current date or time, current page number, or the number of pages in a document. Each field contains a label and a value.
Graph	Graphs are objects that present data from tables in a graphical format in a document.
Graphic	A graphic is an image in a graphic-type field of a table or an independent graphic image in a document. Paradox accepts graphics from the Clipboard and also imports them as .BMP, .GIF, .EPS, .PCX, or .TIF files.
Line	Lines can be created in a document to enhance visual appeal. Arrowheads may be attached to the ends of lines.
Multi-Record	A multi-record object presents a repeating pattern of fields in a document. After the layout of fields from one object is defined, a multi-record object uses the same format to display the values in several records.

OBJECT TYPE	DESCRIPTION
OLE	You can use Window's Object Linking and Embedding (OLE) capabilities to place objects from other applications into a Paradox container. Refer to your Windows documentation for information about OLE.
Table Frame	A table frame is an object that may contain the data in a table. After you place a table frame in a document, you may bind a table to it so that the table frame contains the bound table's data.
Text	Text objects contain text of any length and in any available format in a document. Text objects are contained within a text frame.

Each design object has a number of properties to which Paradox assigns default values, but which you can change. The properties of a box, for example, include the fill color and pattern, and the style, color, and thickness of the frame. See *Properties of Objects*.

The following procedures show how to create these types of objects in documents. You can use the optional grid to help you place objects accurately. See *Properties of Objects* for information about rulers and about grid settings, displaying the grid, and snapping to the grid.

When a document is in Design mode, the Status bar shows the name and type of a selected object.

TO CREATE A BOX DESIGN OBJECT IN A DOCUMENT

A box is a rectangle or square you can place around all or part of a document.

1. Open a document in Design mode.

2. Optionally, use the Properties menu to display rulers, to display a grid, and to turn on Snap To Grid (see *Properties of Objects*).

3. Click the Box tool in the Speedbar, then move the cursor into the work area. The cursor shape changes to a cross with a rectangle below it.

4. Move the center of the cross to position the top-left corner of the box, press the mouse button, drag down to position the bottom-right corner of the box, then release the mouse button. A selected box appears.

5. Right-click the box to display its properties pop-up menu.

6. Click items on the pop-up menu to define the properties of the box.

TO CREATE A BUTTON DESIGN OBJECT IN A FORM

Buttons in Paradox forms act like buttons in most Windows applications—when a user clicks a button, a certain action occurs. In Paradox, the action that occurs as a result of clicking a button is defined by a method written in ObjectPAL, the Paradox programming language. ObjectPAL programming is beyond the scope of this book.

You can place buttons in forms, but not in reports.

1. Open a document in Design mode.

2. Optionally, use the Properties menu to display rulers, to display a grid, and to turn on Snap To Grid (see *Properties of Objects*).

3. Click the Button tool in the Speedbar, then move the cursor into the work area. The cursor shape changes to a cross with a miniature button below it.

4. Move the center of the cross-cursor to position the top-left corner of the button, press the mouse button, drag down to position the bottom-right corner of the button, then release the mouse button. A selected gray button appears with the word LABEL inside it.

5. Right-click the button to display its properties pop-up menu.

6. Click items on the pop-up menu to define the properties of the button. You can attach a method at this point, as described under Objects.

7. To change the label (by default LABEL) within the button, click within the label to select it, then use normal Windows editing techniques to replace it with the appropriate text.

TO CREATE A CROSSTAB
DESIGN OBJECT IN A DOCUMENT

A crosstab is a representation, in spreadsheet format, of data in one or more tables.

1. Open a document in Design mode.

2. Optionally, use the Properties menu to display rulers, to display a grid, and to turn on Snap To Grid (see *Properties of Objects*).

3. Click the Crosstab tool in the Speedbar, then move the cursor into the work area. The cursor shape changes to a cross with a miniature representation of a spreadsheet below it.

4. Move the center of the cross to position the top-left corner of the crosstab, press the mouse button, drag down to position the bottom-right corner of the crosstab, then release the mouse button. A selected crosstab skeleton, with three undefined field labels, appears.

5. Inspect each undefined field label separately, and define a field for each (see *Crosstabs*).

6. Right-click the crosstab to display its properties pop-up menu.

7. Click items on the pop-up menu to define the properties of the crosstab.

TO CREATE AN ELLIPSE
DESIGN OBJECT IN A DOCUMENT

An ellipse is created within a rectangular container.

1. Open a document in Design mode.

2. Optionally, use the Properties menu to display rulers, to display a grid, and to turn on Snap To Grid (see *Properties of Objects*).

D

3. Click the Ellipse tool in the Speedbar, then move the cursor into the work area. The cursor shape changes to a cross with an ellipse below it.

4. Move the center of the cross to position the top-left corner of the ellipse container, press the mouse button, drag down to position the bottom-right corner of the container, then release the mouse button. A selected container appears with the ellipse inside it.

5. Right-click within the ellipse to display its properties pop-up menu.

6. Click items on the pop-up menu to define the properties of the ellipse.

7. Right-click within the container, but outside the ellipse, to display a menu of the properties of the container outside the ellipse.

8. Click items on the pop-up menu to define the properties of the container outside the ellipse.

TO CREATE A FIELD DESIGN OBJECT IN A DOCUMENT

A field is an object that contains a label and a value. A field object can be displayed with or without the label.

1. Open a document in Design mode.

2. Optionally, use the Properties menu to display rulers, to display a grid, and to turn on Snap To Grid (see *Properties of Objects*).

3. Click the Field tool in the Speedbar, then move the cursor into the work area. The cursor shape changes to a cross with a miniature representation of a field below it.

4. Move the center of the cross to position the top-left corner of the field, press the mouse button, drag down to position the bottom-right corner of the field, then release the mouse button. A selected field appears with a label and an outlined area for a value.

5. Right-click the field (outside the label and value) to display the field properties pop-up menu.

6. Click items on the pop-up menu to define the properties of the field.

7. Click the label to select it. Use normal Windows editing techniques to change the characters in the label.

8. Right-click the label to display its properties pop-up menu. Click items on the pop-up menu and change properties as appropriate.

9. Click the outlined value area, then right-click to display the value's properties. Change the properties as appropriate.

TO CREATE A GRAPH DESIGN OBJECT IN A DOCUMENT

A graph object provides a visual representation of data stored in one or more tables.

1. Open a document in Design mode.

2. Optionally, use the Properties menu to display rulers, to display a grid, and to turn on Snap To Grid (see *Properties of Objects*).

3. Click the Graph tool in the Speedbar, then move the cursor into the work area. The cursor shape changes to a cross with a miniature graph below it.

4. Move the center of the cross to position the top-left corner of the graph, press the mouse button, drag down to position the bottom-right corner of the graph, then release the mouse button. A selected, but undefined, graph appears.

5. Right-click the Undefined Graph label to display a properties pop-up.

6. In the properties pop-up, click Define Graph, then click the list header (...) to display the Define Graph dialog box.

7. Use the Define Graph dialog box to define the graph as described in *Graphs*.

TO CREATE A GRAPHIC DESIGN OBJECT IN A DOCUMENT

A graphic is an object, created in another application, that is available to Paradox by way of the Clipboard or as a .BMP, .GIF, .EPS, .PCX, or .TIF file.

1. Open a document in Design mode.

D

185

2. Optionally, use the Properties menu to display rulers, to display a grid, and to turn on Snap To Grid (see *Properties of Objects*).

3. Click the Graphic tool in the Speedbar, then move the cursor into the work area. The cursor shape changes to a cross with a miniature graphic below it.

4. Move the center of the cross to position the top-left corner of the graphic, press the mouse button, drag down to position a temporary bottom-right corner for the graphic, then release the mouse button. A selected container appears with the words *Undefined Graphic* inside it. The size of the container is unimportant, because Paradox adjusts the size to suit the graphic you place within it.

5. Right-click the container to display its properties pop-up menu.

6. Click Define Graphic.

7. To place the contents of the Clipboard into the graphics container, click Paste (Paste is dimmed if the Clipboard is empty).

8. To place the contents of a file into the container, click Paste From to display the Paste From Graphic File dialog box. Use this box to select the graphic file.

9. After step 7 or 8, the graphic appears on the form, with the size of the container adjusted to fit the graphic.

10. Right-click the graphic to display its properties pop-up menu.

11. Click items on the pop-up menu to define the properties of the graphic.

TO CREATE A LINE DESIGN OBJECT IN A DOCUMENT

1. Open a document in Design mode.

2. Optionally, use the Properties menu to display rulers, to display a grid, and to turn on Snap To Grid (see *Properties of Objects*).

3. Click the Line tool in the Speedbar, then move the cursor into the work area. The cursor shape changes to a cross with a diagonal line below it.

4. Move the center of the cross to position the top-left end of the line, press the mouse button, drag down to position the bottom-right end of the line, then release the mouse button. A selected line appears.

5. Right-click the box to display its properties pop-up menu.

6. Click items on the pop-up menu to define the properties of the line.

TO CREATE A MULTI-RECORD
DESIGN OBJECT IN A DOCUMENT

A multi-record object displays one or more records within a document. You define the field layout for one record, and the same layout applies to the other records.

1. Open a document in Design mode.

2. Optionally, use the Properties menu to display rulers, to display a grid, and to turn on Snap To Grid (see *Properties of Objects*).

3. Click the Multi-record tool in the Speedbar, then move the cursor into the work area. The cursor shape changes to a cross with a representation of two records below it.

4. Move the center of the cross to position the top-left corner of the multi-record container, press the mouse button, drag down to position the bottom-right corner of the container, then release the mouse button. A selected container appears with rectangular regions for four records within it. The unfilled region is the master; changes you make here are automatically applied to the repeating regions.

5. Click the master region to select it.

6. Drag the handles around the master region to change its size. The repeating regions also change size.

7. Right-click anywhere within the container to display its properties pop-up menu.

8. Click Define Record and then click the list header (…) to display the Define Multi-Record Object dialog box. Use this dialog box to define the multi-record layout, as described in *Multi-Record Objects*.

D

9. Repeat step 7, and click Record Layout and use the Record Layout dialog box to choose the number and spacing of records within the object, as described in *Multi-Record Objects*.

10. Repeat step 7, and click other items on the properties pop-up to define additional properties.

TO CREATE AN OLE DESIGN OBJECT IN A DOCUMENT

An OLE (Object Linking and Embedding) object is one that exists under the control of another OLE-capable application. Before starting this procedure, cut or copy an object from an OLE server application into the Clipboard.

To change an OLE object, double-click it and the application in which it was created appears. Use that application to make changes, choose File ➤ Exit & Return (or the equivalent) in that application, and click Yes to update the object embedded in the Paradox document. The Paradox document reappears, showing the changed OLE object.

1. Open a document in Design mode.

2. Optionally, use the Properties menu to display rulers, to display a grid, and to turn on Snap To Grid (see *Properties of Objects*).

3. Click the OLE tool in the Speedbar, then move the cursor into the work area. The cursor shape changes to a cross with a representation of OLE below it.

4. Move the center of the cross to position the top-left corner of an OLE container, press the mouse button, drag down to position the bottom-right corner of the container, then release the mouse button. A selected container appears with the words *Undefined OLE* within it.

5. Right-click the container to display the properties pop-up menu.

6. Click Define OLE, click Paste and the object in the Clipboard appears in the container, with the container size automatically adjusted to suit the size of the object.

7. Right-click the container again to display its properties pop-up menu.

8. Click items on the pop-up menu to define the properties of the object.

TO CREATE A TABLE FRAME DESIGN OBJECT IN A DOCUMENT

A table frame looks like a table but is, in fact, a composite object consisting of field objects (the fields from a table), text objects (the field labels), a grid, columns (the vertical fields), and rows (the horizontal records).

1. Open a document in Design mode.

2. Optionally, use the Properties menu to display rulers, to display a grid, and to turn on Snap To Grid (see *Properties of Objects*).

3. Click the Table tool in the Speedbar, then move the cursor into the work area. The cursor shape changes to a cross with a table below it.

4. Move the center of the cross to position the top-left corner of the table frame, press the mouse button, drag down to position the bottom-right corner, then release the mouse button. A selected table frame appears.

5. Right-click the table frame to display its properties pop-up menu.

6. Click Define Table, then click the header (…) to display the Define Table Object dialog box. Use this box to define the table, as described in *Tables*. Alternatively, you can inspect and define individual fields or individual records.

7. Right-click the table frame again, or right-click the object within the table, to choose other properties.

TO CREATE A TEXT DESIGN OBJECT IN A DOCUMENT

A text object contains one or more text characters. A *resizing* text object automatically adjusts its size to accommodate whatever text is placed within it. A *fixed-size* text object remains the same size; if there is more text than can fit within it, the text scrolls vertically.

To create a resizing text object:

1. Open a document in Design mode.

2. Optionally, use the Properties menu to display rulers, to display a grid, and to turn on Snap To Grid (see *Properties of Objects*).

D

3. Click the Text tool in the Speedbar, then move the cursor into the work area. The cursor shape changes to a cross with an A below it.

4. Move the center of the cross to position the first character to be entered and click the mouse button. A flashing vertical insertion marker appears.

5. Type some text. The text extends to the right of the insertion marker until you define a right border by pressing ↵. At this time the insertion marker moves to a position one line below its initial position. As you continue typing, the text wraps at the right border.

6. Click the Selection Arrow button on the Speedbar, and then click the text. A selected container appears surrounding the text.

7. Right-click the text to display its properties pop-up menu.

8. Click the property you want to see or change.

To create a fixed-size text object:

1. Follow steps 1 through 3 in the preceding procedure.

2. Move the center of the cross to position the top-left of the text container, press the mouse button, and drag to position the bottom-right of the text container. A text container appears with a flashing insertion marker at its top-left corner.

3. Type some text. The text wraps automatically at the right edge of the container and scrolls upward when the container is filled. Use the ↑ or ↓ keys to see text that has scrolled outside the container.

4. Follow steps 6 through 8 in the preceding procedure.

TO NAME A DESIGN OBJECT

Paradox automatically names every object using a format that consists of the pound sign (#), a descriptive word, and then a number. In the case of a form, the form itself is named #Form1 and the first page of the form is named #Page2. If you add a box and a line to the form, they are named #Box3 and #Line4. As you add more objects they are named in a similar manner, using consecutive numbers. These names appear in the object tree and also in the Status bar when you select an object.

There is no need to pay much attention to object names when you use Paradox interactively. However, when you use scripts or ObjectPAL methods you may need to refer to objects by name. In this case you can use the names assigned by Paradox, or you can replace these names by more meaningful names you choose. These names may be up to 32 characters long, but must not contain spaces.

1. Select an object. Its current name and type appear in the Status bar.
2. Right-click the object to display its pop-up properties menu. The top item in the menu shows the object name.
3. Click the object name to display the Object Name dialog box.
4. Enter the new object name into the text box, then click OK.
5. The new name appears in the Status bar and, if you inspect the object again, in the properties pop-up menu.

See Also Crosstabs, Forms, Graphics, Major Objects, Methods, Multi-Record Objects, Object Linking and Embedding, Objects, Properties of Objects, Reports, Tables

Desktop

PURPOSE The Desktop is where you start working with Paradox. It contains the conventional Windows title bar and menu bar. The Speedbar, below the title bar, has buttons that provide fast access to many functions. Paradox always shows the buttons that are relevant for the window currently displayed in the Desktop; the inside covers of this book show all of the available sets of Speedbar buttons. The Status bar at the bottom of the window provides status information while you work with Paradox.

TO INSPECT OR CHANGE DESKTOP PROPERTIES

Any changes you make to Desktop properties are saved when you exit from Paradox and are used when you next open it.

1. Choose Properties ➤ Desktop.

2. If you want to change the title in the title bar, enter a new title.

3. If you want to change the Desktop background, type the full path name of a bitmap file, or click Find to find a bitmap file.

4. If you want to change the appearance of the Speedbar, click an option. See *Speedbar* for details.

5. If you want access to the full set of methods that can be attached to objects, click Advanced in the ObjectPAL Level section. The default, Beginner, provides access to only basic methods.

See Also Help, Methods, Speedbar, Status Bar

DIRECTORIES

PURPOSE A directory contains a related group of files, such as those involved in a single Paradox project. The Paradox installation procedure creates two directories as subdirectories of the PDOXWIN directory. These are named WORKING (alias :WORK:) and PRIVATE (alias :PRIV:). Unless you specify otherwise, all the files you create while working with Paradox are written into the WORKING directory, and all the temporary files Paradox creates are written into the PRIVATE directory.

TO CREATE ADDITIONAL WORKING AND PRIVATE DIRECTORIES

You should use a separate working directory for each Paradox project. Also, if more than one person uses Paradox on a single computer, there should be a separate private directory for each person.

1. Use standard Windows or DOS methods to create as many working and private directories as you need.

2. Give each working directory a DOS-compatible name that indicates the project for which it will be used. Give each private directory a name, such as an eight-character abbreviation of the name of the person who will use it.

TO DESIGNATE A PRIVATE DIRECTORY

If two or more people use Paradox on your computer, each person should use a separate private directory. At the beginning of each Paradox session, each user should use these steps to designate the appropriate private directory. After a directory is designated, the user may refer to it by the alias :PRIV:.

1. Choose File ➤ Private Directory.
2. Either enter the full path name of the private directory into the Private Directory text box, or click Browse to use Browser to find the directory.

TO DESIGNATE A WORKING DIRECTORY

After you have designated a directory as your current working directory, you can subsequently refer to it by the alias :WORK:. When you open Paradox, the working directory you most recently selected is remembered.

Paradox automatically creates a file named PDOXWORK.INI in the working directory. This file is used to remember which windows were open, together with their position and size, whenever you change working directories or exit Paradox. It also remembers preferences you choose in the Desktop Properties dialog box. If you delete PDOXWORK.INI, Paradox uses default Desktop settings and creates a new PDOXWORK.INI as soon as you change a Desktop property.

1. Choose File ➤ Working Directory.
2. If you know the full path name of the directory you want to select, enter it in the Working Directory text box, otherwise click Browse and then use Browser to find the directory.

See Also Aliases, Browser, Desktop

D

DOCUMENTS (FORMS AND REPORTS)

PURPOSE Paradox can create two types of documents: forms and reports. Forms are used for such purposes as providing a convenient format for entering data into tables, linking tables, creating scripts, and creating automated routines with ObjectPAL. Reports are primarily used to provide printed information based on data in tables.

The information in this section applies to both forms and reports. See *Forms* for information that applies only to forms. See *Reports* for information that applies only to reports.

TO CLOSE A DOCUMENT

Use the following procedure to close a form or report.

1. Double-click the Control-menu box in the document's title bar. If you have saved the document since you last made changes to it, the document is immediately closed.

2. If you have not saved the document since you last changed it, a Paradox warning appears. Click Yes if you want to save the changed document before closing it, or click No if you want to save the document without the changes.

TO CREATE A NEW DOCUMENT

Use the following procedure to create a new form or report.

1. Choose File ➤ New.

2. Choose Form (to create a new form) or Report (to create a new report) to display the Data Model dialog box.

3. Define the data model for the new document. See *Data Models*.

TO DISPLAY A DOCUMENT'S DESIGN

Use one of the following steps, as appropriate.

- ◆ Open a form or report in Design mode.
- ◆ If a form or report is already open in View Data mode, click the Design button on the Speedbar.

TO MOVE AMONG RECORDS

When a document containing table fields is first displayed in View Data mode, it shows the values in the first record of the master table. You can move among records by clicking Speedbar navigation buttons, pressing function keys, or selecting commands from the Record menu.

MOVEMENT	SPEEDBAR BUTTON	FUNCTION KEY	RECORD MENU COMMAND
First record		Ctrl+F11	First
Up 10 records		Shift+F11	Previous Set
Previous record		F11	Previous
Next record		F12	Next

MOVEMENT	SPEEDBAR BUTTON	FUNCTION KEY	RECORD MENU COMMAND
Down 10 records	▶▶	Shift+F12	Next Set
Last record	▶▶	Ctrl+F12	Last

TO OPEN A DOCUMENT

This procedure opens a form as a form or a report as a report. See *Forms* for information about opening a report as a form, and see *Reports* for information about opening a form as a report.

As an alternative to this procedure, you may open a folder to display icons representing documents in the current working directory, and then double-click a document's icon to open that document.

1. Click the Open Form or Open Report button on the Speedbar to display the Open Document dialog box which shows a list of forms or reports in the current working directory.

2. If you want to open the document in Design mode, click the Design button.

3. Double-click the name of the document to open it.

TO SAVE A DOCUMENT WITH A NEW NAME

Use this procedure to save a document either for the first time, or to a different directory or disk. The document must be in Design mode before it can be saved. Paradox saves forms with the default file-name extension .FSL, and reports with the extension .RSL.

1. If the document is in View Data mode, click the Design button on the Speedbar to switch to Design mode.

2. Choose File ➤ Save As to display the Save File As dialog box. If you are saving the document for the first time, File ➤ Save also displays the Save File As dialog box.

3. To save the file in any directory other than your current working directory, click Browse, then use Browser to select a directory.

4. Enter the name under which you want to save the document in the New File Name text box. Do not type a file-name extension unless you have a specific reason for using an extension different from the Paradox default. If you want to save the file anywhere other than in your current working directory, type the full path name.

5. Click OK. If the selected directory already contains a file with the name you typed in step 4, Paradox asks your permission before overwriting that file. Otherwise, the document is immediately written to disk.

D

TO SAVE A DOCUMENT WITH ITS EXISTING NAME

Use this procedure if you have previously saved the document to disk and want to save it again with the same name, overwriting the existing file. The document must be in Design mode before you can save it.

If you follow this procedure for a document that has not previously been saved and, therefore, is not named, Paradox responds to step 2 as if you had chosen the Save As command. See the preceding procedure for information.

1. If the document is in View Data mode, click the Design button on the Speedbar to switch to Design mode.

2. Choose File ➤ Save to immediately save the file.

TO SWITCH BETWEEN VIEW DATA AND DESIGN MODES

Use the View Data mode to see or edit the values of fields in a document, or to add records to or delete records from tables. Use Design mode to place, move, change, or delete design objects in a document.

To switch from View Data mode to Design mode, click the Design button on the Speedbar.

To Switch from Design mode to View Data mode, click the View Data button on the Speedbar.

See Also   Data Models, Forms, Objects, Reports, Tables

ENCRYPTING DATA

See *Password Protection.*

EXPORTING AND IMPORTING DATA

PURPOSE Paradox can export data from a table and import data into a table so that you can interchange data with other DOS and Windows applications and with applications maintained on other platforms. The supported file formats are:

1-2-3 (versions 1A and 2.x)

Excel

Quattro

Quattro Pro (DOS)

Quattro Pro for Windows

Text (delimited and fixed length)

TO EXPORT DATA
FROM A TABLE—GENERAL PROCEDURE

1. From the Desktop, choose File ➤ Utilities ➤ Export to display the Table Export dialog box.
2. Click the name of the file to export in the Table Name list.
3. Click an export format in the Export File Type list.
4. Click OK to display the Export dialog box.
5. If you want the name of the exported file to be other than Paradox proposes, enter a name in the New File Name text box. Do not use a file-name extension unless you specifically need one different from the default.
6. Use the steps in the following procedures to export in specific formats.

199

TO EXPORT DATA FROM
A TABLE AS A DELIMITED TEXT FILE

By default, commas separate fields in the exported file, and nonnumeric values are enclosed in double quotation marks. Use steps 3, 4, and 5 if you need to export in a different format. Also, by default, the exported file uses the OEM character set, but you can use step 6 to select the ANSI character set.

1. Follow steps 1 through 5 in *To Export Data from a Table—General Procedure.*

2. Click Options to display the Text Options dialog box.

3. Specify the field separating character.

4. Specify the field delimiting character.

5. Choose whether only text fields or all fields are to be delimited.

6. Choose between the OEM and ANSI character-sets.

7. Click OK to return to the Export dialog box.

8. Click OK. Paradox saves the table data in a file with the extension .TXT.

TO EXPORT DATA FROM
A TABLE AS A FIXED-LENGTH TEXT FILE

By default, Paradox creates a text file in which field lengths are the same as those in the table, but you can choose different field lengths. Also by default, Paradox uses the OEM character set, but you can select the ANSI character set.

1. Follow steps 1 through 5 in *To Export Data from a Table—General Procedure.*

2. If you want to use a previously saved export configuration, click Load, click the name of the specification file, click OK, and then proceed to step 6. Otherwise skip this step.

3. Make any changes you require to the field start positions and field lengths.

4. Click the character-set you want to use.

5. Click Save if you want to save the export file specifications. By default, Paradox saves the specifications as a table with the name EXPORT.DB in your private directory, overwriting any existing file with this name.

6. Click OK.

TO EXPORT DATA FROM A TABLE AS A SPREADSHEET FILE

Paradox can export data in 1-2-3 (version 1A or 2.x), Excel, Quattro, Quattro Pro (DOS), or Quattro Pro for Windows formats. By default, Paradox assigns an exported file the file-name extension appropriate for the chosen spreadsheet format.

1. Follow steps 1 through 5 in *To Export Data from a Table—General Procedure*.

2. Clear the "Make row headers from field names" check box if you want the spreadsheet to be created without row headers.

3. Click OK.

TO IMPORT DATA INTO A TABLE—GENERAL PROCEDURE

When Paradox imports data, it automatically creates a new table with the appropriate structure and then writes the data into that table. You cannot import data into an existing table. However, you can import data into a new table and then add that data into an existing table (see *Tables*).

1. From the Desktop, choose File ➤ Utilities ➤ Import to display the File Import dialog box.

2. Click the name of the file you want to import and click OK. If the file is in a directory other than your working directory, use Browser to find and select it. The Import dialog box appears.

3. Enter a name for the imported table.

4. Select Paradox or dBASE format for the table.

5. Follow the steps in the subsequent procedures according to the type of file you are importing.

TO IMPORT DATA FROM A DELIMITED TEXT FILE INTO A TABLE

1. Follow steps 1 through 3 in *To Import Data into a Table—General Procedure*.

2. Click Options to display the Text Options dialog box.

3. Specify the field-separating character used in the file to be imported.

4. Specify the field-delimiting character used in the file to be imported.

5. Choose whether only text fields or all fields are delimited in the file to be imported.

6. Choose whether the file to be imported employs the OEM or ANSI character set.

7. Click OK to return to the Import dialog box.

8. Click OK to create the new table and import the data.

TO IMPORT DATA FROM A FIXED-LENGTH TEXT FILE INTO A TABLE

1. Follow steps 1 through 3 in *To Import Data into a Table—General Procedure*.

2. Click OK to create the new table and import the data.

TO IMPORT DATA FROM A SPREADSHEET FILE INTO A TABLE

Paradox automatically assigns field types to imported data, using the most restrictive field type that can accommodate every value in a column.

Any formatting characters, such as lines or boxes, in a column of a spreadsheet are interpreted as alphanumeric data. You should remove any such characters from a spreadsheet before importing it into Paradox.

1. Follow steps 1 through 3 in *To Import Data into a Table—General Procedure*.

2. Specify the range of cells to be imported or open the Named Ranges list box and choose a named range.

3. Click OK to create the new table and import the data.

See Also Fields in a Table, Files, Tables

FIELDS IN A DOCUMENT

PURPOSE Fields are objects that consist of a label and a value. The label is a name for the value. The value is obtained from other sources such as a value that exists in a table. Some fields contain special values that have information about the database environment. Fields can contain individual values or can contain calculated values that consist of data from several sources.

TO ADD CALCULATED ALPHANUMERIC FIELDS INTO A DOCUMENT

Paradox uses calculated alphanumeric fields to concatenate (join) strings that exist in other alphanumeric fields. When such fields are displayed in View Data mode (or are printed), each field is automatically right-trimmed so that there are no spaces between the fields.

1. Display the document in Design mode.
2. Click the Field tool in the Speedbar.
3. Create a container of any size for the field.
4. Right-click the container to display its properties pop-up menu.
5. Click Define Field. Another pop-up menu lists the names of all fields currently associated with the document and also a header (...), which provides access to other field sources. A check mark shows that the field is currently undefined.
6. Click the header to display the Define Field Object dialog box.
7. Click the Data Model button close to the top left of the dialog box.
8. Click the name of the table that contains the fields you want to use in the calculated field, click the right-pointing arrow, then click OK to return to the Define Field Object dialog box.
9. Click the Calculated box.

10. Open the list of fields in the table, click the first one you want to use in the calculated field, and click Copy Field. The field name appears in the text box under the Calculated button.

11. Click an insertion marker to the right of the field name in the text box, type + (the plus sign), then repeat step 10 to bring an additional field into the calculated field.

12. Click OK to return to the document design window. The calculated field is shown in Design format.

13. Click the View Data button on the Speedbar to see an example of the calculated field.

TO ADD CALCULATED NUMBER FIELDS INTO A DOCUMENT

Calculated number fields are numeric values derived from other fields.

1. Follow steps 1 through 10 in *To Add Calculated Alphanumeric Fields into a Document*.

2. Open the Summary list and click the type of calculation to be made.

3. Follow steps 12 and 13 in *To Add Calculated Alphanumeric Fields into a Document*.

TO ADD CONSTANTS WITHIN A CALCULATED ALPHANUMERIC FIELD

You may want to use a calculated alphanumeric field to place a person's first name, middle initial, and last name in a single field. When you do this, you need to include space and punctuation characters, which are examples of constants.

1. Follow steps 1 through 10 in *To Add Calculated Alphanumeric Fields into a Document*.

F

2. Click an insertion marker to the right of the field name in the text box, type + (the plus sign), then the constant (space, punctuation mark, or other character) within double quotation marks.

3. Type another plus sign, then bring the next field into the calculated field.

4. Click OK to return to the document design window. The calculated field is shown in Design format.

5. Click the View Data button on the Speedbar to see an example of the calculated field.

TO ADD FIELDS FROM A TABLE INTO A DOCUMENT

1. Follow steps 1 through 7 in *To Add Calculated Alphanumeric Fields into a Document*.

2. Click the name of the table that contains the field you want to add, click the right-pointing arrow, and then click OK to return to the Define Field Object dialog box.

3. Open the list of fields in the table. A list of fields appears, followed by a list of table parameters.

4. Click the name of the field you want to use, then click OK. The document design window reappears, with the new field displayed. Paradox automatically adjusts the size of the field container.

TO ADD SPECIAL FIELDS INTO A DOCUMENT

Special fields have values that relate to the document's environment. These are the current date, the current time, the number of pages in the document, and the current page number.

1. Follow steps 1 through 6 in *To Add Calculated Alphanumeric Fields into a Document*.

2. In the Define Field Object dialog box, open the list of special fields, click one of those fields, and then click OK. The document design window reappears with the new field displayed.

TO CREATE A DOCUMENT
CONTAINING FIELDS FROM A TABLE

This procedure creates a document and brings all the fields from a table into it. After you have created the document you can delete fields that you do not need.

1. Choose File ➤ New ➤ Form or File ➤ New ➤ Report to display the Data Model dialog box.
2. Click one of the tables in the list of file names, click the right-pointing arrow to bring a table into the data model, then click OK to display the Design Layout dialog box with the table field shown in a vertical format.
3. Click OK to display the document in Design mode.

TO DELETE FIELDS FROM A DOCUMENT

If you have brought all the fields from a table into a document, you can use this procedure to delete those fields you do not need.

1. Display the document in Design mode.
2. Select the field to be deleted.
3. Press the Delete key.

See Also Fields in a Table, Forms, Objects, Reports, Tables

FIELDS IN A TABLE

PURPOSE All records in a table contain identical fields, each of which provides space for a specific item of data. You must give every field a name and designate it as a specific type.

TO ADD A FIELD TO A TABLE

You may add fields while creating a new table or while restructuring an existing table. This procedure creates fields without setting field properties. See *To Define Field Properties* for information about setting properties.

1. Open a Create Paradox for Windows Table dialog box to create a new table, or open a Restructure Paradox for Windows Table dialog box to restructure an existing table.

2. With the Field Name column of the Field Roster highlighted for a blank record, type a field name. Each field name must:

   ◆ consist of one to 25 characters;
   ◆ not start with, but can include, blank spaces;
   ◆ be unique within each table;
   ◆ contain only printable characters except brackets, braces, and parentheses;
   ◆ not contain –> as two adjacent characters;
   ◆ not contain # by itself.

3. Press Tab or ↵ to highlight the Type column.

4. Designate the field type by typing the single character shown below. Alternatively, press the spacebar or right-click to display a list of types and select a type from the list.

The following field types are available:

FIELD TYPE	CHAR-ACTER	RANGE OF SIZES IN TABLE	DESCRIPTION
Alpha-numeric	A	1–255	Any printable characters.
Binary	B	1–255	Any data that Paradox cannot directly interpret, such as sound. ObjectPAL can access binary data.

FIELD TYPE	CHAR-ACTER	RANGE OF SIZES IN TABLE	DESCRIPTION
Currency	$	Default	Same range as Number fields. The currency format is defined in Windows.
Date	D	Default	Valid date from January 1, 100 to December 31, 9999. Leap years and leap centuries are correctly handled. All dates are checked for validity. Date formats are defined in Windows.
Formatted Memo	F	1–255	Same as Memo fields, with the addition that text attributes are stored (typeface, size, style, color).
Graphic	G	1–255	Graphics created in a paint or draw application, or obtained by scanning.
Memo	M	1–240	Any printable characters and print control characters. The size defines the number of characters stored in the table. The remaining characters of each memo field are stored outside the table in a .MB file.

F

FIELD TYPE	CHAR-ACTER	RANGE OF SIZES IN TABLE	DESCRIPTION
Number	N	Default	Positive or negative numbers in the range 10^{-307} to 10^{308} with 15 significant digits.
OLE	O	1–255	Objects placed from other Windows applications that support OLE as a server.
Short Number	S	Default	Positive or negative whole numbers in the range −32,767 to 32,767.

5. Press Tab or ↵ to move to the next column. If the field type is one that requires a size to be specified, the size column is highlighted; otherwise, that column is skipped.

6. If the Size field is highlighted, enter the size, then press Tab or ↵.

7. If the field being defined could be a key field, the key column becomes highlighted. Press any key or double-click to make the field a key field. If the field cannot be a key field, the empty Field Name field in the next row of the Field Roster is highlighted.

8. Repeat steps 2 through 7 to add more fields.

TO DEFINE FIELD VALIDITY CHECKS

You can define field validity checks at the time you create a table or, subsequently, when you restructure it. When you are adding or editing a record, the validity checks for every field must be satisfied before you can move to another record or leave Edit mode. You may define the following validity checks:

VALIDITY TYPE	EXPLANATION
Required Field	Any type of field may be marked as required. If a field is marked as required, every record must have a value in that field.
Minimum and Maximum	Alphanumeric, currency, date, number, and short fields may have minimum, maximum, or minimum and maximum values defined.
Default	Most types of fields may have a default value. When you add a record to a table, Paradox automatically enters default values. If necessary, you can override default values in individual fields.
Picture	A picture is a template that formats the value you enter into a field. See *Pictures* for detailed information.

The following procedure sets all validity checks. Use only those steps that apply when setting validity checks for a specific field.

1. With a table's structure displayed in a Create Paradox for Windows Table or Restructure Paradox for Windows Table dialog box, click anywhere on the field definition in the Field Roster.

2. If the text box below Table Properties does not contain the words *Validity Checks*, open the list of table properties and choose Validity Checks.

3. To mark the field as required, click the Required Field box.

4. To set a minimum value, click an insertion marker inside the Minimum text box, then type the minimum value.

5. To set a maximum value, click an insertion marker inside the Maximum text box, then type the maximum value.

F

6. To define a default value, click an insertion marker inside the Default text box, then type the default value.

7. To define a picture, click an insertion marker inside the Picture text box, then type the Picture. Alternatively, click Assist for help in constructing a picture (see *Pictures* for more information).

TO CUT OR COPY A FIELD VALUE TO THE CLIPBOARD

The Clipboard provides a convenient way to copy or move values between records within a table. You can also copy or move values from one table to another.

1. Open the table that contains the value to be copied or moved.

2. Highlight the value.

3. Click the Cut to Clipboard button on the Speedbar or the Copy to Clipboard button on the Speedbar to cut or copy the value to the Clipboard.

TO PASTE A VALUE FROM THE CLIPBOARD INTO A TABLE

You can cut or copy a value from a Paradox table or from another Windows application into the Clipboard, and then paste it into a field in a table. The target field must be compatible with the value; otherwise, an error message appears in the Status bar. The pasted value overwrites any value currently in the target cell.

1. Copy or cut a value into the Clipboard.

2. Highlight the field into which the value is to be pasted.

3. If necessary, click the Edit Data button on the Speedbar to turn on the Edit mode.

4. Click the Paste from Clipboard button on the Speedbar.

See Also Fields in a Document, Pictures, Tables

FILES

The files generated and read by Paradox are identified by the file-name extensions listed here.

EXTENSION	CONTENTS
.BAK	Backup files
.BMP	Windows bitmap
.DB	Paradox table
.DBF	dBASE table
.DBT	dBASE memos
.EPS	Encapsulated PostScript
.FDL	Form in delivered format (without source code)
.FSL	Form in development format (with source code)
.FTL	Form stored temporarily
.GIF	Bitmap
.INI	Initial conditions
.LCK	File-locking information
.MB	Paradox memos
.MDX	dBASE maintained index
.NDX	dBASE non-maintained index
.QBE	Saved query
.PCX	Bitmap
.PX	Paradox primary index
.RDL	Report in delivered format (without source code)

EXTENSION	CONTENTS
.RSL	Report in development format (with source code)
.RTL	Report stored temporarily
.SSL	Saved script
.STL	Script saved temporarily
.TIF	Tag image file format graphic
.TV	Paradox table-view settings
.TVF	dBASE table-view settings
.TXT	Text
.VAL	Validity checks and referential integrity for Paradox table
.Xnn	Secondary index for Paradox table; nn is any two-digit number from 01 to 99
.Ynn	Secondary index for Paradox table; nn is any two-digit number from 01 to 99

Browser provides a convenient way to look for and access files.

See Also Browser

FOLDERS

PURPOSE A folder is a window that, by default, shows icons representing major objects in the current working and private directories and provides quick access to them. Paradox automatically adds tables, forms, queries, and reports to the folder. You can add other objects from the working directory, or from any other directory, to a folder.

TO ADD A FOLDER ITEM

You can add Paradox and non-Paradox objects, such as text files, graphics files, or spreadsheet files, to a folder. It is not necessary to open a folder before you add an item to it.

1. From the Desktop, click the Add Folder Item button on the Speedbar. The Select File dialog box appears with a list of tables displayed. Unless you have previously deleted a table from the folder, the tables listed are already in the folder.

2. In the Select File dialog box, open the Type list box and click the type of file you want to add. A list of available files appears in the File Name list box. Alternatively, click Browse to use Browser to find the object to add.

3. Double-click the name of the object you want to add to the folder. Alternatively, select one or more objects to add, and then click OK.

TO OPEN A FOLDER

An open folder window displays icons representing the major objects in the current working and private directories, together with any other objects you have added to that folder. The name of the working directory on which the folder is based appears in the window's title bar.

1. Select the working directory you want to display.

2. Click the Open Folder button on the Speedbar.

TO PERFORM AN ACTION
ON AN OBJECT IN A FOLDER

To perform an action on an object represented by an icon in a folder window, right-click the icon and a menu of actions appropriate for the type of object appears. Click an action to initiate it. The highlighted action at the top of the menu (View in most cases) is the default action. To perform an object's default action directly from the Folder window, double-click the object's icon. The default action of a

215

Query object is Run. This allows you to run a query by double-clicking on its icon in the Folder window.

TO REMOVE A FOLDER ITEM

You can remove objects from a folder. It is not necessary to open a folder before you remove items from it. After an object is removed from a folder, the object still exists as a file and may be accessed from File List boxes and by using Browser.

1. From the Desktop, click the Remove Folder Item button on the Speedbar. The Remove Item From Folder dialog box appears with a list of items in the folder.

2. To remove an object, double-click the name of that object. To remove two or more objects, select the names of those objects.

TO SHOW ALL OBJECTS IN THE WORKING DIRECTORY

A folder normally includes only major objects in the working and private directories, but you can take the following steps to make a folder show all files in the working directory (until you change working directories). Use the same steps to return to showing only major and added objects.

1. Click the Open Folder button on the Speedbar.

2. Choose Folder ➤ Show All Files. Icons appear in the folder representing all objects in the working directory.

TO TIDY ICONS IN A FOLDER

If icons overlap in a folder, use these steps to rearrange them.

1. Click the Open Folder button on the Speedbar.

2. Choose Folder ➤ Tidy Icons.

See Also Browser, Major Objects, Queries

FORMS

PURPOSE Forms are used for such purposes as providing a convenient format for entering data into tables, linking tables, creating scripts, and creating automated routines with ObjectPAL. A form can consist of one or more pages.

The procedures listed here apply specifically to forms. See *Documents (Forms and Reports)* for procedures that are used with reports as well as forms.

TO ADD A PAGE TO A FORM

By default, a form consists of a single page. If necessary, a form can consist of several pages. Use this procedure to add a page to the end of a form. You cannot insert a page between existing pages.

1. Display a form in Design mode.
2. Choose Form ➤ Page ➤ Add.

TO ADD A RECORD TO A TABLE

When the fields in one or more tables are shown in a form, you can use this procedure to add records to the tables. When two tables are linked by a one-to-one relationship, the table at the receiving end of the link is read-only by default. You must turn off read-only status before you can add a record to that table. See *Linking Tables*.

1. Display the form in View Data mode.
2. Click the Last Record button on the Speedbar to go to the last record in the document.
3. Click the Edit Data button to access Edit mode.
4. Click the Next Record button to open an empty record.
5. Click the first field into which you want to enter data, then enter the data into that field.

F

6. Press ↵ (more than once if necessary), or press ↓, to move to the next field into which you want to add data, then add data into that field.

7. Repeat step 6 as many times as necessary.

8. If you want to add another record, repeat steps 4 through 7. If an error message appears in the Status bar when you try to move to the next record or leave Edit mode, the data you have entered is not consistent with the type or properties of one or more fields. You must make any necessary corrections before you can leave the new record.

9. After you have completed adding new records, click the Edit Data button on the Speedbar to leave Edit mode.

TO COPY A PAGE IN A FORM

Use this procedure to copy a page of a form to another position in the same form or to another form.

1. Select the page to be copied.

2. Choose Edit ➤ Copy to copy the page and all objects on it to the Clipboard

3. Select the page before which you want to place the copied page.

4. Choose Edit ➤ Paste.

TO CREATE A QUICK FORM

A default quick form shows the fields from a single table arranged in a column. You can designate a specific form as a preferred form, in which case this procedure displays the preferred form instead of the default quick form.

1. Open the table on which the form is to be based.

2. Click the Quick Form button on the Speedbar.

TO DELETE A PAGE FROM A FORM

1. Open a form in Design mode.
2. Display the page to be deleted.
3. Press Delete to delete the page and all objects on it.

TO DELETE RECORDS FROM A TABLE

1. Display the document in View Data mode.
2. Display the record to be deleted.
3. Click the Edit Data button on the Speedbar to access Edit mode.
4. Press Ctrl+Delete.
5. Click the Edit Data button on the Speedbar to leave Edit mode.

TO DELIVER A FORM WITHOUT SOURCE CODE

A delivered form is one that can be accessed only in View Data mode, not in Design mode. You can supply delivered forms to other people so that they can use the forms, but not change the design.

1. Open the form in Design mode.
2. Choose Form ➤ Deliver. Paradox saves a delivered form with the file-name extension .FDL.

TO DISPLAY A FORM'S SOURCE TABLE

Use this procedure to display a single-table form's source table, or a multi-table form's master table. The form must be in View Data mode.

1. If the form is in Design mode, click the View Data button on the Speedbar.
2. Click the Table View button on the Speedbar.

F

TO DISPLAY A SPECIFIC
PAGE OF A MULTI-PAGE FORM

1. With the document in View Data mode, choose Form ➤ Page.

2. Click First, Last, Next, or Previous as required. Alternatively, choose Go To and then type the page number.

TO DISPLAY ALL THE PAGES OF A FORM

1. Display the form in View Data mode or Design mode.

2. Choose Properties ➤ Zoom ➤ Best Fit.

TO EDIT A RECORD IN A TABLE

When the fields in one or more tables are shown in a form, you can use this procedure to edit records in those tables. When two tables are linked by a one-to-one relationship, the table at the receiving end of the link is read-only by default. You must turn off read-only status before you can edit a record in that table. See *Linking Tables*.

1. Display the form in View Data mode.

2. Click the Edit Data button on the Speedbar to access Edit mode.

3. Use the navigation buttons in the Speedbar to find the record to be edited. Alternatively, locate the record by value (see *To Locate a Record in a Table*).

4. Click the field you want to edit.

5. Either type a new value for the field, or click where you want to edit the existing value to create an insertion marker and then use standard Windows techniques to delete and insert characters.

6. Repeat steps 4 and 5 to edit other fields.

TO INSPECT OR CHANGE A FORM'S PROPERTIES

Properties are modifiable attributes of objects. This procedure deals with properties that apply to a form as a whole. For information about properties of objects contained within a form, see *Properties of Objects*.

1. With a form displayed in Design mode, choose Properties to display a menu of properties.

2. Click the property you want to change.

    ◆ **Desktop**: see *Desktop*.

    ◆ **Designer**: see *Selecting and Deselecting Objects* and *Objects*.

    ◆ **Form:** allows you to change the way a form's window appears and also provides access to methods that may be attached to a form.

    ◆ **Current Object**: provides access to the currently selected object on the form.

    ◆ **Form Options**: allows you to save the form's current properties as defaults and to restore the initial default properties.

    ◆ **Zoom:** allows you to reduce or increase the magnification of the form.

    ◆ **Snap To Grid:** turns on or off the ability to snap the top-left corner of an object to a grid, whether the grid is displayed or not.

    ◆ **Show Grid:** turns on or off a display of non-printing grid points on the screen.

    ◆ **Grid Settings:** allows you to change grid spacing.

    ◆ **Horizontal Ruler:** displays or hides the horizontal ruler.

    ◆ **Vertical Ruler:** displays or hides the vertical ruler.

    ◆ **Expanded Ruler:** turns on or off an addition to the horizontal ruler which allows you to format text.

F

TO LOCATE A RECORD IN A TABLE

You can locate a record in a table by searching for a specific field value.

1. With a form displayed in View Data mode, click the Locate Field Value button on the Speedbar to display the Locate Value dialog box.

2. Enter the value to search for in the Value text box. You may use wildcard characters. See *Wildcards*.

3. Click Case Sensitive if you want a case-sensitive search.

4. Click Exact Match if you want to search for whole words only and are not using a pattern.

5. Click @ and .. if you have used either or both of these characters as wildcards in step 2.

6. Click Advanced Pattern Match if you have used advanced pattern matching in step 2.

7. Open the Fields list box and click the name of the field in which to search.

8. Click OK to start searching from the beginning of the table. If the value is found in a record, the form displays that record. A message appears in the Status bar if no matching record is found.

9. To locate the next record that contains the value, click the Locate Next button on the Speedbar.

TO MOVE PAGES IN A FORM

Use this procedure to move a selected page to the end of a form.

1. Display the form in Design mode.

2. Optionally, choose Properties ➤ Zoom ➤ Best Fit so that you can see the entire form.

3. Select the page to be moved, or select an object on the page to be moved.

4. Choose Form ➤ Page ➤ Rotate to move the selected page to the end of the form.

TO OPEN A REPORT AS A FORM

If you've created a report and then determine that you need to use it as the basis of a form, you can use these steps to open an existing report as a form.

1. From the Desktop, choose File ➤ Open ➤ Report to display the Open Document dialog box.

2. Open the Open As list box and click Form.

3. Double-click the name of the report in the File Name list box.

See Also Documents (Forms and Reports), Preferred Objects, Wildcards

F

GRAPHS

PURPOSE Graphs display data from tables in an easy-to-understand visual format. Paradox can generate tabular, one-dimensional summary, and two-dimensional summary graphs. It creates graphs by first cross-tabulating the data and then generating a visual display.

You can also import graphs generated in other applications (see *Design Objects*).

TO CREATE A QUICK TABULAR GRAPH

A tabular graph is a column (vertical bar) graph that displays values from one or more fields in a table.

1. Open the table on which you want to base the graph.

2. Click the Quick Graph button on the Speedbar to display the Define Graph dialog box.

3. Open the list of fields in the table. Fields that cannot be used for the horizontal axis, such as Memo fields, are dimmed. Click the field to be used for the horizontal axis of the graph. The field name appears under X-Axis in the Field Used section of the dialog box.

4. Click Y-Value.

5. Open the list of fields again. Fields that cannot be used as quantities to be plotted vertically, such as Memo and Alphanumeric fields, are dimmed. Click the fields to be used for vertically plotted quantities. The field names appear under Y-Value in the Field Used in section of the dialog box.

6. If two or more fields are selected for Y-Value, the Change Order buttons are brightened. To change the order of fields, highlight one of them, then click the up-arrow or down-arrow to move that field.

7. By default, Tabular is selected in the Data Type section of the dialog box. Click OK to display the graph as an object on a new form.

TO CREATE A QUICK ONE-DIMENSIONAL SUMMARY GRAPH

A one-dimensional summary graph is a column (vertical bar) graph that displays summarized values from one or more fields in a table. Summaries can be the sum of field values, the number of field values, or the minimum, maximum, or average field value.

1. Open the table on which you want to base the graph.
2. Click the Quick Graph button on the Speedbar to display the Define Graph dialog box.
3. Click the 1-D Summary button in the Data Type section of the dialog box.
4. Follow steps 3 through 6 in *To Create a Quick Tabular Graph*.
5. Click one of the fields in the Y-Value list to highlight it.
6. Open the summary list box and choose the type of summary you want for that field.
7. Repeat steps 5 and 6 for other fields in the Y-Value list.
8. Click OK to display the graph as an object on a new form.

TO CREATE A QUICK TWO-DIMENSIONAL SUMMARY GRAPH

A two-dimensional summary graph is similar to a one-dimensional summary graph, with the additional capability of grouping the plotted values according to values in a defined field.

1. Open the table on which you want to base the graph.
2. Click the Quick Graph button on the Speedbar to display the Define Graph dialog box.
3. Click the 2-D Summary button in the Data Type section of the dialog box.
4. Follow steps 4 through 7 in *To Create a Quick One-Dimensional Summary Graph*.

G

5. Click the Group By button in the Fields Used In section of the dialog box.

6. Open the list of fields again and click the field on which columns in the graph are to be grouped.

7. Click OK to display the graph as an object on a new form.

TO CUSTOMIZE A GRAPH

Paradox displays a graph as an object in a new form, initially displayed in View Data mode. You can customize the form by switching to Design mode and inspecting the graph or individual parts of it. You can also add such graphic objects as lines (perhaps with arrows) and labels to embellish the graph.

To customize the graph as a whole:

1. With a graph displayed as an object in a form, click the Design button on the Speedbar to switch to Design mode.

2. To inspect the graph, right-click a blank area within the graph container (not within the graph itself). A pop-up menu of graph properties appears.

3. Click the property you want to change, and choose from the selections offered.

You can also customize the following individual elements of a graph:

- the X-axis;
- the Y-axis;
- the graph background;
- each series in the graph;
- the grid.

In each case, with the graph displayed in a form in Design mode, right-click the element you want to customize, then choose from the pop-up properties menu.

See Also Crosstabs, Design Objects, Forms, Objects, Tables

HELP

PURPOSE Help provides online guidance as you work with Paradox.

Paradox provides a comprehensive online reference by way of a help menu system, and also provides context-sensitive help.

TO ACCESS CONTEXT-SENSITIVE HELP

At any time while you are using Paradox, you can press F1 to display a Help window showing information about your current task.

When you have a dialog box displayed, you can click the Help button in the box to display a Help window which shows information about that dialog box.

TO USE THE HELP MENU

The Paradox Help menu, accessed by clicking Help in the Menu bar, is similar to that in other Windows applications.

IMPORTING DATA

See *Exporting and Importing Data.*

INDEXES

PURPOSE The main purpose of an index is to display or access records in a specific order. Paradox allows you to define a single key (primary index), and one or more secondary indexes for each table.

See *Keys* for information about keys.

A secondary index serves two purposes:

- It allows you to display the records in a table in an order based on one or more fields in the table;

- When a master table is linked to a detail table, and the linking field in the detail table is not a key field, that field must be identified as a secondary index so that the appropriate record in the detail table can be found (see *Linking Tables*).

A single field may be used as a simple (noncomposite) secondary index. Two or more consecutive fields may be used as a composite secondary index.

TO DESIGNATE A SINGLE FIELD AS A SECONDARY INDEX

You can designate one or more secondary indexes at the time you create a table structure (as in this procedure) or, subsequently, when you restructure the table. A noncomposite secondary index is based on a single field. A table must have a key (primary index) before any field can be designated as a secondary index.

1. From the Desktop, choose File ➤ New ➤ Table.

2. Click OK in the Table Type dialog box to display the Create Paradox for Windows Table dialog box.

3. In the Field Roster, enter a name, type, and size for each field in the table.

4. Designate the first field as a key (see *Keys*).

5. Open the list box close to the top of the Table Properties section of the dialog box, then click Secondary Indexes.

6. Click Define to display the Define Secondary Index dialog box.

7. In the Fields list, click the name of the field that is to be a secondary index, then click the right-pointing arrow. The field name appears in the Indexed fields list.

8. Click OK and the Save Index As dialog box appears.

9. Enter a name (up to 25 characters) for the secondary index and click OK. The name you enter must not be the same as a field name. The Restructure dialog box appears with the new index name listed.

TO DESIGNATE TWO OR MORE FIELDS AS A COMPOSITE SECONDARY INDEX

You can designate one or more composite secondary indexes at the time you create a table (as in this procedure) or, subsequently, when you restructure the table. A composite secondary index is based on two or more consecutive fields. A table must have a key (primary index) before any field can be designated as a secondary index.

1. Follow steps 1 through 6 in *To Designate a Single Field as a Secondary Index*.

2. In the Fields list, click the name of the field that is to be a first secondary index field, then click the right-pointing arrow. The field name appears in the Indexed fields list.

3. Repeat step 2 to add one or more consecutive fields to the indexed fields list.

4. To change the order of fields in the composite secondary index, select a field in the Indexed Fields list, then click the up-arrow or down-arrow to move that field.

5. Follow steps 8 and 9 in *To Designate a Single Field as a Secondary Index*.

TO CREATE SECONDARY INDEXES BY RESTRUCTURING A TABLE

To create a secondary index in an existing table, follow the procedure in *Tables* to restructure a table. With the Restructure Paradox for Windows Table displayed, follow the steps in the preceding two procedures.

TO DISPLAY A TABLE IN INDEX ORDER

A table with no key is displayed in the order in which records have been entered. A table with a key is, by default, displayed in key order. A table with one or more secondary indexes may be displayed in secondary-index order.

1. Open the table.

2. Choose Table ➤ Order/Range to display the Order/Range dialog box. The Index List list box shows the name of all existing indexes, with an asterisk by the key index. The index that controls the current record display order is highlighted.

3. Click the key or secondary index to be used to control the display order, then click OK to display the table in the new record order.

TO ERASE A SECONDARY INDEX

1. Display the Restructure Paradox for Windows Table dialog box for the table from which a secondary index is to be erased.

2. Open the Table Properties list box, then click Secondary Indexes. A list box shows the names of all existing secondary indexes.

3. Click the name of the secondary index to be deleted, then click the Erase button. The selected secondary index name disappears from the list box.

See Also Keys, Tables

INSPECTING OBJECTS

PURPOSE Inspect an object to examine, and perhaps change, its properties. Use the procedure here to inspect the properties of objects within a document in Design mode, and also to inspect tables.

TO INSPECT OR CHANGE THE PROPERTIES OF AN OBJECT IN A DOCUMENT

As an alternative to the procedure for inspecting an object given here, you can also start from an object tree to inspect objects in a document. See *Object Trees* for details.

1. Display a document in Design mode.

2. Right-click an object to display a pop-up menu that lists the object's properties. Three types of properties are shown in pop-up menus:

   ◆ a property name followed by an ellipsis (three dots)—a dialog box appears when you select one of these properties;

   ◆ a property name followed by a right-pointing triangle—a secondary pop-up menu appears when you select one of these properties;

   ◆ a property name with nothing following it—a check mark before this type of property shows that it is turned on, the absence of a check mark shows that it is turned off.

3. If the property name you want to change is followed by an ellipsis or a triangle, click it to see the dialog box or next pop-up menu. Then select items from the dialog box or pop-up menu. If the property name is not followed by an ellipsis or triangle, click the name to turn the property on or off.

TO INSPECT GROUPED OBJECTS IN A DOCUMENT

When objects are grouped (see *Objects*), you can inspect either the group as a whole or individual objects within the group. Use the preceding procedure, right-clicking within an individual object to inspect that object. Right-click within the group, but not within an individual object, to inspect the group as a whole. When you inspect the group as a whole, the pop-up properties menu shows only those properties that all objects within the group have in common.

TO INSPECT A TABLE

See *To Inspect or Change a Table's Properties* in *Tables*.

See Also Object Trees, Objects, Properties of Objects, Tables

KEYS

PURPOSE Each Paradox table may have a single key consisting of one or more fields. A key:

- determines the primary order in which records are displayed;
- prevents entry of duplicate records because the value of the key field in each record must be unique;
- when a master table is linked to a detail table, the key field (or a secondary index field) in the detail table is used to locate records.

If a single field is to be a key, it must be the first field in the table structure. If two or more fields are used as a composite key, the first must be the first field in the table structure and additional fields must be consecutive in the structure.

You can designate a key at the time you create a table structure or, subsequently, when you restructure a table.

TO CREATE A SINGLE-FIELD KEY

Use this procedure to designate a key field.

1. From the Desktop, choose File ➤ New ➤ Table.
2. Click OK in the Table Type dialog box to display the Create Paradox for Windows Table dialog box.
3. In the Field Roster, enter the field name, type, and size for the first field of the table, then press Tab or ↵ to highlight the Key column.
4. Double-click the highlighted area, or press any character-key, to designate the field as a key. An asterisk appears in the key column, indicating the field is a key field.
5. If you want to remove the key designation, repeat step 4.

TO CREATE A COMPOSITE KEY

1. Follow steps 1 through 4 in *To Create a Single-Key Field*.

2. Repeat steps 3 and 4 in that procedure to add consecutive fields to the key.

See Also Indexes, Tables

LINKING TABLES

PURPOSE Linking tables allows a record in one table access to records in another table.

Most databases consist of several linked tables. When two tables are linked, a field in one table, the *master* table, is linked to a corresponding field in the second table, the *detail* table. Except for Memo, Formatted Memo, Graphic, Binary, and OLE fields, the link can originate from any master-table field. The field in the detail table must be either a key or a secondary index. When Paradox accesses a record in the master table, it searches the detail table to locate a record in which the linking field value is the same as that in the master table. Consequently, the master-table record has access to all fields in the linked record of the detail table.

Tables may be linked in:

- *one-to-one relationships*, in which each master table record is linked to no more than one record in the detail table;

- *one-to-many relationships*, in which each master table record is linked to any number of records in the detail table.

By combining one-to-one and one-to-many relationships, you can also link tables in many-to-many relationships.

Each table in a multi-table database may have many links to other tables. Each link is created separately between a master table and a detail table. Any table may act as a master table in some relationships and as a detail table in others.

Tables may also be linked to lookup tables (see *Lookup Tables*) and to referential integrity tables (see *Referential Integrity*).

TO LINK TWO TABLES
IN A ONE-TO-ONE RELATIONSHIP

A link provides a relationship between a master table and a detail table. When two tables are linked in a one-to-one relationship, the link terminates at the key field of the detail table. The fact that key fields have unique values ensures that no more than one record in the detail table is linked to a master-table record.

1. Create a master table structure containing the field from which the link is to originate.

2. Create a detail table structure with the first field designated as a key. That field must have the same type and size (but not necessarily the same name) as the field in the master table from which the link will originate.

3. Choose File ➤ New ➤ Form to display the Data Model dialog box.

4. Click the name of the master table in the File Name list, then click the right-pointing arrow to move that table into the data model.

5. Click the name of the detail table in the File Name list, then click the right-pointing arrow to move that table into the data model.

6. Point onto the master-table name in the data model, press the mouse button, drag into the detail-table name, and release the mouse button to display the Define Link dialog box, which shows the master-table field Paradox proposes to link to the detail table. If this field is correct, jump to step 8, otherwise continue with step 7.

7. If the master-table field proposed is not correct, click the correct field in the Field list, and then click the right-pointing arrow. The clicked field replaces the previous one displayed in the link display.

8. Click OK and the Data Model dialog box reappears with the two tables displayed one above the other and a line with a single arrowhead pointing from one table to the other. This format indicates a one-to-one link.

9. Click OK to proceed to the Design Layout dialog box. See *Documents (Forms and Reports)* for information about designing a layout.

TO LINK TWO TABLES IN A ONE-TO-MANY RELATIONSHIP

In a one-to-many relationship, the link from the master table terminates at a secondary index field of the detail table. The fact that secondary index fields may have the same values in any number of records allows many detail-table records to be linked to a master-table record.

1. Create a master table structure containing the field from which the link is to originate.

2. Create a detail table structure with a field designated as a secondary index. That field must have the same type and size (but not necessarily the same name) as the field in the master table from which the link will originate.

3. Follow steps 3 through 7 in *To Link Two Tables in a One-to-One Relationship*.

4. If the proposed detail-table index is not correct, click the correct index and then click the left-pointing arrow. The clicked index name replaces the one previously displayed.

5. Click OK and the Data Model dialog box reappears with the two tables displayed side-by-side and a line with a double arrowhead pointing from one table to the other. This format indicates a one-to-many link.

6. Click OK to proceed to the Design Layout dialog box. See *Documents (Forms and Reports)* for information about designing a layout.

TO UNLINK TWO TABLES

1. Open, in Design mode, the form that links the two tables.

2. Choose Form ➤ Data Model to display the Data Model dialog box.

3. Right-click the arrowhead at the end of the line that shows the link you want to remove. This displays the Define Link dialog box.

4. Click Unlink and then click OK to redisplay the Data Model dialog box with the link removed.

5. Click OK.

See Also Documents (Forms and Reports), Forms, Indexes, Keys, Tables

LOOKUP TABLES

PURPOSE Lookup tables simplify data entry and reduce the possibility of entering erroneous data. By using lookup tables, you can:

- ◆ require that the values entered into a field of one table, the *child* table, exist in the first field of another table, the *parent lookup* table;

- ◆ enter values into fields of a child table by copying them from the parent lookup table.

The link between a field in a child table and a field in a parent table controls data entry only. Any change made to values in the parent table do not affect values already in the child table. When referential integrity is used, however, changes to values in the parent table do affect values in the child table. See *Referential Integrity*.

TO CREATE A LOOKUP TABLE

A lookup table is similar to any other table. The values you want to look up must be in the first field. Other fields may contain values that may or may not be involved in the lookup process.

1. Create the structure for a new table with the first field assigned for lookup values. This field must be of the same type as the fields in the tables that will use the lookup values.

2. Enter lookup and other values into the table.

3. Save the table.

TO REQUIRE THAT VALUES ENTERED INTO A FIELD EXIST IN A LOOKUP TABLE

This is useful when only certain values are permissible in a field. For example, you can use it to ensure that only valid abbreviations for names of states appear in a database that contains addresses.

After following this procedure, when you enter a value into the field linked to the lookup table, Paradox will only accept blank values or values that are listed in the lookup table.

1. Create a lookup table with one record for each permitted entry value, and with the permitted entry values in the first fields of those records.

2. Create the table that will use the lookup values. The field or fields that will use the lookup values must have the same type as the corresponding field in the lookup table.

3. In the Create Paradox for Windows Table dialog box, or the Restructure Paradox for Windows Table dialog box displaying the structure of the table that will use the lookup table, open the Table Properties list box, click Table Lookup, then click Define to display the Table Lookup dialog box.

4. In the Fields list box, click the field that will refer to the lookup table, and then click the right-pointing arrow.

5. In the Lookup Table list box, click the name of the lookup table, and then click the left-pointing arrow.

6. Accept the default selection (Just Current Field) in the Lookup Type box and (Fill No Help) in the Lookup Access box, then click OK.

TO FIND VALUES IN A LOOKUP TABLE

You can use a lookup table to search for a code that represents certain attributes of an item you want to add to a table, so that you do not have to remember codes or risk using them incorrectly.

After you follow the steps in this procedure, start entering values into the table. When you come to the field that is linked to the lookup table, press Ctrl+Space, and a box containing the lookup table is superimposed. Scroll, if necessary, to find the descriptive text, and then click OK. The lookup table disappears, and the lookup value you chose is written into your table.

1. Create a lookup table with one record for each permitted entry value, with those permitted entry values in the first fields of those records, and with descriptive text as values in the second field. Make the first field a key, and

make the second field a secondary index. Index the table on the second field (see *Indexes*).

2. Create the table that will use the lookup values. The field or fields that will use the lookup values must have the same type as the corresponding field in the lookup table.

3. In the Create Paradox for Windows Table dialog box, or the Restructure Paradox for Windows Table dialog box displaying the structure of the table that will use the lookup table, open the Table Properties list box, click Table Lookup, then click Define to display the Table Lookup dialog box.

4. In the Fields list box, click the field that will refer to the lookup table, and then click the right-pointing arrow.

5. In the Lookup Table list box, click the name of the lookup table, and then click the left-pointing arrow.

6. Accept the default selection (Just Current Field) in the Lookup Type box.

7. Click Help and Fill in the Lookup Access box, then click OK.

TO FIND VALUES IN A LOOKUP TABLE AND WRITE CORRESPONDING FIELD VALUES INTO A TABLE

A lookup table can contain several fields, all of which are copied into another table when Paradox finds a match in the lookup fields. For example, a table might contain fields for employee ID numbers, names, and internal telephone numbers. If a lookup table contains these three fields and contains the values for all employees, a user entering data into another table that has matching fields need only type a valid ID number, and Paradox automatically copies the values from the other two field into the new table.

1. Create a lookup table with one record for each permitted entry value, with those permitted entry values in the first fields of those records, and with other fields containing supplementary values.

2. Create the table that will use the lookup values. The table structure must have fields that correspond to those in the lookup table.

3. In the Create Paradox for Windows Table dialog box, or the Restructure Paradox for Windows Table dialog box showing the structure of the table that will use the lookup table, open the Table Properties list box, click Table Lookup, then click Define to display the Table Lookup dialog box.

4. In the Fields list box, click the field that will refer to the lookup table, and then click the right-pointing arrow.

5. In the Lookup Table list box, click the name of the lookup table, and then click the left-pointing arrow.

6. Click All Corresponding Fields in the Lookup Type box.

7. Accept the default (Fill No Help) in the Lookup Access box, then click OK.

See Also Indexes, Referential Integrity, Tables

MAILING LABELS

See *Multi-Record Objects*.

MAJOR OBJECTS

PURPOSE Paradox uses major objects to store, display, print, and manipulate data.

The major objects are:

OBJECT TYPE	DESCRIPTION
Forms	Forms define relationships between objects. They are used to control the display of data on the screen and to link tables. Forms are also vehicles in which you create scripts and ObjectPAL methods.
Queries	Queries are questions about data in tables. You can also use queries to insert data into, or delete data from, a table, edit data in a table, and perform calculations on data in a table.
Reports	Reports are primarily used to design the way data stored in tables appears when printed. You can use reports to sort and group data, and also to calculate values based on data in tables.
Scripts	Scripts are segments of programming code written in ObjectPAL (the Paradox programming language). You can use scripts to automate operations on a database.

OBJECT TYPE	DESCRIPTION
Tables	Tables contain data arranged in rows and columns. Each row of a table, called a record, contains information about one item. Each column, called a field, contains one category of information about items.

See Also Design Objects, Forms, Objects, Queries, Reports, Scripts, Tables

METHODS

PURPOSE Methods are instructions that are executed whenever a specific event occurs in a Paradox environment. When you inspect an object in a document, you see a pop-up menu which contains a list of properties. The last of these properties is Methods. Click this to see a list of the Paradox Built-In methods. These methods are skeletons you can use to construct your own methods. The methods you see depend on whether you have chosen Beginner or Advanced in the Desktop Properties dialog box (see *Properties of Objects*). Refer to *Mastering Paradox for Windows*, by Alan Simpson (SYBEX, 1993) for further information.

MULTI-RECORD OBJECTS

PURPOSE A multi-record object in a document displays the values in one or more records. For example, multi-record objects in a report are used to print mailing labels (see *Reports*). Paradox does not offer a separate single-record object. If you need a single-record object, create a multi-record object with a single row and single column of records.

TO CHANGE THE NUMBER OF
RECORDS IN A MULTI-RECORD DOCUMENT

A multi-record object initially has regions for four records in two rows and two columns. The top-left region is known as the *master* region and shows the report layout, which applies to all regions. The other regions, known as *repeating* regions, show only the positions of records. Use this procedure to change the number of rows and columns.

1. Display a document, containing a multi-record object, in Design mode. The procedure below shows how to create such a document.
2. Right-click an empty space within the master region to display a properties pop-up menu, then click Record Layout.
3. In the Record Layout dialog box, enter the number of columns (Across), the number of rows (Down), the space between columns, and the space between rows.
4. Also in this dialog box, click a box to choose the sequence in which records are displayed, then click OK. If the document is large enough, it is displayed. Otherwise, an error message appears.

TO CREATE A DOCUMENT
BASED ON A MULTI-RECORD OBJECT

A document in Design mode initially shows a multi-record document as four regions. The layout you create in the master region applies to all repeating regions.

1. Choose File ➤ New ➤ Form or File ➤ New ➤ Report to display a Data Model dialog box.
2. Click the name of the table on which you want to base the document, click the right-pointing arrow, and click OK to display the Design Layout dialog box.
3. In the Style section of the dialog box, click Multi-Record.
4. Click Page Layout to specify a page size suitable for the multi-record object and other objects in the document.

5. Click OK to display the new document in Design mode. A master region at the top left shows the field layout.

6. Modify the field layout in the master region.

M

OBJECT TREES

PURPOSE An object tree shows relationships between objects in a document. As you develop progressively more complex databases, particularly when you attach ObjectPAL code to objects, you will find that object trees provide invaluable information about document structure, names of objects, and the containership relationships between objects. An object tree also provides a convenient means of selecting objects, particularly in complex documents.

TO PRINT AN OBJECT TREE

Paradox provides no direct way to print an object tree. However, you can display an object tree, press the Print Screen key to copy it to the Clipboard, paste it into another Windows application (Word for Windows, for example), and then print it. This method only allows you to print as much of an object tree as can be displayed in a single window.

TO SHOW THE RELATIONSHIPS BETWEEN ALL OBJECTS IN A DOCUMENT

When no objects within a document are selected, a document's object tree shows the document as the root object at the left side of the tree. Progressively to the right, the object tree shows the first level of objects contained by the form, the next level of objects contained by the first-level objects, and so on.

1. Open a document in Design mode.

2. If the right end of the Status bar shows an object name (meaning that an object is selected), press Esc until the right end of the Status bar is blank (meaning that the underlying form object or report object is selected).

3. Click the Object Tree button on the Speedbar.

4. To close the object tree, click its Control-menu button, and then click Close.

TO SHOW OBJECTS
CONTAINED BY A SELECTED OBJECT

1. Open a document in Design mode.

2. Select an object. The right end of the Status bar shows the type of object selected.

3. Click the Object Tree button on the Speedbar to display the selected object and the objects contained by it.

4. To close the object tree, click its Control-menu button, and then click Close.

TO INSPECT AN OBJECT'S PROPERTIES

1. Open an object tree that contains the object, using one of the preceding procedures.

2. Right-click the object in the object tree to open a pop-up menu with a list of properties. Proceed as described in *Inspecting Properties*.

NOTE The only way to inspect or change a form's properties is to use the procedure *To Show the Relationships between All Objects in a Document* to display an object tree that includes the form object, and then right-click the form object. If you display a form and right-click its background, you access the properties of the page, not those of the form.

See Also Containers, Documents (Forms and Reports), Forms, Inspecting Objects, Properties of Objects, Reports, Selecting Objects

OBJECTS

PURPOSE Paradox works with objects, which are classified as major objects and design objects. See *Major Objects* and *Design Objects*.

TO CHANGE AN OBJECT'S SIZE

When you place a design object into a document, you give it a preliminary size. By default, graphic, OLE, field, table frame, multi-record, graph, and crosstab objects have the Size To Fit property turned on so that Paradox automatically adjusts the object's size to suit whatever you subsequently place into it. If you turn off Size to Fit, you can make the object whatever size you want. You can also use this procedure to change the size of objects that do not have a Size To Fit property.

1. Open a document in Design mode.

2. Click an object to select it. Eight dark squares (handles) appear around the object to indicate it is selected.

3. Drag the handles to change the object's size. Use the handles in the center of the vertical edges to change its width, the handles in the center of the horizontal edges to change its height, or the handles at the corners to change its width and height.

TO CHANGE THE WAY OBJECTS ARE STACKED

Design objects may be placed one on top of another. If an object is opaque, it conceals any objects (or parts of objects) below it. You can change the order in which objects are stacked so that a document appears as you want it. This procedure shows how to place an object on top of others. You can also place an object behind all others.

See *Colors* for information about making objects transparent.

1. Open a document in Design mode.

2. Move objects, or place new objects, so that the objects overlap.

3. Make the objects opaque by filling them with a color.

4. Click an object that is partly obscured by another object.

5. Choose Design ➤ Bring To Front to place the selected object on top of all other objects.

TO CUT OR COPY AN OBJECT TO THE CLIPBOARD

Use the Clipboard to move design objects between Paradox forms, or between a Paradox form and another Windows application. Cut or copy an object from one application and then paste it into the other. The Copy and Cut commands place the selected object and all objects it contains into the Clipboard.

1. Open a Paradox document or another Windows application.

2. Select an object.

3. Choose Edit ➤ Cut to move the object to the Clipboard, or choose Edit ➤ Copy to copy the object to the Clipboard.

TO DUPLICATE AN OBJECT

Use this procedure to duplicate a design object (together with all other objects it contains) within one container, such as a form. You cannot use cut (or copy) and paste to duplicate an object within one container. For example, if you have a line object in a form, you cannot use copy and paste to create a second line object in the same form. However, if a box object in a form contains a line object, you can use copy and paste to copy the line into another box (or other object) in the same form.

1. Open a document in Design mode.

2. Select one or more objects.

3. Choose Design ➤ Duplicate. A duplicate of the originally selected object appears immediately below that object.

4. Move the duplicate to the appropriate position.

TO GROUP OBJECTS

Grouped objects behave as a single object. When you inspect a group of objects, the properties pop-up menu shows only those properties all objects have in common (see *Inspecting Objects*). Grouped objects remain as a group until they are ungrouped.

You can create many levels of groups. The first group can be grouped with another object, or with another group of objects, to form a second-level group, and so on.

1. Open a document in Design mode.

2. Select two or more objects.

3. Choose Design ➤ Group. A single set of handles surrounds the group.

TO MOVE AN OBJECT

A design object's default properties allow it to be moved in any direction. If you want to move an object horizontally while keeping it in the same vertical position, or if you want to move an object vertically while keeping it in the same horizontal position, use the procedure described in *To Prevent an Object from Moving*.

When you move an object, the contained objects also move.

1. Open a document in Design mode.

2. Select one or more objects.

3. Point into the selected object, or into one of the selected objects, press the mouse button, and drag.

TO PASTE AN OBJECT FROM
THE CLIPBOARD INTO A DOCUMENT

You can cut or copy an object from a Paradox document or from another Windows application into the Clipboard. Subsequently, in the same Windows session, you can paste that object into a document other than the Paradox document from which the object was originally cut or copied. If you want to make a copy of an object within a Paradox document, use the Duplicate procedure described in *To Duplicate an Object*.

1. Cut or copy an object into the Clipboard.

2. Open the document into which the object is to be pasted in Design mode.

3. Choose Edit ➤ Paste.

TO PLACE A DESIGN OBJECT INTO A DOCUMENT

You can create any of the Paradox design objects in a document. This procedure applies to design objects in general. See *Design Objects* for information about specific design objects.

1. Open a document in Design mode.

2. Click the button on the Speedbar that corresponds to the design object you want to place and move the cursor into the work area. The shape of the cursor changes to a cross with a symbol representing the design object below it.

3. Place the center of the cross at the top-left corner of the space to be occupied by the design object, press the mouse button, drag to the lower-right corner of the space and release the mouse button. When you release the mouse button, the Selection Arrow button on the Speedbar and the design object are automatically selected.

TO PREVENT AN OBJECT FROM MOVING

An object can be *pinned* vertically so that it can only move horizontally, horizontally so that it can only move vertically, or in both directions so that it cannot move in any direction.

Use this procedure to set one or both pin properties for an object. Use the same procedure to unset one or both properties.

1. Open a document in Design mode.

2. Right-click an object to inspect it, and a pop-up properties menu appears.

3. Click Design and another pop-up menu appears.

4. Click Pin Vertical to prevent vertical movement, or click Pin Horizontal to prevent horizontal movement. In either case, the pop-up menus disappear.

5. Repeat steps 2 through 4 to pin the object in both directions.

TO UNGROUP OBJECTS

When there is only one level of groups in a document, ungrouping restores all the objects as individual objects. When there are two or more levels of groups, ungrouping starts at the highest level of grouping.

1. Open a document in Design mode.

2. Select a group of objects.

3. Choose Design ➤ Ungroup. The objects, or groups of objects, within the group appear as separately selected objects.

See Also Containers, Design Objects, Methods, Object Trees

PAGE LAYOUT

PURPOSE Page layout allows you to specify the size of a document so that it is suitable for displaying on screen or printing.

TO DESIGN A FORM PAGE LAYOUT FOR DISPLAY

1. Open a form in Design mode.
2. Choose Form ➤ Page ➤ Layout to display the Design Layout dialog box.
3. If Screen is not checked in the Design For region, click it.
4. In the Custom Size text boxes, enter the size of the form as you want to see it on the screen, then click OK. The page appears with its top-left corner at the top-left of the form window.

TO DESIGN A REPORT PAGE LAYOUT FOR PRINTING

1. Open a report in Design mode.
2. Choose Report ➤ Page ➤ Layout to display the Page Layout dialog box.
3. If Printer is not checked in the Design For region, click it.
4. Click either Portrait or Landscape, as appropriate.
5. Click one of the standard paper sizes or, for a custom size, choose Centimeters or Inches, then enter the width and height in the Custom Size text boxes.
6. Choose Centimeters or Inches, then enter dimensions for the four margins.
7. Click OK to display the document. If the paper size and margins do not provide sufficient space for the objects in the document, an error message is displayed.

P

NOTE To display a page, centered on the screen with the form the same size as the page, turn on the form's Size To Fit property, save the form, and then reopen the form.

See Also Data Models

PASSWORD PROTECTION

You can assign password protection to a table or to individual fields. You can also assign access rights to specific users. When people try to access a password-protected table or record, or to use protected rights, they are prompted for a password and must supply it before proceeding.

TO ASSIGN A PASSWORD TO A TABLE

You can assign a master password to a table at the time you create it or, as in this procedure, when you restructure it. Everyone who accesses the table in any way must use this password.

1. With the table to be restructured displayed, open the Restructure Paradox for Windows Table dialog box.

2. Open the Table Properties list, click Password Security, and then click Define to display the Password Security dialog box with a flashing insertion marker in the Master Password dialog box.

3. Enter the master password. As you type, each character is displayed as an asterisk. The password may contain one to 31 characters and may include spaces. Terminate the password by pressing Tab and the insertion marker moves to the Verify Master Password dialog box.

4. Enter the password a second time.

5. Click OK. If there were any differences between the two times you typed the password, an error message appears. Otherwise, Paradox accepts the password.

TO ASSIGN TABLE RIGHTS

For any password-protected table, you can assign auxiliary passwords that give different users:

- all rights to a table
- the rights to insert and delete individual records, but not to empty or delete the table
- the right to insert records, but not to delete them
- the right to update records by changing field values, but not to insert or delete records
- read-only rights.

Begin by following steps 1 through 4 in *To Assign a Password to a Table*.

1. Click the Auxiliary Password button to access the Auxiliary Passwords dialog box.
2. Enter an auxiliary password.
3. Click one of the Table Rights buttons and then click Add.
4. Repeat steps 2 and 3 to assign additional auxiliary passwords.
5. Click OK.

Each auxiliary password can provide access to only one type of table rights.

TO ASSIGN RIGHTS TO INDIVIDUAL FIELDS

For any field in a password-protected table, you can assign auxiliary passwords that give different users:

- All rights to access that field, subject to the limits of their rights to that table
- ReadOnly access to that field
- None—no access to that field

Begin by following steps 1 through 3 in *To Assign Table Rights*.

1. Click a field name in the Field Rights list. The field is initially shown with All rights.

2. Click the Field Rights button once or twice to select ReadOnly or None.

TO REMOVE A PASSWORD

1. Open the Restructure Paradox for Windows Table dialog box.

2. Open the Table Properties list, click Password Security, and then click Modify to display the Password Security dialog box.

3. Click Delete, type the password to be deleted in the two text boxes, then click OK.

See Also Tables

PICTURES

PURPOSE A picture is a template that can format and control the value entered into a field of a table.

TO CONSTRUCT A PICTURE

A picture consists of a string of characters, some of which have a special meaning and others of which are used literally.

The special characters are:

CHARACTER	SPECIAL MEANING
#	Any digit
?	Any uppercase or lowercase letter

CHARACTER	SPECIAL MEANING
&	Uppercase letter—converts lowercase letters to uppercase
@	Any letter
!	Any character—converts lowercase letters to uppercase
;	Interpret next character as literal, not a special character
*	The character that follows may be repeated any number of times
[ ]	Characters within brackets are optional
{ }	Characters within braces are grouped
, (comma)	Alternative values

All other characters are interpreted literally.

TO PROVIDE A PICTURE FOR A FIELD

A picture may be provided at the time a table structure is created or, subsequently, when the table is restructured. See *To Define Field Validity Checks* in *Fields in a Table*.

TO USE A BUILT-IN PICTURE

Paradox provides some frequently used built-in pictures you can use as they are in your tables, or modify to satisfy similar requirements.

1. Open a Restructure Paradox for Windows Table dialog box and select a field for which you want to define a picture.
2. Click the Assist button to open the Picture Assistance dialog box.
3. Open the list of sample pictures.
4. Click the sample you want to use, click Use, and then click OK. The selected picture appears in the Restructure dialog box.

P

257

TO USE ASSIST TO VERIFY A PICTURE'S SYNTAX

When you create your own pictures, you can use Assist to verify their syntax before you place them into tables.

1. Open a Restructure Paradox for Windows Table dialog box and select a field for which you want to define a picture.

2. Click the Assist button to open the Picture Assistance dialog box.

3. Enter the picture you propose using into the Picture text box.

4. Click the Verify button. If the syntax is correct, the message *The picture is correct* appears; otherwise, an error message appears.

5. Correct the syntax if necessary, then repeat step 4.

6. Click OK. The picture appears in the Restructure dialog box.

See Also Tables

PREFERRED OBJECTS

PURPOSE When you display a table, the Speedbar contains buttons you can use to display a Quick Form, a Quick Report, a Quick Graph, or a Quick Crosstab. When you click one of these buttons, Paradox displays a default version of the object. As an alternative, you can designate a form, a report, a graph, or a crosstab you've created as *preferred*, in which case clicking the button displays the preferred object, rather than the default.

TO DESIGNATE A PREFERRED FORM, REPORT, GRAPH, OR CROSSTAB

1. Display a table.

2. Choose Properties ➤ Preferred and then choose Form, Report, Graph, or Crosstab to display the appropriate Choose Preferred dialog box, which displays the objects of that type in the current working directory.

3. Click the object you want to designate as preferred, then click OK.

See Also Forms, Reports

PRINTING

PURPOSE The Print command in the File menu allows you to make a printed copy of forms, reports, and tables as they appear on screen. To present information, you should normally design a report and print that.

TO SET UP THE PRINTER

Printer setup allows you to choose from printers already installed under Windows. For information about installing different printers, consult your Windows documentation. You should check, and perhaps modify, your printer setup before printing from Paradox.

1. From the Desktop, choose File ➤ Printer Setup to display the Printer Setup dialog box.

2. Click the name of the printer you want to use.

3. Click Modify Printer Setup to display the setup dialog box for the printer you have chosen.

4. Make whatever changes are necessary in the dialog box, click OK to return to the Printer Setup dialog box, then click OK to accept the setup.

TO PRINT A FORM

This procedure prints the form with values from one record. If you want to print values from all records, you should print a report instead.

1. Display a form in View Data mode.

2. Choose File ➤ Print to display the Print File dialog box. The printer section at the top of the box confirms which printer will be used.

3. By default, all pages of a multi-page form will be printed. If you want to print a specific range of pages, make appropriate From: and To: entries in the Print section of the box.

4. By default, one copy will be printed. If you want to print more than one copy, enter the number of copies in the Copies section of the box.

5. Click OK to start printing.

TO PRINT A FORM'S DESIGN

Use this procedure to make a printed copy of a form's design.

1. Display a form in Design mode.

2. Use steps 2 through 5 in *To Print a Form*.

TO PRINT A REPORT

1. Display a report in View Data mode.

2. Choose File ➤ Print and then choose Page to print a sample page, or Report to print the entire report. The Print File dialog box appears.

3. By default, the complete report will be printed. If you want to print only a specific range of pages, make appropriate entries in the Print section of the dialog box.

4. By default, one copy of the report will be printed. If you want to print more than one copy, enter the number of copies in the Copies section of the dialog box.

5. By default, only the fields in the report that fit within the width of the paper are printed. If you want to print fields that overflow the width of the paper, click an appropriate button in the Overflow Handling section of the box.

6. Click OK to start printing.

TO PRINT A TABLE

For best results, you should create a report in order to print the values of fields in a table (see *Reports*). This allows you to optimize the format of fields. However, you can use the following procedure to print a table directly.

1. Display a table.

2. Follow steps 2 through 4 in *To Print a Form*.

3. By default, only the fields in the table that fit within the width of the paper are printed. If you want to print fields that overflow the width of the paper, click an appropriate button in the Overflow Handling section of the box.

4. Click OK to start printing.

TO PRINT A TABLE'S STRUCTURE

Use this procedure to make a printed copy of a table's structure. The printed pages contain one row for each field in the structure. Within each row, columns show the elements of the field's structure. Because there are many possible elements, four landscape pages are required.

1. Choose File ➤ Utilities ➤ Restructure to display a list of tables.

2. Double-click the name of a table to show the table's structure.

3. Click Save to save the structure and also to save a file named STRUCT.DB in your private directory.

4. Choose File ➤ Open ➤ Table, then double-click :PRIV:STRUCT.DB to display a table that contains the structure of the table you selected in step 2.

P

5. To make a printed copy of the structure, follow steps 2 through 4 in To *Print a Form.*

See Also Forms, Queries, Reports, Tables

PROPERTIES OF OBJECTS

A Paradox database consists of major objects (tables, forms, etc.) and design objects (fields, text, graphics, and so on). See *Design Objects* and *Major Objects*.

Every object has a set of modifiable attributes called properties. A table, for example, has such properties as background color or pattern, text has a certain type-style, color, and size, lines have a certain width and color. There are some properties that all objects have, and some that are specific to certain types of objects.

Every property has a default value that Paradox uses unless you change the value.

For information about inspecting or changing an object's properties, see *Inspecting Objects.*

See Also Color, Desktop, Forms, Reports, Speedbar, Tables

QUERIES

PURPOSE Queries allow you to obtain information from databases interactively. The result of a query is an answer, which appears as a table named ANSWER.DB in your private directory. Each time you make a query, the new answer overwrites any existing ANSWER.DB table. When you exit from Paradox, ANSWER.DB is deleted.

QUERY OPERATORS The following is a list of operators used in defining queries. To use the name of an operator as literal text, enclose it in double quotation marks.

CATEGORY	OPERATOR	MEANING
Reserved symbols	Checkmark	Display unique field values in ascending order in answer
	Checkplus	Display all field values in ascending order in answer
	Check-descending	Display unique field values in descending order in answer
	Check Group	Specify a group for set operations
Reserved words	CALC	Calculate a new field
	INSERT	Insert records with specified values
	DELETE	Remove records with specified values
	CHANGETO	Change specified values in fields

Q

CATEGORY	OPERATOR	MEANING
Reserved words (continued)	FIND	Find specified values in a table
	SET	Define specific records as a set for comparisons
Arithmetic operators	+	Addition or alphanumeric string concatenation
	−	Subtraction
	*	Multiplication
	/	Division
	()	Group operators
Comparison operators	=	Equal to (optional)
	>	Greater than
	<	Less than
	>=	Greater than or equal to
	<=	Less than or equal to
Wildcard operators	@	Any single character
..		Any series of consecutive characters
Special operators	LIKE	Similar to
	NOT	Does not match
	BLANK	No value
	TODAY	Today's date
	OR	Specify OR condition in a field

CATEGORY	OPERATOR	MEANING
Special operators (continued)	,	Specify AND condition in a field
	AS	Specify the name of a field in answer table
	!	Display all values in a field regardless of matches
Summary operators	AVERAGE	Find the average of values in a field
	COUNT	Find the number of values in a field
	FIRST	Find the value in the first record of a group
	LAST	Find the value in the last record of a group
	MIN	Find the least positive or most negative value in a field
	MAX	Find the most positive or least negative value in a field
	SUM	Find the total of all values in a field
	ALL	Calculate summary of all values in a group
	UNIQUE	Calculate the summary of unique values in a group
	VAR	Calculate the variance of all values in a group

Q

CATEGORY	OPERATOR	MEANING
Set comparison operators	ONLY	Display records that match only members of set
	NO	Display records that match no members of set
	EVERY	Display records that match every member of set
	EXACTLY	Display records that match members of set and no others

To construct queries, you work within a query editor window.

TO ADD A TABLE TO A QUERY

You can add tables to a query editor window, up to a maximum of 24.

1. Display a query editor window (see *To Create a New Query*).
2. Click the Add Table button on the Speedbar to display the Select File dialog box with a list of tables in the current working directory.
3. Double-click the name of a table to add it to the query editor window.

TO CHANGE ANSWER TABLE PROPERTIES

1. With a query editor window open, choose Properties ➤ Answer Table ➤ Options.
2. If you wish, replace the default ANSWER.DB name for the answer table with another name.
3. Click dBASE if you want the answer table to be in dBASE, rather than Paradox, format.

4. Change the properties (data dependency, alignment, color, and font) of the answer table, just as you change the properties of any other table, using the image of the table in the dialog box (see *Tables*).

5. Click OK to accept the changes.

TO CHANGE THE ORDER OF FIELDS IN AN ANSWER TABLE

By default, the order of fields in the answer table is the same as that in the table from which values are taken. You can change the order of fields in the answer table using this procedure. The procedure does not change the order in which fields appear in the query editor window.

1. Follow steps 1 through 3 in *To Change Answer Table Properties*.

2. Using the image of the answer table, drag the name of a field horizontally to a new position.

3. Repeat step 2 to move other fields, then click OK to accept the changes.

TO CONTROL THE ORDER OF RECORDS IN AN ANSWER

There are two ways to control the order of records in an answer table: by using check mark operators and by changing the properties of the answer table.

When check mark operators are used, the order of records in an answer table is controlled by the leftmost selected field. You can use four different types of check marks, as listed among the query operators at the beginning of this entry.

1. From the Desktop, choose File ➤ New ➤ Query and then double-click the name of the table you want to query.

2. Point onto the check box below the leftmost field you want in the answer, then press and hold down the mouse button to see the four possible check marks.

3. Drag down to highlight the type of check mark you want to use, then release the mouse button. The selected check icon appears in the check box.

4. Click check boxes in other fields you want to include in the answer.

5. Click the Run Query button on the Speedbar.

When you want a greater degree of control over record order, change the properties of the answer table:

1. Open a query editor window.

2. Select the fields to be included in the answer table by clicking to place a check mark in the appropriate check boxes.

3. Choose Properties ➤ Answer Table ➤ Sort to display the Sort Answer dialog box.

4. One at a time, click the names of the fields to be used as the sort criteria, then click the right-pointing arrow to move them into the Sort By list. Select the fields in order, starting with the primary sort field.

5. If necessary, change the priority of fields in the Sort By list by clicking a field name and then clicking the upward- or downward-pointing arrow.

6. If necessary, remove a field from the Sort By list by clicking it, and then clicking the left-pointing arrow.

7. Click OK.

TO CREATE A NEW QUERY

You create a query by displaying the fields of a table, or of several tables (up to a maximum of 24), in a query editor window and selecting which of the fields are to appear in the answer. The answer appears in a table with the name ANSWER.DB. If fields from two or more tables are selected, the tables must be linked.

1. From the Desktop, choose File ➤ New ➤ Query to display the Select File dialog box.

2. Click the name of a table you want to query, or the names of several tables, to display a query editor window. The query editor window has one row for

each table. Each row starts with the name of the table with a check box below it, and also shows all the fields in the table with a check box below each.

3. Click the check box under a table name if you want all fields in that table to appear in the answer, or click the individual check boxes under the field names if you want only some fields to appear.

4. If there are two or more tables in the query editor window, establish a link between the fields (see *To Link Fields in a Query*).

5. Click the Run Query button on the Speedbar. An answer appears in the form of a Paradox table with the name ANSWER.DB. Records are sorted in the order determined by the type of check mark in the leftmost selected field. ANSWER.DB is written into your private directory, overwriting any existing file with that name.

TO CREATE A QUERY WITH ALREADY-LINKED TABLES

1. Choose File ➤ New ➤ Query. The Select File dialog box appears.

2. Open the Type list box and click <Forms>. The Select File dialog box reappears with a list of forms in your working directory.

3. Double-click the form on which you want to base the query. The query editor window appears, showing the tables in the form, with links represented by example elements.

TO LINK FIELDS IN A QUERY

When fields from two or more tables are selected in a query editor window, the tables must be linked before a query can be run. You can link fields in the query editor window, or you can bring tables that are already linked into a query editor window. See *Linking Tables* for background information.

To link tables in a query editor window:

1. Display a query editor window containing two or more tables.

2. Select the fields to be included in the answer.

3. Click the Join Tables button on the Speedbar.

4. Click the linking field in the master table and then click the linking field in the detail table. A red (or highlighted) example element appears next to the check box in each field.

5. Run the query.

TO OPEN A QUERY

1. Choose File ➤ Open ➤ Query to display the Select File dialog box.

2. Double-click the name of a query to display a query editor window containing the selected query.

TO PERFORM A QUERY ON A GROUP OF RECORDS

You can use the summary operators listed at the beginning of this entry to make a calculation based on field values in a group of records. By default, Paradox uses all values in the group. If you add UNIQUE to the query statement, only unique values are used.

Suppose you have a table of addresses, and you want to list those states for which there is only one record:

1. Open a query window containing the address table.

2. Click the check box in the State field to group the records by state and to display selected states in the answer.

3. In any other field, not the State field, type COUNT = 1.

4. Click Run Query. The answer table contains the states for which there is only one record.

TO REMOVE A TABLE FROM A QUERY EDITOR WINDOW

You can remove a table from a query editor window, even if that table is linked to other tables.

1. Display a query editor window.

2. Click the Remove Table button on the Speedbar to display the Remove Table dialog box showing the names of all tables in the query editor window.

3. Click the name of the table to be deleted, then click OK.

TO RENAME A FIELD IN AN ANSWER TABLE

Paradox normally displays fields in an answer table with the same name as in the original table. You can use the AS operator to provide a different name in the answer table.

1. Display a query editor window.

2. Check a field so that it will be displayed in the answer table.

3. In the space to the right of the check box, type AS followed by the new name. For example, if you want a field named Co. No. to be named Company Number in the answer table, type AS Company Number.

TO RUN A QUERY

You can run a query from the folder window or from the query editor window.

To run a query from the folder window:

1. Open the folder window.

2. Double-click the query icon.

To run a query from the query editor window:

1. Choose File ➤ Open ➤ Query. The Select File dialog box appears.

2. Double-click the name of the query you want to run.

3. Click the Run Query button in the Speedbar.

TO SAVE A QUERY

You can save a query so that you can reuse it. Paradox saves a query with the extension .QBE.

1. Create a query.
2. Choose File ➤ Save or File ➤ Save As. See *Documents* for information about the difference between these options.
3. If the Save File As dialog box appears, enter a name for a query and then click OK.

TO SAVE QUERY PROPERTIES

After you have changed query properties, you can save them as a default so that they will be used for all subsequent queries unless you specify otherwise. You can also return to the original properties.

1. With a query editor window displayed, choose Properties ➤ Query Options.
2. Click Save as Default to save the current properties, or click Restore Default to return to the original properties.

TO SELECT QUERY RESTART OPTIONS

Restart options allow you to control what happens if the data changes while you are making a query.

1. With a query editor window displayed, choose Properties ➤ Restart Options to display the Query Restart Options dialog box.
2. Click one of the buttons in the dialog box. You can choose to do any of the following:

   - restart your query whenever data changes;
   - lock all the tables accessed by your query so that no change is permitted;
   - ignore data changes and continue with the query.

TO SELECT EXACTLY MATCHING RECORDS

You can create a query that will produce an answer that contains only records with fields that exactly match examples. Examples are case-sensitive and must exactly match field values.

When examples are provided for several fields, only those records containing values that match all fields are selected. You can choose whether the matching fields should appear in the answer.

1. Display a query editor window containing one or more tables.
2. Check the fields you want in the answer table.
3. Click an insertion point to the right of the check box in a field where you want to place an example, then type the example. This field can be checked if you want its values to appear in the answer, or not checked if you do not want its values in the answer. The space where you type the example automatically expands if you type more characters than will fit.
4. Repeat step 3 if you want to place examples in additional fields.
5. Run the query.

TO SELECT INEXACTLY MATCHING RECORDS

Use the LIKE operator with an example to find fields having values similar to the example. In this way you can find records in which capitalization is different from that in the example, or in which spelling is somewhat different.

A match is found only if the value in the record starts with the same letter as the example. Also, more than half the characters in the record must be the same as the characters in the example, and they must be in the same order.

You can place exact examples in some fields and inexact examples in other fields.

1. Display a query editor window containing one or more tables.
2. Check the fields you want in the answer table.
3. Click an insertion point to the right of the check box in a field where you want to place an example, then type the word LIKE, a space, and then the

Q

273

example. This field can be checked if you want its values to appear in the answer, or not checked if you do not want its values in the answer.

4. Repeat step 3 if you want to place examples in additional fields.

5. Run the query.

TO SELECT INEXACTLY MATCHING RECORDS USING WILDCARDS

Follow the steps in *To Select Inexactly Matching Records*, using one or both of the wildcard operators listed at the beginning of this entry.

TO SELECT RECORDS THAT DO NOT CONTAIN CERTAIN VALUES

You can create an answer that contains all records except those in which the values in a certain field match an example. Follow the steps in *To Select Inexactly Matching Records*, replacing LIKE with NOT. You can also use NOT LIKE to give an inexact example.

TO SELECT RECORDS THAT DO NOT CONTAIN VALUES IN CERTAIN FIELDS

You can create an answer that contains all records in which the values in a certain fields are empty or are not empty. Follow the steps in *To Select Inexactly Matching Records*, entering EMPTY, or NOT EMPTY, in the fields to be matched.

TO SELECT RECORDS IN WHICH FIELD VALUES MATCH A RANGE OF EXAMPLE VALUES

You can use comparison operators to look for a range of matching values in alphanumeric, currency, date, number, and short fields. These operators are listed in the table at the beginning of this entry.

Place comparison operators immediately to the left of the value.

You can use two comparison operators within a sample to place lower and higher limits on the range. Enter the lower limit, a comma, and then the upper limit. For example >=100,<=200 instructs Paradox to include records in which a field has values in the range 100 through 200.

TO SELECT RECORDS THAT CONTAIN ALTERNATIVE VALUES IN A FIELD

You can create a query to look for records with a field that contains any one of several values. Using a table of addresses, for example, you might want to find all records in which the state abbreviation is CA or MN.

The OR operator allows you to specify two or more alternative values in the same field. In this case, enter the example as CA OR MN.

If you want Paradox to interpret OR (or any other operator) as a value, enclose it within double quotation marks. To look for records containing CA or OR in the state field, enter the example as CA OR "OR".

TO SELECT RECORDS THAT CONTAIN SPECIFIC VALUES IN DIFFERENT FIELDS

You can create a query to look for records in which more than one field contains specific values. Using a table of addresses, for example, you might want to find all records in which the state abbreviation is CA together with all records in which the city is Oldtown.

This procedure shows how to search for specific values in two different fields. You can extend it to look for values in more than two fields; you can also use inexact examples in any of the fields.

1. Display a query editor window showing a row of fields from a table.
2. Enter an example in one field (CA in the state field, for example).
3. Press ↓ to display a second row of fields from the same table.

4. In the second row of fields, enter an example in a different field (Oldtown in the city field, for example).

5. Check the fields to be included in the answer table. The same fields must be checked in both rows of fields.

6. Run the query.

TO USE EXAMPLE ELEMENTS TO REPRESENT FIELD VALUES

Queries frequently make use of field values to perform calculations, to link tables, and to define sets. Paradox uses *example elements* as a means of referring to field values. An example element is a name for a value; it is distinct from the field name and from the value itself.

Suppose a table contains a field named Type, and that field in the first three records of the table has values CP, WP, and SS. If an example element EE1 is assigned to the field, EE1 has the value CP when the first record is selected, WP when the second record is selected, and SS when the third record is selected.

To assign an example element to a field:

1. Open a query window.

2. Click the field to which you want to assign an example element.

3. Press F5, then type the example element characters. The example element is displayed in red on a color monitor, or is highlighted on a monochrome monitor.

See Also Fields in a Table, Linking Tables, Tables

RECORDS

PURPOSE A record is a single row of fields in a table, containing all the information about one item.

TO ADD RECORDS FROM ONE TABLE TO ANOTHER

You can add records already existing in one table (the *source* table) to another table (the *target* table). The fields in the two tables must be in the same order and must be compatible. Fields are completely compatible if they are the same type and the field in the target table is at least as large as the field in the source table. If the fields are of the same type, but the field in the target table is smaller than the field in the source table, Paradox warns you that you may lose some data.

Certain different types of fields are also compatible. For example, Paradox can add currency field values in the source table to number fields in the target table.

You can choose to append records to the target table, update records in the target table, or both. Appended records are placed at the end of a non-keyed target table. They are placed in the correct position in a keyed target table. If the key field of a record in the source table is identical to the key field of a record already in the target table, that record is placed in a temporary KEYVIOL table (see *Temporary Tables*).

If you choose to update records in the target table, that table must be keyed. A record in the source table containing a field value identical to that in the key field of a record in the target table replaces the corresponding target-table record.

1. Choose File ➤ Utilities ➤ Add to display the Table Add dialog box.
2. Click the name of the table from which you want to add records. The name appears in the Add Records From Source Table dialog box.
3. Click an insertion marker in the To Target Table text box.
4. Click the name of the table to which you want to add records. The name appears in the To Target Table text box.
5. Click Append, Update, or Append & Update, according to how you want records to be placed in the table.

R

6. Click View Source Table or View Target Table (or both) if you want the tables to be displayed.

7. Click Add.

TO APPEND RECORDS TO A TABLE

You can append records directly into a table, as this procedure describes, or you can use a form to add records (see *Forms*).

1. Open a table.

2. Click the Last Record button on the Speedbar.

3. Click the Edit Data button on the Speedbar.

4. Click the Next Record button on the Speedbar to open a blank record with the first field highlighted.

5. Enter values for as many records as required. As you complete each record it moves to a position in the table controlled by the current primary or secondary index.

6. Click the Edit Data button on the Speedbar.

TO DELETE RECORDS FROM A TABLE

You can delete records directly from a table, as in this procedure, or delete records using a form (see *Forms*).

1. Open a table.

2. Click the Edit Data button on the Speedbar.

3. Click the record number of the record you want to delete.

4. Press Ctrl+Delete.

5. Click the Edit Data button.

TO INSERT RECORDS INTO A TABLE

You can insert records directly into a table, as in this procedure, or insert records using a form (see *Forms*). If you want to place records in a specific position in a table, the table must not have a key.

1. Open an unindexed table.
2. Click the record before which you want to insert the new record, then press Insert to open a blank record in the table.
3. Enter values for the new record.

See Also Fields in a Table, Indexes, Keys, Tables

REFERENTIAL INTEGRITY

PURPOSE When two tables, a *parent* and a *child*, are linked by referential integrity, Paradox prevents anyone from entering a value in the child table unless that value already exists in the key field of the parent table. This field might, for example, contain abbreviations for state names. In this case, users can enter only valid state abbreviations in the child table. The parent and child tables must be in the same directory.

When you establish a referential integrity link between child and parent tables, you choose between Cascade (the default) and Prohibit update rules:

- Cascade—when you change a reference in the parent table, the change immediately occurs in all records of the child table that contain that reference value;
- Prohibit—you can change a reference in the parent table only if no records in the child table contains that reference.

R

TO CREATE A PARENT TABLE

A parent table contains records in which the first field, which is a key, contains reference values.

1. Define the structure of a table in which the first field will contain reference values. Other fields may contain whatever values you need.

2. Mark the first field as a key.

3. Save the table structure.

4. Open the table and enter reference values into the first field of as many records as are needed.

5. Close the table.

TO REQUIRE A REFERENTIAL INTEGRITY CHECK OF A FIELD'S VALUE USING DEFAULT UPDATE RULES

Use this procedure when only certain values are permissible in a field. For example, you can use it to ensure that only valid abbreviations for state names appear in a database.

After following this procedure, when you enter a value into the field linked to the lookup table, a child table will only accept blank values or values which exist in the parent table. For alphanumeric fields, values entered into the child table must match the capitalization of values in the parent table.

1. Create a parent table with one record for each permitted entry value, and with the permitted entry values in the first fields of those records.

2. Create the structure of a table that will use the reference values. The field or fields that will use the reference values must be the same type as the field which contains reference values in the parent table.

3. In the Create Paradox for Windows Table dialog box, or the Restructure Paradox for Windows Table dialog box displaying the structure of the child table, open the Table Properties list box, click Referential Integrity, then click Define to display the Referential Integrity dialog box.

4. In the Fields list box, click the field that will refer to the parent table, and then click the right-pointing arrow.

5. In the Table list box, click the name of the parent table, and then click the left-pointing arrow.

6. Click OK to accept the default update rules and display the Referential Integrity Name dialog box.

7. Enter a referential integrity name and click OK.

8. Save the table.

See Also Tables

REPORTS

PURPOSE Reports are used to provide printed information based on data in tables.

The procedures listed here apply specifically to reports. See *Documents (Forms and Reports)* for procedures that are used with forms as well as reports.

TO CHANGE THE SIZE OF BANDS

The header, group, and footer bands in a printed report are the same size as those you see when you design the report on screen. When you place objects into a band, the band automatically expands, if necessary, to provide space for the object. However, a band does not contract if objects do not fill it. If a band is empty, or is larger than needed, it will appear as blank space in the printed report. You should, therefore, adjust the size of bands as part of the process of formatting a report.

Do the following to change the size of a header band or an upper group band:

1. Display the report in Design mode.

2. If band labels are not visible, choose Properties and click Band Labels.

3. If the vertical ruler is not visible, click Vertical Ruler in the Properties menu.

4. Click the band label above the band to be changed. The band becomes highlighted to show it is selected.

5. Point into the band label at a position where the cursor changes to a double-headed arrow.

6. Press and hold down the mouse button.

7. Drag up to increase the size of the band, or drag down to decrease the size of the band, then release the mouse button. While you are dragging, a short line at the left of the ruler shows you the position of the band label.

Use a similar procedure to adjust the size of a footer band or a lower group band.

TO CHOOSE RESTART OPTIONS

When you create a report based on tables to which other people have access, there is a risk that someone will change the data in those tables while the report is being generated. Paradox provides choices to control this situation.

1. Choose Report ➤ Restart Options to display the Restart Options dialog box.

2. Click one of the buttons in the dialog box.

You have the following choices:

- **Restart report if data changes:** if any change occurs to the data, report generation starts again;

- **Lock tables to prevent changes:** as soon as you start generating a report, all involved tables are locked so that changes cannot be made;

- **Lock and copy tables:** as soon as you start to generate a report, Paradox makes a copy of all involved tables and uses those copies for the report, while allowing other users to make changes to the original tables;

- **Ignore data changes and continue:** Paradox uses the original data, even if changes are made while the report is being generated.

TO CREATE A CUSTOM REPORT

A custom report is a report you design, rather than a quick report that Paradox designs.

There are three possible starting points for a custom design:

- ◆ a quick report, which you can modify (see *To Create a Quick Report*);
- ◆ a form, which you can open as a report (see *To Open a Form as a Report*);
- ◆ a new report, which you design completely (see *To Create a New Report*).

Start with a quick report if you want a report based on a single table, with a form if you want a report based on tables that are already linked by a report, or with a new report if you want a report based on several tables that are not already linked by a form.

TO CREATE MAILING LABELS

You can use names and addresses in a table to create mailing labels.

1. From the Desktop, choose File ➤ New ➤ Report to display the Data Model dialog box.
2. Click the name of the table that contains the values to appear on the mailing labels, click the right-pointing arrow, and then click OK to display the Design Layout dialog box.
3. Click Multi-Record.
4. Click Select Fields to display the Select Fields dialog box.
5. Remove any fields that should not appear in the mailing labels from the Selected Fields list, by clicking each field and then clicking the Remove Field button. Then click OK to return to the Design Layout dialog box. Click OK to display the Report Design window.
6. Remove the fields that Paradox placed in the page header band by clicking each field and then pressing Delete.
7. Remove the space for the page header and page footer bands by dragging the band labels (see To *Change the Size of Bands*).

R

8. Choose Report ➤ Page Layout to display the Page Layout dialog box.

9. Select the orientation and paper size, and enter the margin sizes as appropriate, then click OK.

10. Click the master record twice to select it, then drag the right handle to set the width to match the width of the labels.

11. Make any necessary changes to the layout of the master label (see *Fields in a Document*).

12. Click the master record twice to select it, then drag the bottom handle to set the height to suit the height of the labels.

13. Right-click the master record to display the pop-up properties menu, then click Record Layout to display the Record Layout dialog box.

14. Enter the number of labels across and down the page, and the horizontal and vertical separation. Select the order in which records are to appear, and click OK.

15. Click the View Data button on the Speedbar to preview the label layout.

16. Click the Design button on the Speedbar to return to the Report Design window and make any necessary modifications.

17. Choose File ➤ Save to save the report.

TO CREATE A NEW REPORT

1. Choose File ➤ New ➤ Report to display a Data Model dialog box.

2. Define the data model for the new report. See *Data Models*.

TO CREATE A QUICK REPORT

A quick report is based on a displayed table.

1. Open the table on which the report is to be based.

2. Click the Quick Report button on the Speedbar.

TO DEFINE SUMMARY FIELDS

Summary fields in a report show values calculated from fields in tables. To include a summary field in a report:

1. Display a report in Design mode.

2. Click the Field tool in the Speedbar, and create a field in the report.

3. Right-click the field to display a pop-up properties menu.

4. Click Define Field and, in the secondary pop-up menu, click the header (...) to display the Define Field Object dialog box.

5. Open the list of fields and click the field from which the summary is to be calculated.

6. Open the list of summary operators, click one of the operators, and click OK. Then click View Data. The report reappears showing the summary field.

The summary operators are:

OPERATOR	FUNCTION
Avg	Divides the total of all values in a set by the number of non-null values in the set.
Count	Counts the number of non-null values in a set
Max	Finds the maximum value in a set
Min	Finds the minimum value in a set
Std	Finds the standard deviation of values in a set
Sum	Finds the total of values in a set
Var	Finds the variance of values in a set

R

TO DELIVER A REPORT WITHOUT SOURCE CODE

A delivered report is one that can only be accessed in View Data mode, not in Design mode. You can supply delivered reports to other people so that they can use the reports, but not change the design.

1. Open the report in Design mode.

2. Choose Report ➤ Deliver. Paradox saves a delivered report with the extension .RDL.

TO DISPLAY A SPECIFIC PAGE OF A REPORT

Printed reports usually consist of many pages. Use this procedure to preview pages on the screen.

1. Open a Report in View Data mode.

2. Click the Speedbar navigation buttons to display the first page, previous page, next page, or last page of the report. Alternatively, click the Go To Page button on the Speedbar to display the Go To Page dialog box and type the number of the page you want to display.

TO GROUP RECORDS BY ALPHANUMERIC VALUES

By default, a report has five bands: the report header band, the page header band, the data band, the page footer band, and the report footer band. Band labels, which are visible in Design mode if they are turned on, indicate where each band begins and ends.

You can add a group band, as in this procedure, so that a report contains items grouped by a range of values. If a table contains an alphanumeric field, you can group items by one, two, or more characters at the beginning of the field.

1. Display a report in Design mode.

2. If band labels are not visible, choose Properties and click Band Labels.

3. Click the Add Band button on the Speedbar to display the Define Group dialog box.

4. If you want to see the data model on which the report is based, click the Data Model button at the top-left of the dialog box. You can modify the data model at this stage (see *Data Models*). In the Data Model dialog box, click Cancel to return to the Define Group dialog box without keeping changes, or click OK to return with changes.

5. Click the alphanumeric field on which you want the report to be grouped.

6. Click the Range Group button.

7. In the text box under Range Group, enter 1 to group on the first character in the selected field, 2 to group on the first two characters, and so on.

8. Click OK and a new group band appears.

9. Edit the group band as required.

10. Scroll down to the bottom of the report and to see a group band between the bottom of the data band and the page footer band. You can place objects in this band, or move the group band label up to the bottom record band so that the empty group band does not occupy space in the report.

TO GROUP RECORDS BY DATE

If a table contains a date field, you can add a group band so that a report contains items grouped by ranges of days, weeks, months, quarters, or years.

1. Follow steps 1 through 4 in *To Group Records by Alphanumeric Values*.

2. Click the Range Group button.

3. Click a field of type Date in the Field list. A list of available groupings appears.

4. Click one of the grouping options.

5. Click OK and a new group band appears.

6. Modify the upper and lower group bands as appropriate.

R

TO GROUP RECORDS BY NUMBER OR CURRENCY

If a table contains a number or currency field, you can add a group band so that a report contains items grouped by ranges of values in those fields.

1. Follow steps 1 through 4 in *To Group Records by Alphanumeric Values*.

2. Click the Range Group button.

3. Click a field of type Number or Currency in the Field list. A list of available groupings appears.

4. In the text box under Range Group, type a number representing the range of the groups you want in the report. The first group starts with zero and ends at the value you enter. Subsequent groups contain same-size ranges.

5. Click OK and a new group band appears.

6. Modify the upper and lower group bands as appropriate.

TO OPEN A FORM AS A REPORT

When you have designed a form, particularly one that links tables, you can use that form as the basis of a report.

1. From the Desktop, choose File ➤ Open ➤ Form to display the Open Document dialog box.

2. Click the name of the form you want to open.

3. Click View Data if you want to see the values in a report, or click Design if you want to see the layout of the report.

4. Open the Open As list and click Report, then click OK.

TO OPEN A REPORT

1. From the Desktop, choose File ➤ Open ➤ Report to display the Open Document dialog box.

2. Click the name of a report in the File Name list.

TO PLACE FIELDS WITHIN BANDS

You can place fields from tables, calculated fields, or special fields within bands.

1. Open a report in Design mode.
2. Click the Field tool in the Speedbar, and create a field in a band of a report.
3. Right-click the field to display its properties pop-up menu.
4. Click Define Field.
5. Click one of the listed special fields, or click the list header (…) to display the Define Field Object dialog box.
6. Use the dialog box to choose a field from a table, or to create a calculated field (see *Fields in a Document*), then click OK.

TO SAVE A REPORT

You can save a report with its current name or under a new name.

1. Display the report in Design mode.
2. Choose File ➤ Save to save the report with its current name, or choose File ➤ Save As to provide a new name for the report. In either case, the report is saved as a file in the working directory. By default, the file-name extension is .RSL.

See Also Data Models, Design Objects, Documents (Forms and Reports), Fields in a Document, Forms, Tables

R

SCRIPTS

PURPOSE Scripts are instructions, written in ObjectPAL, that you can use to make something happen within the Paradox environment. A script is often used when an operation involving many keystrokes or mouse clicks has to be performed often. After the script is written, the operation can be performed by simply running the script.

To take advantage of scripts, you must be somewhat familiar with ObjectPAL. Consult the Paradox documentation for more information.

SELECTING AND DESELECTING OBJECTS IN A DOCUMENT

PURPOSE When you work with a design object, you must select it before you can perform an operation on it. You may select individual objects or groups of objects. You may select objects in a document displayed in Design mode, or you may select objects in an object tree.

TO CONTROL THE ORDER IN WHICH OBJECTS ARE SELECTED

A document consists of objects within objects, organized as shown in its object tree. Normally, when you click an object to select it, Paradox selects the outermost object. When you click repeatedly, Paradox progressively selects contained objects until it reaches the innermost object. You can change this so that Paradox immediately selects the object on which you click, regardless of whether it is contained. If you have difficulty selecting objects in a complex tree, you may find it helpful to switch between these two modes of selection.

1. With a document displayed in Design mode, choose Properties ➤ Designer to display the Designer Properties dialog box. If Select From Inside is unchecked, Paradox is in the normal mode in which objects are progressively selected from the outside.

2. Click Select From Inside to switch between the two selection modes, then click OK. The selection mode remains in effect after you close and reopen Paradox.

TO DESELECT AN OBJECT

An object, or more than one object, is always selected. When you deselect objects, you always select a higher-level object, eventually reaching the underlying form or report object.

Use any one of the three following methods to deselect objects:

- Click outside the selected object. Wherever you click you select another object, either another design object, an object contained within a design object, or the underlying page object (if the document is a form) or band object (if the document is a report). The Status bar indicates which object is selected. You cannot select the underlying form or report object by clicking.

- Press the Esc key. Each time you press this key, you move one level to the left in the object tree, eventually reaching the underlying form or report object.

- Click the Object Tree button on the Speedbar to display the object tree with the currently selected objects highlighted. Click an object in the object tree to deselect currently selected objects and to select a new object. You can select any object, including the underlying form or report object, in this way.

TO SELECT ONE OBJECT

You can use this procedure to select a single object when Select From Inside is not active.

1. Display a document in Design mode.

2. Click an object. Handles appear around the outermost object on which you clicked to indicate it is selected. Also, the right end of the Status bar shows the type of object selected.

3. To select a contained object, click repeatedly. Each time you click, the next contained object is selected.

TO SELECT MULTIPLE OBJECTS BY CLICKING

1. Display a document in Design mode.

2. Click an object to select it.

3. Hold down the Shift key while you click other objects to select them. When two or more objects are selected, the Status bar shows the most recently selected object.

4. To deselect one of several selected objects, hold down the Shift key and click that object.

TO SELECT MULTIPLE OBJECTS BY DRAGGING

1. Display a document in Design mode.

2. Point above and to the left of a group of objects, then press and hold down the mouse button.

3. Press and hold down the Ctrl key while you drag to a position below and to the right of the group of objects, then release the mouse button and the Ctrl key. All outer-level objects (but not the objects contained within them) are selected.

TO SELECT ALL OBJECTS CONTAINED BY AN OBJECT

Use this procedure to select all objects that an object directly contains.

1. Display a document in Design mode. The document is initially displayed with the form object or report object selected.

2. If objects in the document are already selected, press Esc one or more times to select the form object or report object.

3. To select all first-level objects contained by the form or report, choose Edit ➤ Select All.

4. To select all objects contained by another object, select that object and then choose Edit ➤ Select All.

TO USE THE OBJECT TREE TO SELECT OBJECTS

Although using an object tree takes a little more effort than clicking on objects, it provides a very clear picture of which objects are selected. An object tree also provides an easy way to select or deselect specific objects in a complex structure.

1. Display a document in Design mode.

2. Click the Object Tree button on the Speedbar to display the object tree with selected objects highlighted.

3. Click an object to select it and, at the same time, deselect all other selected objects. Alternatively, hold down the Shift key while you click an object to add that object to those currently selected.

4. Close the object tree to return to the document in Design mode with the objects selected.

See Also Documents (Forms and Reports), Forms, Object Trees, Reports

SPACING OBJECTS IN A DOCUMENT

PURPOSE The Adjust Spacing command automatically spaces objects uniformly.

TO SPACE OBJECTS UNIFORMLY

1. Open a document in Design mode.

2. Select objects that are to be spaced uniformly.

3. Choose Design ➤ Adjust Spacing.

4. Choose Horizontal to adjust spacing horizontally, or choose Vertical to adjust spacing vertically. In either case, the innermost objects of the selected group move to equalize spacing.

See Also Selecting and Deselecting Objects

SPEEDBAR

PURPOSE Buttons in the Speedbar provide fast access to many operations. Paradox always shows the buttons that are relevant for the window currently displayed in the Desktop. The inside covers of this book show all of the available sets of Speedbar buttons.

TO CHANGE A SPEEDBAR TOOL'S PROPERTIES

When a document is displayed in Design mode, the Speedbar contains buttons that represent tools you can use to create design objects within a document. Each tool creates a design object with specific properties.

You can change the default properties Paradox assigns to each tool either by defining properties or by copying properties from an object in the document. The new properties become defaults for the current Paradox session.

To define a tool's properties:

1. Open a document in Design mode.

2. Right-click a tool in the Speedbar to display its properties pop-up menu.

3. Click any of the properties in the menu to display a secondary pop-up menu.

4. Use this menu to specify new default properties for the tool.

To copy properties from an object to a tool:

1. Open a document in Design mode.
2. Use a Speedbar design tool to create an object.
3. Inspect the object and change its properties.
4. With the object selected, choose Design ➤ Copy To Speedbar. This copies the object's properties to the tool so that subsequent objects created by the tool have the same properties.

TO FORMAT THE SPEEDBAR

By default, the Speedbar appears as a single row of buttons under the menu bar. You can change the Speedbar to a single or double row or column of buttons which can be placed anywhere on the screen. The new Speedbar format remains in effect after you close and reopen Paradox.

1. Choose Properties ➤ Desktop to display the Desktop Properties dialog box.
2. In the Speedbar section of the box, click Floating, click 1 Column, 2 Columns, 1 Row, or 2 Rows, then click OK. The Speedbar appears in the new format with a blank area at its top-right corner.
3. Point onto the blank area in the Speedbar and drag to move the Speedbar.
4. To restore the Speedbar to its original position and format, repeat step 1, click Floating, and click OK.

TO IDENTIFY SPEEDBAR BUTTONS

Whenever you point onto a button on the Speedbar the name of that button appears at the left end of the Status bar.

See Also Status Bar

STATUS BAR

The Status bar, a single row at the bottom of the work area, contains four regions. The Status Window at the left shows current information such as the name of a Speedbar button, and which record of a table is accessed. Three smaller Mode Windows at the right provide information about current modes. It is here that Paradox displays *Edit* when that mode is selected and, when a document is displayed in Design mode, the type of object currently selected.

TABLES

PURPOSE Tables provide storage for the data handled by Paradox.

TO BORROW THE STRUCTURE OF A TABLE

When you want to create a new table that has a structure similar to that of an existing table, you can copy (Paradox calls it "borrow") the structure of the existing table.

1. Choose File ➤ New ➤ Table to display the Table Type dialog box.
2. Click OK to accept the default table type and display the Create Paradox for Windows Table dialog box.
3. Click Borrow to display the Borrow Table Structure dialog box.
4. Click the name of the table structure you want to use.
5. Click any of the options you want to include with the table structure.
6. Click OK to copy the structure and options into the new table.

TO CHANGE THE WIDTH AND ORDER OF COLUMNS, AND THE DEPTH OF ROWS

You can change the width of individual columns, change the order of columns, and change the depth of all rows.

1. Open a table.
2. To change the width of a column, place the cursor on and close to the top of a vertical grid line. Adjust the position until the cursor changes to a double-headed arrow. Drag the grid line horizontally to change the width of the adjacent column.
3. To change the order of columns, place the cursor on the heading of a column, then drag the heading to a new position.

297

4. To change the depth of all rows, move the cursor onto the horizontal line under the first record number. Adjust the position until the cursor changes to a double-headed arrow. Drag the line up or down to decrease or increase the depth of all rows.

TO CLOSE A TABLE

Paradox provides no explicit way to save a table, because values entered into, or changed in, records are automatically saved when you move to a new record and when you leave Edit mode. **Warning:** If you have a table in Edit mode and make changes to a record or enter a new record, you must move to another record or switch out of Edit mode before closing the table. Otherwise, you will lose the changes you made to the record.

To close a table, double-click its Control-menu box, or click the Control-menu box and then click Close.

TO COPY A TABLE

Always copy tables from within Paradox to ensure that related files are also copied. If you use DOS or Windows to copy a table to another directory, related files will be missing in the new directory.

1. Choose File ➤ Utilities ➤ Copy to display the Copy dialog box.
2. Click the name of the table you want to copy. The name appears in the Source File text box.
3. Enter the name, with extension, for the copied file in the Destination File text box.
4. Click Copy.

TO CREATE A NEW TABLE

You create a new table by creating a structure that lists the fields in the table and, optionally, defines table properties.

1. From the Desktop, choose File ➤ New ➤ Table to display the Table Type dialog box.

2. Click OK to accept the default Paradox for Windows table type and to open the Create Paradox for Windows Table dialog box.

3. Add fields to the table (see *To Add a Field to a Table* in *Fields in a Table*).

4. Define table properties (see *To Define Field Validity Checks* in *Fields in a Table*), Table Lookup (see *Lookup Tables*), Secondary Indexes (see *Indexes*), Referential Integrity (see *Referential Integrity*), Password Security (see *Password Protection*).

5. Click Save As to open the Save Table As dialog box.

6. Enter a DOS-compatible name for the table, then click OK to save the table structure.

TO DEFINE A TABLE IN A DOCUMENT

After you use the Table tool to place a table frame in a document, you choose a table and Paradox assigns that table's fields to the table frame.

1. Open a document in Design mode and create a table frame in it (see *Design Objects*).

2. Right-click the table frame to display its pop-up properties menu.

3. Choose Define Table to display a table pop-up menu, which lists tables already associated with the document and also has a header (…) item.

4. If the table you want is listed, click it and the table appears within the table frame. Otherwise, proceed to the next step.

5. Click the header, and the Define Table Object dialog box appears.

6. Click the Data Model icon at the top left of the dialog box to display the Data Model dialog box containing a list of tables.

7. Click the table you want to use, click the right-pointing arrow, and then click OK. The Define Table Object dialog box reappears, showing the name of the table you selected.

8. Open the list of fields in the table and select those you want to appear in the table within the table frame. The names of the listed fields appear in the Included Fields section of the dialog box.

9. By default, Size to Fit is checked. This means that the size of the table frame will change to suit the size of the fields in the table. Click the check box if you want the size of the table frame to remain unchanged.

10. By default, Replace Layout is checked. This means that the fields from the table will replace all fields currently in the table frame. Click the check box if you want the fields from the table to be added to the fields already in the table frame (including undefined fields).

11. Click OK. The Form (or Report) Design window reappears with the selected fields within the table frame.

TO EDIT RECORD VALUES

You can edit record values directly in a table, as described here, or in a form (see *Forms*).

1. Open a table.
2. Click the Edit Data Speedbar button.
3. Click the field you want to edit to highlight the field.
4. To replace the entire value of the field, type the new value. As soon as you type the first character, the original value disappears and is replaced by the typed character.
5. To change, delete, or insert characters within the existing value, click an insertion marker, then use conventional Windows editing techniques.
6. Press ↵ or Tab to move to the next field.

TO DELETE A FIELD

When you are about to delete a field, Paradox warns that you may lose some data. It does not warn you that the field may appear in a document.

1. From the Desktop, choose File ➤ Utilities ➤ Restructure to display the Select File dialog box.

2. Double-click the name of the table from which you want to delete a field to display the Restructure Paradox for Windows Table dialog box.

3. Click the number of the field to be deleted.

4. Press Ctrl+Delete to remove the field from the structure.

5. Click Save to save the table. A message appears to warn you that you may lose data if you continue.

6. Click OK.

TO DELETE A TABLE

Delete a table from within Paradox, rather than from DOS or Windows. By using this technique, you delete all files related to a table as well as the table file. If you delete a table from DOS or Windows, various related files will be left on your hard disk.

1. Choose File ➤ Utilities ➤ Delete to display the Delete dialog box.

2. Click the name of the table you want to delete. The name appears in the File Name text box.

3. Click Delete. A warning message appears telling you that the file you selected and related files will be deleted.

4. Click OK to delete the files.

TO EMPTY A TABLE

When you empty a table, you remove all records from a table, leaving its structure intact.

1. Choose File ➤ Utilities ➤ Empty to display the Table Empty dialog box.

2. Click the name of the table you want to empty. The name appears in the File Name text box.

3. Click the View Table button if you want to view the table before you empty it.

4. Click Delete. A warning message appears telling you that all the data in the table will be lost.

5. Click OK to empty the table.

TO EXAMINE A TABLE'S STRUCTURE

This procedure allows you to examine, but not change, a table's structure.

1. Choose File ➤ Utilities ➤ Info Structure to display the Select File dialog box.

2. Double-click the name of the table you want, to display the Structure Information Paradox for Windows Table dialog box.

3. After you have examined the structure, click Done.

TO INSPECT OR CHANGE A TABLE'S PROPERTIES

You can change the following properties of table components:

INSPECTED COMPONENT	POPUP MENU ITEM	PROPERTY AFFECTED
Grid	Color	Background color of grid lines
	Grid lines	Presence of heading lines
		Presence of column lines
		Presence of row lines
		Line style
		Line color
		Spacing between multiple grid lines

INSPECTED COMPONENT	POPUP MENU ITEM	PROPERTY AFFECTED
Grid	Current record marker	Presence
		Line style
		Color
Headings	Alignment	Horizontal alignment
		Vertical alignment
	Color (background)	
	Font	Typeface
		Size
		Style
		Color
Data	Data dependent	Data dependent conditions (see below)
	Alignment	Horizontal alignment
		Vertical alignment
	Color (background)	
	Font	Typeface
		Size
		Style
		Color

Use the following steps to inspect or change these properties:

1. Open a table.
2. Right-click a component of the table to display a pop-up properties menu.
3. Click an item in the pop-up menu and make changes to those properties.
4. Repeat steps 2 and 3 to change other properties.

The data-dependent property, which can be chosen for field values, allows you to change the appearance of a value according to its data. For example, you can display positive values in black and negative values in red. The data-dependent property can be set for alphanumeric, currency, date, number, and short fields.
Use the following steps to set the data dependent property of a field value so that values less than zero have a red background and values of zero or greater have a gray background.

1. Open a table.
2. Right-click within a field column to display the pop-up properties menu.
3. Click color and then click the red sample in the color palette. The background in every record becomes red.
4. Right-click within the same field column again, and in the pop-up properties menu, click Data Dependent to display the Data Dependent Properties dialog box.
5. Click New Range and enter the beginning of the range. To set the beginning of the range as >=0, click >= and click Apply Changes, delete <*blank*> in the upper text box, type 0 and click Apply Changes. This places the beginning of the range in the Ranges box.
6. Click the Set Properties button to display the properties pop-up menu.
7. Click Color and then click the light gray sample in the color palette. This will make the background color to gray for all the fields that satisfy the condition established in step 5.
8. Click OK. The table reappears with the background of values in the selected field shown in red if they are less than zero, otherwise in gray.

TO LOCATE A RECORD

You can locate a field, locate a record number, or locate a record that contains a specific value in a specific field.

1. Open a table.
2. Choose Record ➤ Locate to display a popup menu.
3. Do one of the following:

   ◆ Click Field, click a field name, then click OK to highlight the selected field in the current record.

   ◆ Click Record Number, type a record number, then click OK to highlight the current field in the selected record.

   ◆ Click Value to display the Locate Value dialog box, then follow steps 2 through 9 in *To Locate a Record in a Table* in *Forms*.

TO MOVE A FIELD

You can change the order of fields in a table.

1. Display the structure of a table in the Create Paradox for Windows Table dialog box or in the Restructure Paradox for Windows Table dialog box.
2. Point onto the field number of the record you want to move, then press and hold down the mouse button. The cursor changes to a double-headed arrow, and gray lines appear above and below the field definition.
3. Drag up or down until the cursor is on the field before which you want to move the selected field, then release the mouse button. The field structure reappears with the fields in the new order.

TO MOVE AMONG RECORDS IN A TABLE

You can move among records in a table by using the Speedbar navigation buttons, function keys, or the Record menu, as shown in the table under *Documents*.

TO OPEN A TABLE FROM THE MAIN MENU

1. Choose File ➤ Open ➤ Table to display the Open Table dialog box.

2. Double-click the name of the file you want to open.

TO OPEN A TABLE FROM THE FOLDER

1. Click the Open Folder button on the Speedbar to open the Folder.

2. Double-click the icon representing the table you want to open.

TO PLACE A BINARY OBJECT IN A TABLE

You can place a binary object, such as a sound file, into a binary-type field in a table, but you must use ObjectPAL methods to do so. Paradox does not allow you to place or access binary files interactively.

TO PLACE A GRAPHICS OBJECT IN A TABLE

You can place a graphics object into a graphic-type field in a table.

1. Cut or copy a graphics file from its source application into the Clipboard.

2. In Paradox, open a table that includes a graphics field.

3. Click the Edit Data Speedbar button.

4. Highlight the field into which the graphics object is to be placed.

5. Choose Edit ➤ Paste.

TO PLACE AN OLE OBJECT IN A TABLE

You can place an object from an OLE server application into a table. To edit the object in the table, double-click it to open it in the server application.

1. Open a table that includes an OLE field.

2. Click the Edit Data Speedbar button.

3. Highlight the field into which the OLE object is to be placed.

4. Cut or copy an object from an OLE server into the Clipboard.

5. Choose Edit ➤ Paste Link.

TO RENAME A TABLE

Always rename a table from within Paradox to ensure that all associated files are renamed along with the table.

1. Choose File ➤ Utilities ➤ Rename to display the Rename dialog box.

2. Click the name of the table you want to rename, and that name appears in the Source File text box.

3. Enter the new name with the .DB extension into the Destination File text box. If you omit the extension, the file name will have no extension and, consequently, Paradox will not recognize the file as a table.

4. Click OK.

TO RESTRUCTURE A TABLE

You can modify a table structure by adding, removing, or changing fields, and by changing table properties. When you save a restructured table, Paradox warns you if the changes would cause loss of data.

1. Choose File ➤ Utilities ➤ Restructure to display the Select File dialog box.

2. Double-click the name of the table you want to restructure to display the Restructure Paradox for Windows Table dialog box.

3. Make changes to the table structure.

4. Click Save to save the table structure with its current name, or click Save As to save it with a different name.

TO SEARCH A TABLE FOR A FIELD VALUE

Use the steps in *To Locate a Record in a Table* in *Forms*. Start with a table, rather than a form, displayed.

TO SORT A TABLE

You can sort a table into an order determined by any fields except binary, formatted memo, graphic, memo, and OLE, in ascending or descending order. In the case of an unkeyed table, you can choose to sort the actual table and retain the same file name, or you can sort a copy of the table giving the copy a different name. In the case of a keyed table (which is always in key order), you can only sort a copy of the table with the key and secondary indexes removed.

1. Open a table.
2. Choose Table ➤ Sort to display the Sort Table dialog box.
3. If the table is unkeyed, choose between sorting the same table or a new table.
4. If the table is keyed, or if the table is unkeyed and you choose a new table, enter the name of the new table.
5. Click the name of the field to be used as the basis of the primary sort, then click the right-pointing arrow to place this field in the Sort Order list. By default, 123 appears at the left of the field name to indicate that the sort is in ascending order.
6. If you want the sort to be in descending order, click Sort Direction to change 123 to 321.
7. Repeat steps 5 and 6 to add fields to the sort list.
8. To change the sort priority, click a field in the sort list, then click one of the Change Order arrows.
9. Click Sort Just Selected Fields if you want to sort only on the fields in the Sort Order list. Otherwise, Paradox automatically adds all other sortable fields to the Sort Order list in the order they occur in the Fields list.

10. Click Display Sorted Table if you want the table to be displayed after the sort.

11. Click Sort.

TO SUBTRACT RECORDS FROM A TABLE

You can subtract records that occur in one table (the target) from records that are in another table (the source). The target table must be keyed.

1. From the Desktop, choose File ➤ Utilities ➤ Subtract to display the Table Subtract dialog box.

2. Click the name of the source table. The name appears in the Subtract Records in Source text box.

3. Click an insertion marker in the From Target Table text box.

4. Click the name of the target table. The name appears in the From Target Table text box.

5. Click OK and a message appears to warn you that records will be deleted.

6. Click OK.

See Also Design Objects, Fields in a Table, Forms, Indexes, Keys, Linking Tables, Lookup Tables, Password Protection, Referential Integrity, Temporary Tables

TEMPORARY TABLES

PURPOSE Paradox automatically creates two types of temporary tables in which it stores records that are incompatible with a normal table.

TO USE A PROBLEM TABLE

When you change a field's type while restructuring a table, there may be values which Paradox cannot convert to the new type. In this case, Paradox prompts you to confirm the change and, if you do confirm, moves the records that cannot be converted into a table named PROBLEMS.DB which it creates in the same directory as the restructured table.

If a PROBLEMS.DB table already exists, Paradox renames the new table PROBLEM1.DB. Up to 99 sequentially numbered problem tables can be created.

You can access the problem tables, manually change values in the records so that they become consistent with the new structure, and then use File ➤ Utilities ➤ Add to return the records to the original table.

TO USE A KEY VIOLATION TABLE

When you add or change keys in a table, there may be key violations because previously existing field values do not comply with the key rules. For example, there may be identical values in the new key field of two or more records. In this case, Paradox moves all the records that violate the key to a table named KEYVIOL.DB which it creates in the same directory as the restructured table.

If a KEYVIOL.DB table already exists, Paradox renames the new table KEYVIOL1.DB. Up to 99 sequentially numbered key violation tables can be created.

You can access the key violation tables, manually change values in the records so that they become consistent with the new key, and then use File ➤ Utilities ➤ Add to return the records to the original table.

See Also Keys, Tables

UNDOING OPERATIONS

PURPOSE Undo provides an easy way to recover from certain mistakes.

TO UNDO AN OPERATION

In table and document windows you can choose Edit ➤ Undo to undo all changes to the current record. You cannot undo changes after you have moved to another record, nor can you use undo the retrieve deleted records.

In design windows, you can choose Edit ➤ Undo to undo to most recent operation on an object.

See Also Documents (Forms and Reports), Forms, Reports, Tables

311

WILDCARDS

PURPOSE Wildcard operators, special characters that represent unknown characters, may be used in queries and also when locating records in tables.

TO USE BASIC WILDCARDS

The basic wildcards are:

WILDCARD	REPRESENTS
@	Any single character
..	A series of characters

These operators may be used in queries and when locating records.

When you want to use one of these operators literally in a query, enclose it within quotation marks. If you want to use them literally when locating records, the @ and .. check box in the Locate Value dialog box must be unchecked.

TO USE ADVANCED WILDCARDS

The advanced wildcards, which may be used when locating records but not in queries, are:

WILDCARD	REPRESENTS
^	Start of line
$	End of line
( )	Encloses a series of literals as a group
[ ]	Encloses a series of alternatives
[^]	Encloses a series of exceptions
|	Separates two alternatives

WILDCARD	REPRESENTS
?	Zero or one repeats of the preceding character or group
*	Zero or many repeats of the preceding character or group
+	One or more repeats of the preceding character or group
\	Identifies the next character as a literal rather than an operator

See Also Forms, Queries, Tables

APPENDIX A

INSTALLING PARADOX FOR WINDOWS

SYSTEM REQUIREMENTS

Paradox runs under Windows on IBM-compatible personal computers. The minimum hardware requirements are:

- Microprocessor—80286
- RAM—4 MB
- Hard disk—20 MB free space (more for large databases). Paradox system files occupy approximately 12 MB. The sample files supplied with Paradox occupy approximately 3 MB of additional space.
- Video system—EGA (CGA is not supported)
- Mouse—Windows compatible
- Printer—Windows compatible

As with all Windows applications, the performance of Paradox improves significantly when it runs on a computer with a more advanced and faster microprocessor, with more than the minimum RAM, with a hard disk that has a short access time, and with a more sophisticated video system.

The software requirements are:

- DOS—version 3.1 or later
- Windows—version 3.0 or later running in standard or 386 enhanced mode (real mode is not supported).

Paradox requires that your CONFIG.SYS file defines the following minimum values:

FILES=60

BUFFERS=40

However, if you are using SMARTDRV you may reduce the BUFFERS setting to 10.

This book covers the use of Paradox on a stand-alone computer. However, Paradox may also be used on any network that is 100 percent compatible with Windows.

UP-TO-DATE INFORMATION

The Paradox distribution disks contain one or more README files which contain information that became available after the documentation and this book were written. These files may contain information about installation, and so you will probably save yourself a lot of time if you read them before you start installing Paradox. You can use Windows Notepad to do so.

INSTALLING PARADOX

Borland gives you permission to make a backup copy of the distribution disks and recommends that you do so before installing Paradox. Use the DOS Diskcopy command to be sure that you copy files in all the subdirectories on the disks.

Installing Paradox for Windows is similar to installing many other Windows applications. You must use the installation process described here because many of the files on the distribution disks are compressed, so you cannot just copy them to your hard disk.

The installation process automatically:

♦ creates a directory on your hard disk for the Paradox program files and the sample files supplied with the program;

♦ copies the Paradox files do your hard disk;

♦ adds a Paradox for Windows group to the Windows Program Manager window;

♦ modifies your Windows WIN.INI file so that Paradox runs properly.

Follow these steps to install Paradox:

1. Start Windows.
2. Insert the Paradox Program Disk #1 into one of your floppy disk drives.
3. Display the Program Manager File menu.
4. Choose the Run command to display the Run dialog box.
5. In the Command Line text box, type:

   A:INSTALL

if you are installing from a floppy disk drive A, or:

   B:INSTALL

if you are installing from a floppy disk drive B.

6. Click OK.

After a few moments, you will see a status window that tells you the names of files that are being copied into your Windows directory. Then you will see a dialog box that suggests a name (PDOXWIN) for a directory to be created for the Paradox system files. The dialog box also suggests that the ODAPI files (ODAPI is the database engine used by Paradox) be installed in your WINDOWS\SYSTEM directory.

You should use the suggested directory names unless you already have a good reason for choosing other names.

The dialog box also allows you to choose whether you want the installation process to create a Paradox group within the Program Manager window, whether you want to install the help files, and whether you want to install the sample files. You should choose all of these because:

- the Paradox group in the Program Manager window provides a convenient way to run Paradox;
- the help files provide valuable information that is instantly available while you are working with Paradox;
- the sample files provide useful examples of Paradox techniques.

After you have set the choices to your liking, a message at the bottom of your screen tells you how much disk space is required and how much you have available. If you have enough space on your disk, click the Install button to continue the installation process. If you do not have enough space, you can choose not to install the sample files so that less space is needed.

From this point on, messages on the screen tell you which Paradox disks to insert into your floppy disk drive. Just follow the instructions.

When the installation process is complete, the Program Manager displays the Paradox group with the Paradox Desktop icon.

Click on this icon to start Paradox. To exit from Paradox type Alt-F4, or use one of the other methods described in Lesson 1 in this book.

WARNING

The installation process adds certain files to your WINDOWS\SYSTEM directory, and it modifies your AUTOEXEC.BAT file to include that directory in your path. Paradox must have access to these files in order to run. If you see an error message telling you that Paradox cannot find certain files, you probably need to modify the PATH statement in your AUTOEXEC.BAT file.

INSTALLING SHARE

SHARE is a memory-resident DOS utility that permits file sharing and locking. A message displayed at the end of the installation process instructs you to load SHARE before running Windows. In fact, however, you do not generally need to install SHARE if you are using Paradox on a stand-alone computer.

If you are using Paradox on a network, or if you are using Paradox on a stand-alone computer and expect to need multiple access to tables, you should install SHARE before starting Paradox.

The simplest way to ensure that Share is always loaded is to add

SHARE/F:4096/L:400

to your AUTOEXEC.BAT file. The /F parameter allocates space for file-sharing information; the /L parameter sets the number of files that can be simultaneously locked.

Alternatively, you can type SHARE↵ at the DOS prompt before starting Windows.

INDEX

Note: In this index, page numbers in **boldface** type identify the primary source of information about a major topic; citations in regular type refer to less important topics or incidental information. Citations in *italic* type refer to illustrations.

N

names
   aliases for, 19, **164**
   for design objects, **190–191**
   for documents, **196–197**
   for fields, 5, **208**
      in ANSWER.DB, **149–150**, 271
      defining, **8–9**
      editing, 26
      entering, 21
      form frames for, 50
      for linking, 77, 79–80
      list of, 113, *114*
      in structures, 26
   for reports, 289
   for saving query answers, 137, 139
   for secondary indexes, 31
   for tables, 23, 137, 307
navigating through records, **44–45**, 68, **195–196**, 305
.NDX extension, 213
networks, 11, 319
New command for tables, 20, *20*
next record, moving to, 45, 195, 217
NO operator, 266
NOT operator, 145, 264, 274
number data type and fields, 210
   aligning, 42
   calculated, 205
   default properties for, 41
   formatting, **41–42**, *42*, **63–64**
   grouping records by, **288**
   in queries, 146
number of pages, special field for, 206
number signs (#)
   for object names, 190
   in pictures, 256

O

Object Linking and Embedding (OLE)
      data type and objects, 181, 210
   creating, **188**

placing, in tables, 306–307
Object Name dialog box, 191
ObjectPAL language, 182, 290
Object Tree button, 246, 293
Object Trees, 56, 57, **246–247**, 293
objects, 40, **247**
   aligning, **63–64**, 165
   boxes around, **64**
   color of, **168–169**
   contained, **56–57**, **170–171**, 247, 292–293
   cutting and copying, **249**
   design, **179–191**
   displaying, 216, 247
   on forms, **55–64**
   grouping, 231–232, **249–250**
   inspecting, **231–232**
   major, **242–243**
   moving, **61–63**, **250–251**
   multi-record, 180, **187–188**, **243–245**
   placing, **251**, 306–307
   preferred, **258–259**
   properties of, 181, **247**, 262
   relationships between, **246–247**
   selecting, **57–59**, **290–293**
   size of, **248**
   spacing, **293–294**
   stacking, **248**
   in tables, 306–307
   ungrouping, **252**
ODAPI.CFG file, 164
OEM character set, 200, 202
OLE data type and objects, 181, 210
   creating, **188**
   placing, in tables, 306–307
OLE tool, 188
one-dimensional crosstabs, **171–172**
one-dimensional summary graphs, **225**
one-to-many relationships, 75, *75*, **81–83**, **236–237**
one-to-one relationships, 75, *75*, **77–81**, **235–236**
ONLY operator, 266
Open a Table dialog box, 32, 34, 167

SYBEX

FREE BROCHURE!

Complete this form today, and we'll send you a full-color brochure of Sybex bestsellers.

Please supply the name of the Sybex book purchased.

_____

How would you rate it?

_____ Excellent   _____ Very Good   _____ Average   _____ Poor

Why did you select this particular book?

_____ Recommended to me by a friend

_____ Recommended to me by store personnel

_____ Saw an advertisement in _____

_____ Author's reputation

_____ Saw in Sybex catalog

_____ Required textbook

_____ Sybex reputation

_____ Read book review in _____

_____ In-store display

_____ Other _____

Where did you buy it?

_____ Bookstore

_____ Computer Store or Software Store

_____ Catalog (name: _____)

_____ Direct from Sybex

_____ Other: _____

Did you buy this book with your personal funds?

_____ Yes   _____ No

About how many computer books do you buy each year?

_____ 1-3   _____ 3-5   _____ 5-7   _____ 7-9   _____ 10+

About how many Sybex books do you own?

_____ 1-3   _____ 3-5   _____ 5-7   _____ 7-9   _____ 10+

Please indicate your level of experience with the software covered in this book:

_____ Beginner   _____ Intermediate   _____ Advanced

Which types of software packages do you use regularly?

_____ Accounting	_____ Databases	_____ Networks
_____ Amiga	_____ Desktop Publishing	_____ Operating Systems
_____ Apple/Mac	_____ File Utilities	_____ Spreadsheets
_____ CAD	_____ Money Management	_____ Word Processing
_____ Communications	_____ Languages	_____ Other _____

(please specify)

Which of the following best describes your job title?

_____ Administrative/Secretarial   _____ President/CEO

_____ Director   _____ Manager/Supervisor

_____ Engineer/Technician   _____ Other _____

(please specify)

Comments on the weaknesses/strengths of this book: _____

_____

_____

_____

_____

_____

Name _____

Street _____

City/State/Zip _____

Phone _____

PLEASE FOLD, SEAL, AND MAIL TO SYBEX

SYBEX, INC.
Department M
2021 CHALLENGER DR.
ALAMEDA, CALIFORNIA USA
94501

SYBEX

SEAL

THE FORM (DESIGN) SPEEDBAR

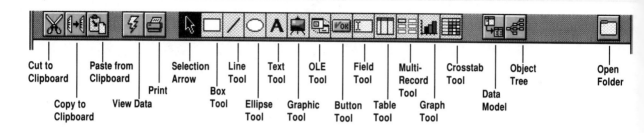

Cut to Clipboard
Copy to Clipboard
Paste from Clipboard
View Data
Print
Selection Arrow
Box Tool
Line Tool
Ellipse Tool
Text Tool
Graphic Tool
OLE Tool
Button Tool
Field Tool
Table Tool
Multi-Record Tool
Graph Tool
Crosstab Tool
Data Model
Object Tree
Open Folder

THE LIBRARY SPEEDBAR

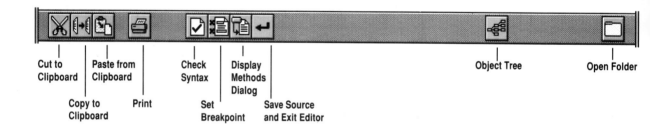

Cut to Clipboard
Copy to Clipboard
Paste from Clipboard
Print
Check Syntax
Set Breakpoint
Display Methods Dialog
Save Source and Exit Editor
Object Tree
Open Folder

THE REPORT (DESIGN) SPEEDBAR

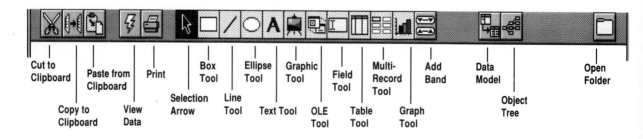

Cut to Clipboard
Copy to Clipboard
Paste from Clipboard
View Data
Print
Selection Arrow
Box Tool
Line Tool
Ellipse Tool
Text Tool
Graphic Tool
OLE Tool
Field Tool
Table Tool
Multi-Record Tool
Graph Tool
Add Band
Data Model
Object Tree
Open Folder